PERSPECTIVES ON INTERNATIONAL FINANCIAL REPORTING AND AUDITING IN THE AIRLINE INDUSTRY

STUDIES IN MANAGERIAL AND FINANCIAL ACCOUNTING

Series Editor: Anne M. Farrell

Recent Volumes:

STUDIES IN MANAGERIAL AND FINANCIAL
ACCOUNTING   VOLUME 35

PERSPECTIVES ON INTERNATIONAL FINANCIAL REPORTING AND AUDITING IN THE AIRLINE INDUSTRY

BY

CAN ÖZTÜRK

Çankaya University, Turkey

LANGUAGE EDITOR

CHARLES RICHARD BAKER

Adelphi University, USA

United Kingdom – North America – Japan
India – Malaysia – China

Emerald Publishing Limited
Howard House, Wagon Lane, Bingley BD16 1WA, UK

First edition 2022

Reprints and permissions service
Contact: permissions@emeraldinsight.com

British Library Cataloguing in Publication Data
A catalogue record for this book is available from the British Library

ISBN: 978-1-78973-760-8 (Print)
ISBN: 978-1-78973-759-2 (Online)
ISBN: 978-1-78973-761-5 (Epub)

ISSN: 1479-3512 (Series)

Printed and bound by CPI Group (UK) Ltd, Croydon, CR0 4YY

ISOQAR certified
Management System,
awarded to Emerald
for adherence to
Environmental
standard
ISO 14001:2004.

ISOQAR
REGISTERED
Certificate Number 1985
ISO 14001

INVESTOR IN PEOPLE

To my wife Oytun and to my daughter Ece
Thank you for their indefatigable support and immense patience.
Can Öztürk
July 2021

CONTENTS

ABOUT THE AUTHOR

Can ÖZTÜRK is an Associate Professor of Financial, International, and Comparative Accounting at the Department of Management, Çankaya University, Turkey where he teaches financial and managerial accounting, financial statement analysis, International Financial Reporting Standards, international trade accounting, and accounting for multinational enterprises. He has obtained PhD in Accounting and Finance from Başkent University, Turkey. In addition, he received his first bachelor's degree in Banking and Finance from Bilkent University, Turkey, as well as his second bachelor's degree in Finance, and his master's degree in Business Administration from the University of Massachusetts Dartmouth, USA. His research interests include financial reporting, financial statement analysis, auditing, and sustainability reporting in the international context. He has published papers in *Accounting in Europe, Journal of Accounting and Management Information Systems*, and *the World of Accounting Science*. He is fluent in English, and French, in addition his native language, Turkish. ORCID ID: https://orcid.org/0000-0003-1587-4707.

FOREWORD

This book is the outcome of the practices of international financial reporting and international auditing in the airline industry. Accountability and responsibility for this book lie with Can Öztürk.

PREFACE

Perspectives on international financial reporting and auditing in the airline industry is a research book which combines international financial reporting and auditing practices in the sector-specific and global context. It has been developed considering the paper of Tan, Tower, Hancock, and Taplin (2002) titled as "Empires of the sky: Determinants of global airlines' accounting-policy choices," the book of Lavi (2016) titled as "the impact of IFRS on industry" and current Accounting Guides and Airline Disclosure Guides of the International Air Transport Association's Industry Accounting Working Group.

The book consists of two sections. First section focuses on observations related to international financial reporting and second section covers observations related to international auditing in the airline industry.

The first section includes four chapters. The first chapter provides an overview of financial reporting in the global airline industry considering the accounting framework adopted by airlines whether they are publicly accountable or not. Following Chapter 1, Chapters 2–4 adopt an IFRS approach in the global context. Chapter 2 focuses on the comparability of financial statements in the airline industry in the context of the diversity of IFRS accounting policy choices; Chapter 3 analyzes the cumulative effect of the adoption of IFRS 15 and IFRS 16 and the compliance level of disclosures of IFRS 16 from a lessee standpoint on the financial statements of Air France – KLM; and Chapter 4 discusses the segment reporting in the airline industry under IFRS 8.

The second section includes one chapter. It analyzes different aspects of International Standards on Auditing in the airline industry considering ISA 570, ISA 700, ISA 701, ISA 701 of the UK, ISA 705, and ISA 706 within the framework of the IFRS adopted airlines.

My wish is that readers whose interests relate to airline financial reporting and auditing find this book informative and inspiring further research.

Can Öztürk
Associate Professor of Accounting
Department of Management
Faculty of Economics and Administrative Sciences
Çankaya University, Turkey
July 2021

ACKNOWLEDGMENTS

As a professor of accounting and a traveler keen on air travel, analysis of the financial statements of airlines in terms of international financial reporting and auditing has been one of my research interests that I have been willing to focus on in my academic career since 2011. However, such an opportunity did not take place until I saw the call for paper announcement of the book serial of Emerald titled as *Studies in Managerial and Financial Accounting* and I submitted my book proposal. This research book took almost three years of mine. In this context, I would like to thank all the Emerald editorial team members that contributed to making this dream come true but particularly to Dr Anne Farrell, Dr Charles Richard Baker, and Aiswarya Mahathma Suritha.

I would like to thank Dr Anne Farrell of Miami University who is the project editor of this book serial, for giving me the opportunity to prepare this research book and for making my dream come true so that I can specialize in airline financial reporting and auditing from a global perspective. In addition, I truly appreciate her patience and support due to my request of deadline extensions.

It has been almost 20 years since I recognize Dr Charles Richard Baker of Adelphi University. I was his MBA student at the University of Massachusetts Dartmouth in 2003. He has been one of my leading accounting professors in my academic career. This book project provided him to contribute to my academic career once again. I would like to thank Dr Baker for his time to check my writing as an experienced researcher on airline accounting. I truly appreciate his support.

I would also like to thank Aiswarya Mahathma Suritha of Emerald who is commissioning assistant of this book serial for her time and contribution during the editorial process of this book.

Last, but certainly not least, I would like to thank all my family and friends for their support during this project.

All errors are my own and come with apologies.

Can Öztürk
July 2021

PART I

INTERNATIONAL FINANCIAL REPORTING

CHAPTER 1

OVERVIEW OF FINANCIAL REPORTING IN THE AIRLINE INDUSTRY

ABSTRACT

This chapter focuses on the diversity of financial reporting frameworks in the airline industry considering past and present. While diversity of financial reporting frameworks existed in the past, currently, the majority of listed and non-listed airlines, whose financial statements are publicly available, are inclined to adopt International Financial Reporting Standards (IFRS), leading toward uniformity in financial reporting frameworks because their country of incorporation or the stock exchange where they are listed either require or permit them to do so. Airlines operating in the United States prepare their financial statements under United States Generally Accepted Accounting Principles and some of Asian-Pacific countries still use their own national accounting standards in financial reporting. In addition, this research points out that the primary determinant of IFRS adoption in the airline industry is the fact that the majority of airlines are listed in national or foreign stock exchanges where IFRS adoption is required, but there are some company-specific determinants for listed and non-listed IFRS adopting airlines. Finally, this chapter also sets forth that there are jurisdictional versions of IFRS in the global context from the perspective of financial statements of airlines leading to some obstacles in understanding the financial reporting framework.

Keywords: Airline industry; financial reporting framework; diversity; uniformity; International Financial Reporting Standards; United States Generally Accepted Accounting Principles

Perspectives on International Financial Reporting and Auditing in the Airline Industry
Studies in Managerial and Financial Accounting, Volume 35, 3–19
Copyright © 2022 by Emerald Publishing Limited
All rights of reproduction in any form reserved
ISSN: 1479-3512/doi:10.1108/S1479-351220220000035001

1. INTRODUCTION

The airline industry is one of the largest global industries served by national firms, with operating profits of $45.9 billion in 2018 and $43.2 billion in 2019 on revenue of $812 billion in 2018 and $838 billion in 2019 (Hanlon, 2007, p. 9; IATA, 2019a, 2020a). The industry provides travel service to almost every country in the global context with aircraft fleet of 29,507 in 2018 and 29,697 in 2019 (IATA, 2019b, 2020b). It has played a crucial role in the creation of a global economy in terms of both its own operations and its impacts on related industries, including but not limited to, aircraft manufacturing and tourism. More than 65 million jobs in 2018 and 88 million jobs in 2020 are globally supported in aviation and related tourism, of which 10.2 million people in 2018 and around 11 million people in 2020 work directly in the aviation industry, including airlines, air navigation service providers, airports, the civil aerospace sector, which manufactures aircraft systems, frames, and engines (ATAG, 2018, 2020).

Historically, major technological developments have occurred during the growth phase of the airline industry such as the introduction of jet airplanes for commercial use in the 1950s, and the development of wide-body "jumbo jets" in the 1970s (Belobaba, 2015, pp. 1–2). Starting from 1978, the economic deregulation of airlines has been in effect leading to cost efficiency, operating profitability, and competitive behavior affecting both domestic air travel within each country and the continuing evolution of a highly competitive airline industry.

The airline industry has its own unique characteristics: (1) high growth rate versus low levels of profitability; (2) highly competitive structure; (3) monopolistic or oligopolistic structure; and (4) capital-intensive structure.

(1) The industry has a high rate of growth accompanied by low levels of profitability (Hanlon, 2007, p. 5; AICPA, 2016). As an evidence of growth, indicators show that airlines transported approximately 960 million passengers in 1986, 1.6 million in 1999, 4.4 billion in 2018 and 4.5 million in 2019 (Yergin, Evans, & Vietor, 2000; Isack & Tan, 2008; IATA, 2019b, 2020b).

On the other hand, profitability of the industry has been sensitive to economic factors such as the ability to attract and retain business and leisure passengers, the effects of political and strategic issues like hostilities, acts of war, terrorist attacks, and expansionism (AICPA, 2016; Isack & Tan, 2008; Lyth, 1996), disease and epidemics like COVID-19, the cost and availability of aircraft insurance, fluctuations in the cost of aviation fuel, competitive pricing policies, and government regulation (AICPA, 2016) as well as high operating costs for wages, jet fuel, maintenance, and depreciation expenses (Straszheim, 1969; Isack & Tan, 2008) versus changes in average fare levels and passenger demand (AICPA, 2016). Profitability indicators show that airlines are less profitable due to increases in expenses of $766 billion in 2018 and $795 billion in 2019 with a particular focus on increases in fuel costs, with net income of $27.3 billion in 2018 and $26.4 billion in 2019 (IATA, 2019a, 2020a).

(2) It is a highly competitive industry due to the following parameters: fare pricing, customer service, routes served, flight schedules, types of aircraft, safety record and reputation, code-sharing relationships, in-flight entertainment systems, and frequent-flyer programs (AICPA, 2016).

(3) It shows a monopolistic or oligopolistic structure. While the paper of Tan, Tower, Hancock, and Taplin (2002) included 80 airlines from 52 countries for an average of 1.5 airlines from each country, this chapter includes 79 airlines from 44 countries for an average of 1.79 airlines from each country. The same structure exists today.

(4) It is capital-intensive. The aircraft fleet is either owned or leased. Before leases were accounted for according to IFRS 16 under International Financial Reporting Standards (IFRS) and ASC 842 under United States Generally Accepted Accounting Principles (US GAAP) (Marşap & Yanık, 2018), airlines had reported approximately 80% of the aircraft fleet on the statement of financial position (i.e., around 80% of airline's aircraft fleet is owned or leased under finance leases) and approximately 20% of its aircraft fleet as well as various buildings (under off balance sheet leases) (Tan et al., 2002). However, currently, all leased assets and liabilities regardless of whether they are under finance or operating lease will be reported on the statement of financial position as soon as an airline adopts IFRS 16 or ASC 842 so that the statement of financial position reflects the liquidity, solvency, and debt/equity structure of an airline.

The objectives of this chapter are to indicate the diversity of the historical financial reporting framework in the airline industry, to determine the trend of IFRS adoption in the airline industry as of the year 2018, to indicate the determinants of IFRS adoption in the industry and set forth the jurisdictional versions of IFRS from the perspective of IFRS financial statements of airlines.

Within the framework of these objectives, this chapter is important because it gives users of airline-related financial information the opportunity to be informed about an industry that is financially sensitive in nature through a common denominator in the reporting of financial situation, financial performance, and cash flows at the financial reporting framework level.

This chapter has the following structure: Section 2 presents a literature review of financial reporting of airlines in the context of diversity and harmonization; Section 3 explains the data, accounting period for the data, constraints of the research and the research methodology; Section 4 discusses the diversity of financial reporting frameworks adopted by airlines considering past and present; Section 5 summarizes the determinants of IFRS adoption in the airline industry and jurisdictional versions of IFRS. Finally, Section 6 presents concluding remarks along with main findings.

2. LITERATURE REVIEW ON FINANCIAL REPORTING CONSIDERING DIVERSITY, HARMONIZATION, AND AIRLINE INDUSTRY

Accounting diversity is the difference between accounting and reporting practices of different countries in (a) accounting measurement, (b) financial disclosure, and (c) auditing practices (Choi & Levich, 1991).

Diversity in accounting has been part of the debate in the airline industry since 1992. Industry-specific primary areas of accounting leading to diversity were determined through KPMG's and International Air Transport Association

(IATA)'s 1992 survey of airlines' annual reports. This survey detected diversity of adopted accounting policies in airline financial reporting in the following areas (Tan et al., 2002): (1) unrealized foreign-exchange differences; (2) frequent-flyer accounting; (3) aircraft depreciation; (4) revenue recognition; (5) maintenance costs; and (6) lease accounting.

As a result of these observations, the IATA Accounting Policy Task Force issued 6 Airline Accounting Guidelines between 1994 and 1997 to minimize diversity and to improve the comparability of financial statements of airlines: (1) AAG 1: Translation of Long-Term Foreign Currency Borrowings; (2) AAG 2: Frequent-Flyer Programme Accounting; (3) AAG 3: Components of Fleet Acquisition Cost and Associated Depreciation; (4) AAG 4: Recognition of Revenue; (5) AAG 5: Accounting for Maintenance Costs; and (6) AAG 6: Accounting for Leases of Aircraft Fleet Assets.

To observe the effects of these guidelines on airline financial reporting, Tan et al. (2002) examined the level of diversity in airline reporting from the perspectives of measurement and disclosure using a sample of 80 airlines considering their 1997/1998 annual reports. The results of this research indicate that airline financial reporting became more uniform, and comparability of airline financial reporting was improved.

In 2016, the IATA Industry Accounting Working Group (IAWG) issued four Airline Disclosure Guidelines to provide comparability of financial statements in the airline industry. These guidelines cover (1) Hedge Accounting under IFRS 9; (2) maintenance accounting; (3) aircraft acquisition cost and depreciation; and (4) segment reporting (IATA, 2016a, 2016b, 2016c, 2016d).

In 2020, IAWG has recently issued three Accounting Guides to ensure comparability of financial statements: (1) IFRS 9 Financial Instruments; (2) IFRS 15 Revenue from Contracts with Customers; and (3) IFRS 16 Leases (IATA, 2020c, 2020d, 2020e).

The objective of former and current guidelines was to try to minimize the diversity and improve uniformity of accounting and financial reporting in the airline industry. However, it should be noted that these guidelines are based on accounting policies, and accounting policies are subsections of financial reporting frameworks like US GAAP and IFRS.

Therefore, the aim of this chapter is to take an overall picture of the financial reporting framework adopted by airlines in the global context considering past and present before moving on to further research.

3. DATA AND RESEARCH METHODOLOGY

3.1 Data

The sample of this research is made up of listed and non-listed airlines whose financial statements are available on their websites without language barrier regardless of whether they are member of IATA. Within the framework of these parameters, a sample of 79 airlines from 44 countries was established using the regional classification of IATA (Table 1). This sample consists of around 6% of

Table 1. Geographical Distribution of the Sample of Airlines.

	Number of Airlines
Americas	22
Europe	22
Africa – Middle East	9
Asia - Pacific	20
China – Northern Asia	6

1.303 commercial airlines whose financial statements are publicly available in the market as of 2018 (ATAG, 2018).

3.2 Accounting Period for the Data

The sample focuses on annual reports of airlines for the accounting period ended on December 31, 2018, to analyze current financial reporting practice in the airline industry. However, the end of accounting periods, sometimes vary from one country to another. In such cases, annual accounting periods ended on January 1, 2019, March 31, 2019, May 31, 2019, June 30, 2019, and September 30, 2019, were equivalent to the annual accounting period ended on December 31, 2018.

In addition, the sample uses the most recently available historical annual reports for analyzing historical financial reporting practice in the airline industry before the IFRS adoption regardless of the end of accounting period.

3.3. Constraint of the Research

A limited number of airlines (Air Malta, Ethiopian Airlines, Oman Air, Precision Air, PNG Air, Qazaq Air, and South African Airways) whose 2018 annual reports were not available were excluded from the sample considering 2018 as the common denominator of the annual accounting period.

3.4 Research Methodology

This research collects data and assesses those data using the frequency of distribution method regarding the financial reporting framework adopted by airlines considering past and present.

4. FINDINGS AND DISCUSSION

4.1 Financial Reporting Framework in the Airline Industry in the Past

Regarding the history of financial reporting framework in airlines, this research detected historical annual reports of 28 airlines (Table 2). By analyzing available historical annual reports of airlines, this research points out the following 4 issues:

1. The majority of airlines prepared their financial statements in accordance with generally accepted accounting principles or national accounting standards of

Table 2. Former Regulation of Financial Reporting in the Airline Industry.

Region	Country	Former GAAP/Standards
Americas		
GOL Linhas Aereas	Brazil (BR)	BR GAAP – US GAAP
Air Transat	Canada	Canadian GAAP
WestJet	Canada	Canadian GAAP
Air Canada	Canada	Canadian GAAP
Cargojet Airways	Canada	Canadian GAAP
Aeromexico	Mexico	Mexican Financial Reporting Standards
Copa Airlines	Panama	US GAAP
China and Northern Asia		
Cathay Pacific Airlines	Hong Kong (HK)	HK GAAP
China Airlines	Chinese Taipei	Chinese GAAP
Europe: EU, EAA, and Others		
Air France – KLM Group	France	French GAAP
Lufthansa	Germany	German GAAP
SAS Group	Sweden	Swedish Accounting Standards
Air Partner	UK	UK GAAP
Easy Jet	UK	UK GAAP
British Airways	UK	UK GAAP
Fast Jet	UK	UK GAAP
Aer Lingus	Ireland	Ireland GAAP
Norwegian Air	Norway	Norwegian GAAP
Turkish Airlines	Turkey	Turkish GAAP
Africa & Middle East		
Comair	South Africa (SA)	SA GAAP
Emirates	UAE	IFRS
Asia – Pacific		
Regional Express	Australia	Australian GAAP
Qantas	Australia	Australian GAAP
Virgin Australia	Australia	Australian GAAP
Korean Air	Korea	Korean GAAP
Asiana Airlines	Korea	Korean GAAP
Air New Zealand	New Zealand (NZ)	NZ GAAP
Singapore Airlines	Singapore	Singapore Accounting Standards

their country of incorporation leading to diversity in measurement and disclosure from one country to another unless countries with similar cultures,
environments, and external factors such as similar background features like
laws and company structures have similar accounting systems and thus similar
accounting practices (Nobes, 1992, 1998).

2. Copa Airlines whose country of incorporation is Panama prepared its financial statements in accordance with US GAAP due to being listed in New York
Stock Exchange (NYSE).

3. GOL Linhas Aereas whose country of incorporation is Brazil had dual reporting in accordance with BR GAAP and US GAAP.

4. Emirates prepared its annual reports in accordance with IFRS since 1994. It
looks like that it is the oldest airline reporting under IFRS. This quite early
adoption of IFRS at this airline compared to other airlines may be explained
by coercive, normative, and mimetic pressures over the United Arab Emirates

(UAE) including the regulatory regimes of the World Bank and multinational corporations, the International Accounting Standards Board (IASB), the influence of the Big 4 accounting firms, and relationships with nations' trading partners (Irvine, 2008, p. 137).

4.2 Financial Reporting Framework in the Airline Industry at Present

Regarding the current trends of financial reporting frameworks adopted by airlines, this research points out that 72.15% of the airlines prepare their financial statements in accordance with IFRS, 15.19% prepare their financial statements in accordance with US GAAP, and the remaining 12.66% use their national accounting standards (Table 3).

In this context, observations show that (1) the majority of airlines have a common denominator by preparing and presenting their financial statements through IFRS adoption; (2) US airlines use US GAAP in financial reporting; and (3) diversity of financial reporting frameworks exists particularly in the Asia-Pacific region because financial reporting practice in India, Indonesia, Japan, Thailand, and Vietnam is still governed by national accounting standards.

4.2.1 Financial Reporting in the Airline Industry in the Americas

In the context of Americas, it is observed that two financial reporting frameworks are used by airline companies in the region depending on financial reporting regulations adopted by their country of incorporation or the stock exchanges where they are listed (Table 4): (1) US GAAP or (2) IFRS as issued by the IASB.

Except for the domestic airlines listed in the USA that are subject to US GAAP within the framework of financial reporting regulated by the US Securities Exchange Commission (SEC) (IASB, 2017c), all other airlines in the region adopt IFRS as issued by the IASB (Table 4) because (1) Air Transat, WestJet, Air Canada, Cargojet Airways, and Aeromexico are listed in their domestic stock exchanges where IFRS adoption is required (IASB, 2016b, 2017a); (2) GOL Linhas Aereas, LATAM Airlines Group, and Volaris are listed in both domestic stock exchange where IFRS adoption is required (IASB, 2016a, 2016b, 2017b) and NYSE where IFRS adoption is permitted for foreign companies without reconciliation to US GAAP (SEC, 2007); and (3) Azul Brazilian Airlines, and Copa Airlines are listed only in NYSE where foreign companies are permitted to adopt IFRS without reconciliation to US GAAP (SEC, 2007) as well as their country of incorporation requires or permits IFRS adoption (IASB, 2016c, 2017b).

Table 3. Global Financial Reporting Framework Adopted by Airlines.

	IFRS	US GAAP	National Accounting Standards	
Americas	10	12	–	22
China and Northern Asia	5	–	1	6
Europe	22	–	–	22
Africa – Middle East	9	–	–	9
Asia-Pacific	11	–	9	20
Total	57	12	10	79

Table 4. Airlines in the Americas.

Airline Company	Country	Listed?	Listed Where?	Single (S) or Dual (D) Listed	Home-country Listing	Foreign-country Listing
GOL Linhas Aereas	Brazil	Yes	Brasil Bolsa Balcão and New York	D	Yes	Yes
Azul Brazilian Airlines	Brazil	Yes	New York	S	No	Yes
Air Transat	Canada	Yes	Toronto	S	Yes	No
WestJet	Canada	Yes	Toronto	S	Yes	No
Air Canada	Canada	Yes	Toronto	S	Yes	No
Cargojet Airways	Canada	Yes	Toronto	S	Yes	No
LATAM Airlines Group	Chile	Yes	Santiago and New York	D	Yes	Yes
Aeromexico	Mexico	Yes	Mexico	S	Yes	No
Volaris	Mexico	Yes	Mexico and New York	D	Yes	Yes
COPA Airlines	Panama	Yes	New York	S	No	Yes
American Airlines	USA	Yes	NASDAQ	S	Yes	No
Alaska Airlines	USA	Yes	New York	S	Yes	No
United Airlines	USA	Yes	NASDAQ	S	Yes	No
Delta Air Lines	USA	Yes	New York	S	Yes	No
FedEx Express	USA	Yes	New York	S	Yes	No
Atlas Air	USA	Yes	NASDAQ	S	Yes	No
UPS Airlines	USA	Yes	New York	S	Yes	No
Hawaiian Air	USA	Yes	NASDAQ	S	Yes	No
JetBlue	USA	Yes	NASDAQ	S	Yes	No
Skywest	USA	Yes	NASDAQ	S	Yes	No
Southwest	USA	Yes	New York	S	Yes	No
Spirit Airlines	USA	Yes	New York	S	Yes	No

4.2.2 Financial Reporting in Airline Industry in China and Northern Asia

In the context of China and Northern Asia, observations show that four financial reporting frameworks are used by airlines in the region (Table 5) depending on financial reporting regulations adopted by their country of incorporation and/or stock exchange where they are listed: (1) Accounting Standards for Business Enterprises of China (ASBE); (2) Hong Kong Financial Reporting Standards (HKFRS); (3) IFRS endorsed by Financial Supervisory Commission (FSC) of Taiwan; and (4) IFRS as issued by the IASB.

Except for Hainan Airlines Group from China that is only listed in domestic stock exchange, and is subject to ASBE of China (IASB, 2018a), all other airlines are also listed but adopt IFRS because stock exchanges where they are listed either require or permit IFRS adoption.

In Hong Kong, the Hong Kong Stock Exchange (HKSE) requires adoption of HKFRS endorsed by the Hong Kong Institute of Certified Public Accountants (HKICPA) for domestic companies (IASB, 2018b). HKFRS is virtually identical to IFRS based on the IASB's declaration. In this context, Cathay Pacific Airlines incorporated in Hong Kong prepares its financial statements in compliance with HKFRS and it meets the national requirements of financial reporting in Hong Kong because it is listed only in HKSE.

Table 5. Airlines in China & Northern Asia.

Airline Company	Country	Listed?	Listed Where?	Single (S), Dual (D) or Triple (T) Listed	Home-country Listing	Foreign-country Listing
Hainan Airlines Group	China	Yes	Shanghai	D	Yes	No
Cathay Pacific Airlines	Hong Kong	Yes	Hong Kong	S	Yes	No
Air China Group	China	Yes	Shanghai, Hong Kong, and London	T	Yes	Yes
China Southern Airlines	China	Yes	Shanghai, Hong Kong, and New York	T	Yes	Yes
China Eastern Airlines	China	Yes	Shanghai, Hong Kong, and New York	T	Yes	Yes
China Airlines	Chinese Taipei	Yes	Taiwan	S	Yes	No

Similar to the practice of Hong Kong, China Airlines, incorporated in Chinese Taipei, prepares its financial statements in compliance with IFRS endorsed by FSC of Taiwan and thus meets the national financial reporting requirements of Taiwan due to its listing only on a domestic stock exchange. IFRS endorsed by FSC of Taiwan is a jurisdictional version of IFRS that eliminates revaluation of property, plant and equipment and intangible assets (IASB, 2016d).

On the other hand, Chinese airlines incorporated in China are examples of a triple listing process. Therefore, not only they are subject to ASBE of China due to their domestic listings in the Shanghai Stock Exchange but also they are subject to financial reporting requirements of other stock exchanges permitting or requiring IFRS adoption: (1) due to the enforcement of being listed in the London Stock Exchange; Air China prepares its financial statements in accordance with IFRS as issued by the IASB; (2) because they are foreign IFRS companies listed in NYSE, China Eastern Airlines and China Southern Airlines prefer the option to prepare their financial statements in line with IFRS as issued by the IASB. Therefore, Air China, China Eastern Airlines and China Southern Airlines also meet the reporting requirement of being listed in HKSE because IFRS adoption is permitted for foreign companies listed in Hong Kong (IASB, 2018b).

4.2.3 Financial Reporting in the Airline Industry in Europe
In the context of Europe, it is observed that three financial reporting frameworks are used by airlines in the region depending on financial regulation adopted by the top international organization like the European Union (EU), their country of incorporation or stock exchange: (1) IFRS as endorsed by the EU and as issued by the IASB, (2) IFRS as issued by the IASB, and (3) Turkish Financial Reporting Standards (TFRS).

Within the borders of the EU, EU's IAS regulation of 1606/2002 regulates IFRS adoption as a requirement for the consolidated financial statements of all publicly traded companies and as an option for the consolidated financial statements of non-publicly traded companies (EU, 2002, p. 243/3).

In the context of the EU, all airlines except Croatia Airlines, Aer Lingus, TAP Group, Virgin Atlantic Group are listed (Table 6). Therefore, they are subject to IFRS as endorsed by EU in preparing their consolidated financial statements. Among the listed ones, it is also observed that Ryanair is the only listed airline both on EU stock exchanges and NASDAQ of the US. In this context, it meets reporting requirements of both exchanges through IFRS adoption.

On the other hand, it is observed that Croatia Airlines, Aer Lingus, TAP, and Virgin Atlantic also prepare their financial statements in accordance with IFRS even though they are non-listed. In this context, it should be noted that the option to require or permit IFRS adoption for the consolidated financial statements of non-publicly traded companies belongs to the national regulatory bodies of accounting standards of the EU countries depending on IAS Regulation 1606/2002 in terms of non-listed companies (EU, 2002, p. 243/3).

Table 6. Airlines in the EU.

Airline Company	Country	Listed?	Listed Where?	Single (S), Dual (D) or Triple (T) Listed	Home-country Listing	Foreign-country Listing
Croatia Airlines	Croatia	No	Non-listed company	–	–	–
Finnair – Finnair Group	Finland	Yes	NASDAQ OMX Helsinki	S	Yes	No
Air France – KLM Group	France	Yes	Euronext Paris & Amsterdam	D	Yes	Yes
Lufthansa Group	Germany	Yes	Berlin, Frankfurt, Hamburg, Stuttgart, Munich, & London	D	Yes	Yes
Aegean Group	Greece	Yes	Athens	S	Yes	No
Aer Lingus	Ireland	No	Non-listed private sector company	–	–	–
Ryanair	Ireland	Yes	Irish, London, & NASDAQ	T	Yes	Yes
Wizz Air	Jersey	Yes	London	S	No	Yes
TAP Group	Portugal	No	Non-listed private sector company	–	–	–
SAS – SAS Group	Sweden	Yes	Stockholm	S	Yes	No
International Airlines Group	Spain	Yes	London, Madrid, Barcelona, Bilbao & Valencia	D	Yes	Yes
Virgin Atlantic Group	UK	No	Non-listed private sector company	–	–	–
Air Partner	UK	Yes	London	S	Yes	No
Easy Jet	UK	Yes	London	S	Yes	No
British Airways	UK	Yes	London	S	Yes	No
Fast Jet	UK	Yes	London	S	Yes	No

In this regard, Croatia Airlines is considered as a large-sized company in Croatia; because it fulfills each of the following parameters in its 2017 financial year to be considered as large-sized company in 2018 in the context of (1) total revenue greater than 260 million HRK (approximately US$45 million); (2) total assets greater than 130 million HRK (approximately US$23 million); and (3) an average number of employees in excess of 250 (IASB, 2016e). Therefore, it is required for Croatia Airlines to prepare IFRS based consolidated financial statements due to being large-sized company.

Non-listed Aer Lingus prepares its financial statements under IFRS in line with its ultimate parent, International Airlines Group. This situation may be explained by a recent research on the IFRS adoption of UK unlisted firms issued by André and Kalogirou (2020) stating that subsidiaries adopt IFRS as part of their group's strategy to improve within group monitoring and raise external debt capital and thus the probability of a subsidiary adopting IFRS increases when the parent company is applying IFRS itself as well as by Guerreiro, Rodrigues, and Craig (2012) stating that IFRS have been part of subsidiaries of listed companies' rationales for accounting practices because it facilitates consolidation of accounts and the harmonization of internal information.

In addition, non-listed TAP and Virgin Atlantic preferred IFRS financial statements. This situation may be explained by Guerreiro et al. (2012) stating that companies belonging to industries that are more organized are more likely to adopt IFRS on a more voluntary basis, considering strong cooperation among firms from the same industry, and organizational interconnectedness leading to consensus regarding the adequacy of IFRS. In this regard, it should be noted that strong cooperation and organizational interconnectedness exist in the airline industry because IATA regulates the airline industry, as well as code-share flights, and airline alliances like Star Alliance, OneWorld, and Skyteam provide the organizational interconnectedness.

Regarding the European Economic Area (EEA), Icelandair, and Norwegian Air consist of listed airlines from Iceland, and Norway that are members of EEA but not EU (Table 7). Therefore, they are required to use IFRS as endorsed by EU (IASB, 2018c).

On the other hand, the European airlines that are not within the borders of the EU, and EAA, are all listed (Table 8). Adoption of IFRS as issued by the IASB is required for El Al and Aeroflot in Israel and Russia (IASB, 2016f, 2016g). In Turkey, Pegasus Airlines and Turkish Airlines adopted TFRS that are fully in compliance with IFRS (IASB, 2018d).

Table 7. Airlines in the EEA.

Airline Company	Country	Listed?	Listed Where?	Single (S), Dual (D), or Triple (T) Listed	Home-country Listing	Foreign-country Listing
Icelandair	Iceland	Yes	NASDAQ OMX Iceland	S	Yes	No
Norwegian Air	Norway	Yes	Oslo	S	Yes	No

Table 8.   Airlines in Europe other than the EU and EEA.

Airline Company	Country	Listed?	Listed Where?	Single (S), Dual (D), or Triple (T) Listed	Home-Country Listing	Foreign-Country Listing
El Al	Israel	Yes	Tel Aviv	S	Yes	No
Aeroflot	Russia	Yes	Moscow	S	Yes	No
Turkish Airlines	Turkey	Yes	Istanbul	S	Yes	No
Pegasus Airlines	Turkey	Yes	Istanbul	S	Yes	No

4.2.4 Financial Reporting in the Airline Industry in Africa and Middle East
In the context of Africa and Middle East, observations show that one financial reporting framework is used by airlines in the region depending on financial reporting regulation adopted by their country of incorporation or stock exchanges where they are listed (Table 9): IFRS as issued by the IASB.

In the region, all airlines except for Qatar Airways and Emirates are all listed. Therefore, being listed requires them to adopt IFRS due to the IFRS adoption in countries where they are incorporated (IASB, 2016h, 2016l, 2016m, 2016n, 2016o) or in stock exchanges where they are listed as it is in the case of Kenya Airlines that has triple listings (IASB, 2016i, 2016j, 2016k).

In the context of Qatar and UAE, IFRS adoption is required for all entities regardless of whether they are listed or not (IASB, 2016o, 2016p). That is why, IFRS adoption is a requirement rather than an option from the perspective of non-listed Qatar Airways and Emirates.

4.2.5 Financial Reporting in the Airline Industry in the Asia-Pacific Region
In the context of Asia-Pacific region, observations show that 12 financial reporting frameworks are used by airlines in the region (Table 10) depending on financial reporting regulation adopted by their country of incorporation and are classified as follows:

National Accounting Standards: (1) Indian Accounting Standards (Ind AS); (2) Indonesian Accounting Standards; (3) Japan GAAP; (4) Thai Financial Reporting Standards; and (5) Vietnamese Accounting Standards, versus
Jurisdictional IFRS: (6) Australian Accounting Standards as issued by Australian Accounting Standards Board; (7) New Zealand equivalents to IFRS; (8) Philippines Financial Reporting Standards; (9) Malaysian Financial Reporting Standards (MFRS); (10) IFRS as adopted by the Republic of Korea; (11) Sri Lanka Financial Reporting Standards; and (12) Singapore Financial Reporting Standards (International) (SFRS(I)).

Because all airlines except for Sri Lankan Airlines, and Air India are listed in their national stock exchanges, they are subject to the accounting standards adopted by their country of incorporation. In this context, SpiceJet, Garuda Indonesia, All Nippon Airways (ANA), Japan Airlines, Bangkok Airways, Thai Airways International, and VietJet prepare their financial statements in

Table 9. Airlines in Africa and Middle East.

Airline Company	Country	Listed?	Listed Where?	Single (S), Dual (D), or Triple (T) Listed	Home-country Listing	Foreign-country Listing
Royal Jordanian	Jordan	Yes	Amman	S	Yes	Yes
Kenya Airways	Kenya	Yes	Nairobi, Dares Salaam, and Uganda	T	Yes	Yes
Jazeera Airways	Kuwait	Yes	Kuwait	S	Yes	Yes
Air Mauritius	Mauritius	Yes	Mauritius	S	Yes	No
Qatar Airways	Qatar	No	Non-listed entity	–	–	–
Comair	South Africa	Yes	Johannesburg	S	Yes	No
Emirates	UAE	No	Non-listed entity	–	–	–
Air Arabia	UAE	Yes	Dubai	S	Yes	No
Abu Dhabi Aviation	UAE	Yes	Abu Dhabi	S	Yes	No

Table 10. Airlines in Asia-Pacific Region.

Airline Company	Country	Listed?	Listed Where?	Single (S) or Dual (D) Listed	Home-country Listing	Foreign-country Listing
Regional Express	Australia	Yes	Australia	S	Yes	No
Alliance Airlines	Australia	Yes	Australia	S	Yes	No
Qantas	Australia	Yes	Australia	S	Yes	No
Virgin Australia	Australia	Yes	Australia	S	Yes	No
Air India	India	No	State-owned company	–	–	–
SpiceJet	India	Yes	Bombay	S	Yes	No
Garuda Indonesia	Indonesia	Yes	Indonesia	S	Yes	No
ANA	Japan	Yes	Tokyo	S	Yes	No
Japan Airlines	Japan	Yes	Tokyo	S	Yes	No
Korean Air	Korea	Yes	Korea	S	Yes	No
Asiana Airlines	Korea	Yes	Korea	S	Yes	No
Air Asia X	Malaysia	Yes	Malaysia	S	Yes	No
Air New Zealand	New Zealand	Yes	New Zealand	S	Yes	No
Cebu Pacific Air	Philippines	Yes	Philippines	S	Yes	No
Singapore Airlines	Singapore	Yes	Singapore	S	Yes	No
Sri Lankan Airlines	Sri Lanka	No	Non-listed company	–	–	–
Bangkok Airways	Thailand	Yes	Thailand	S	Yes	No
Thai Airways International	Thailand	Yes	Thailand	S	Yes	No
Vietnam Airlines	Vietnam	Yes	Ho Chi Minh City	S	Yes	No
VietJet	Vietnam	Yes	Ho Chi Minh City	S	Yes	No

accordance with their national standards (IASB, 2016q, 2017d, 2017e, 2019a, 2019b). However, Regional Express, Alliance Airlines, Qantas, Virgin Australia, Korean Air, Asiana Airlines, Air Asia X, Air New Zealand, Cebu Pacific Air,

Singapore Airlines are required to prepare their financial statements using their country's jurisdictional IFRS (IASB, 2016s, 2017f, 2017g, 2019c, 2019d, 2019e).

On the other hand, non-listed Air India meeting the net worth of INR 250 for the year 2018 reports under Ind AS (IASB, 2019a) as well as non-listed Sri Lankan Airlines that meets one of the specified business enterprises criteria for non-listed entities (liabilities to banks and financial institutions): (1) annual turnover in excess of LKR 500 million; (2) shareholders' equity in excess of LKR 100 million; (3) gross assets in excess of LKR 300 million; (4) liabilities to banks and other financial institutions in excess of LKR 100 million; and (5) staff in excess of 1,000 persons, prepares its financial statements in accordance with Sri Lanka's jurisdictional IFRS (IASB, 2016r).

5. OBSERVATIONS RELATED TO IFRS ADOPTION FROM THE PERSPECTIVE OF AIRLINES' FINANCIAL STATEMENTS

5.1 Determinants of IFRS Adoption in the Airline Industry

This research reveals seven determinants of IFRS adoption from the perspective of airlines (Table 11). In this context, "being listed in a national or foreign stock exchange requiring IFRS based financial reporting" constitutes the primary determinant of IFRS adoption. On the other hand, the remaining six determinants focus on company-specific reasons.

5.2 Jurisdictional Versions of IFRS in the Airline Industry

IFRS as issued by the IASB constitutes the original version of IFRS practice. However, some countries adopt IFRS as issued by the IASB using accounting

Table 11.   Determinants of IFRS Adoption.

Reasons	Number of Airlines	%
Being a listed airline in a requiring national or foreign stock exchange	46	80.70
Required for non-listed entities in Qatar and UAE	2	3.51
Company size (being non-listed and large-sized) in Croatia and Sri Lanka	2	3.51
Being a listed airline in a permitting foreign stock exchange (NYSE) but incorporated in a requiring country (Brazil and Panama)	2	3.51
Being a listed airline in two permitting foreign stock exchanges (HKSE and NYSE) but incorporated in a non-permitting country (China)	2	3.51
Being a non-listed airline from Portugal and UK and operating in an industry where strong cooperation and organizational interconnectedness exist	2	3.51
Being a non-listed subsidiary airline from Ireland whose ultimate parent is a listed IFRS company	1	1.75
Total	57	100

Table 12. Jurisdictional IFRS Observed in the Financial Statements of Airlines.

Title of the IFRS Version	Country	# of Airlines	Compliance with IFRS as Issued by the IASB
IFRS as issued by the IASB + stating just IFRS	–	18	Original version
Australian Accounting Standards adopted by the Australian Accounting Standards Board	Australia	4	Compliance with IFRS as issued by the IASB except for IAS 26 (IASB, 2017f)
IFRS as issued by the IASB	Brazil	2	Compliance with IFRS issued by the IASB with some modifications such as revaluation in IAS 16, and IAS 38 is not allowed (IASB, 2017b)
IFRS as issued by the FSC	Chinese Taipei	1	Compliance with IFRS issued by the IASB with some modifications such as revaluation in IAS 16, and IAS 38 is not allowed (IASB, 2016d)
IFRS as issued by the IASB and as adopted (endorsed) by EU	EU + EEA	18	Compliance with IFRS as issued by the IASB with some modifications on IAS 39, IFRS 9, and IFRS 4 (IASB, 2018c)
HKFRS as issued by the HKICPA	Hong Kong	1	Full Compliance with IFRS as issued by the IASB (IASB, 2018b)
IFRS	Jordan	1	Compliance with IFRS issued by the IASB with some modifications such as revaluation in IAS 16, and IAS 38 as well as fair value in IAS 40 are not allowed (IASB, 2016h)
IFRS as adopted by the Republic of Korea (K-IFRS).	Korea	2	Full compliance with IFRS as issued by the IASB with some additional domestic requirements (IASB, 2017g)
MFRS	Malaysia	1	Full compliance with IFRS as issued by the IASB (IASB, 2019e)
New Zealand equivalents to IFRS ("NZ IFRS")	New Zealand	1	Full compliance with IFRS as issued by the IASB with some additional domestic requirements (IASB, 2019c)
Philippines Financial Reporting Standards	Philippines	1	Full convergence with IFRS as issued by the IASB (IASB, 2019d)
SFRS(I)	Singapore	1	Full Compliance with IFRS issued by the IASB (IASB, 2016s)
Sri Lanka Financial Reporting Standards as issued by the Institute of Chartered Accountants of Sri Lanka.	Sri Lanka	1	Compliance with IFRS issued by the IASB with some modifications such as in IAS 12 and IFRS 7 (IASB, 2016r)
IFRS as issued by the IASB	UAE	3	Full compliance with IFRS as issued by the IASB except for IAS 19 (IASB, 2016o)
TFRS	Turkey	2	Full compliance with IFRS as issued by the IASB (IASB, 2018d)
Total		57	

policy modifications and/or different titles (Table 12). These are called jurisdictional or national versions of IFRS leading to diversity in IFRS adoption (Kvaal & Nobes, 2010, p. 173; Zeff, 2007, p. 292).

Modification of IFRS accounting policies is an ongoing issue in IFRS adoption when financial statements of airlines are observed. Disclosures may state that financial statements are prepared in conformity with IFRS – IFRS as endorsed by EU, IFRS as adopted by the Republic of Korea, or IFRS as issued by FSC. However, users of financial information in the global context should think and question about the version of IFRS because "just stating the title of IFRS" may be considered as "pure IFRS as issued by the IASB" but for other titles of IFRS, it should be noted that there are some differences compared to its original version (Table 12).

On the other hand, treating IFRS as issued by the IASB differently from other forms of IFRS is an ongoing problem in IFRS adoption and has been discussed by Pacter (2005) from the perspective of Hong Kong because Pacter (2005) argued that most investors, money managers, and financial analysts in the world will be unaware that Hong Kong GAAP is identical to IFRS because the basis of presentation, notes, and auditor's reports refers to conformity with HKFRS, not IFRSs. Currently, the same issue applies not only for Hong Kong

Table 13. Statement of Compliance with IFRS as Issued by the IASB.

Airlines	Country	Jurisdictional IFRS Version	Statement of Compliance with IFRS
Regional Express	Australia	Australian Accounting Standards adopted by the AASB	Yes, financial statements comply with IFRS as issued by the IASB.
Alliance Airlines	Australia		
Qantas	Australia		
Virgin Australia	Australia		
Cathey Pacific Airlines	Hong Kong	HKFRS as issued by the HKICPA	No
Air Asia X	Malaysia	MFRS	Yes, financial statements have been prepared in accordance with the MFRS and IFRS
Air New Zealand	New Zealand	New Zealand equivalents to IFRS (NZ IFRS)	Yes, financial statements comply with NZ IFRS and IFRS
Cebu Pacific Air	Philippines	Philippines Financial Reporting Standards	No
Singapore Airlines	Singapore	SFRS(I)	Financial statements have been prepared in accordance with SFRS(I) and IFRS
Sri Lankan Airlines	Sri Lanka	Sri Lanka Financial Reporting Standards	No
Turkish Airlines	Turkey	TFRS	Yes, English translation of annual report states IFRS as issued by the IASB
Pegasus Airlines	Turkey	TFRS	No, English translation of annual report just states TFRS

but also for Philippines, Sri Lanka, and Turkey (Table 13). Since there is no additional statement of compliance with IFRS, foreign users of airline-related financial information cannot know about the financial reporting framework adopted by those airlines.

6. CONCLUSION

This chapter focuses on diversity of accounting at the financial reporting framework level for the airline industry considering past and present and observes that the majority of listed and non-listed airlines whose financial statements are publicly available on their websites prepare their financial statements under IFRS either as a requirement or due to company-specific reasons. US airlines use US GAAP in reporting and around 50% of airlines in the Asia-Pacific region are still using their national accounting standards. Being listed on a national or foreign stock exchange is the primary determinant to adopt IFRS in the airline industry. From the perspective of the airline industry, international financial reporting reflects jurisdictional IFRS leading to some obstacles in understanding the financial reporting framework.

CHAPTER 2

SOME OBSERVATIONS ON IFRS ACCOUNTING POLICY CHOICES: THE CASE OF THE AIRLINE INDUSTRY

ABSTRACT

This chapter deals with the patterns of International Financial Reporting Standards' accounting policy choices that have been analyzed by several authors in a country-specific context. Instead of a country-specific context, this chapter adopts a sector-specific approach in terms of the airline industry in a regional and global context in order to observe the patterns of cosmetic and non-cosmetic policy options. Cosmetic policy options are related to the presentation of financial information which is not expected to impact the comparability of financial information versus non-cosmetic policy options are considered to be policy options that are related to measurement and, therefore, if there is more than one allowable accounting treatment, the comparability of financial information weakens. In the context of the airline industry, this chapter considers the patterns of policy choices related to IAS 1 Presentation of Financial Statements, IAS 2 Inventory, IAS 7 Statement of Cash Flows, IAS 16 Property, Plant and Equipment, IAS 38 Intangible Assets, and IAS 40 Investment Property, within the framework of frequently observed policy options as well as taking depreciation methods and expected useful life into consideration in terms of industry-specific policy options in order to observe whether there is uniformity rather than diversity in the airline industry for presentation and measurement.

Keywords: Accounting policy choice; International Financial Reporting Standards; comparability; uniformity; diversity; airline

Perspectives on International Financial Reporting and Auditing in the Airline Industry
Studies in Managerial and Financial Accounting, Volume 35, 21–50
Copyright © 2022 by Emerald Publishing Limited
All rights of reproduction in any form reserved
ISSN: 1479-3512/doi:10.1108/S1479-351220220000035002

1. INTRODUCTION

As stated by IAS 8, accounting policies refer to the specific principles, bases, conventions, rules, and practices applied by an entity in preparing and presenting financial statements [IAS 8.5] (IASB, 2018h). In this context, International Financial Reporting Standards (IFRS) provide alternative accounting policy choices. These policy options have led to the survival of international differences of practice under IFRS in addition to Nobes (2006) has noted that these are different versions of IFRS, different translations of IFRS, gaps in IFRS, covert options, vague criteria, interpretations in IFRS, estimations in IFRS, transitional or first-time adoption issues, and imperfect enforcement of IFRS.

From an historical perspective, Nobes (2006) states that the International Accounting Standards Committee (currently International Accounting Standards Board (IASB)) prepared its international standards by inserting policy options from its inception to the project of Comparability of Financial Statements because many standards had been issued before the former conceptual framework (1989) was prepared. In addition, the members of the committee and their representatives had diverse backgrounds and were subject to political pressures. As part of the Comparability of Financial Statements Project, these options were gradually removed from practice, such as removal of completed contract method in 1995, elimination of Last-in First-out in 2003, elimination of choice of expensing for interest costs on constructed assets (qualifying assets) in 2007, and removal of proportionate consolidation in 2012 (Doupnik & Perera, 2014; Nobes 2006, 2013).

In terms of IFRS policy options, Nobes (2006) suggests a framework for the further research on accounting policy choices by focusing on 18 clear overt options, 21 covert options, and 12 estimates. Following Nobes (2006), KPMG and von Keitz (2006) analyzed policy options for the year 2005 in terms of listed entities from France, Germany, Hong Kong, Italy, the Netherlands, South Africa, Spain, Sweden, Switzerland, and the UK. Thereafter, Kvaal and Nobes (2010) examined the patterns of 16 accounting policy options, of which nine relate to presentation and seven relate to measurement, in the context of the largest listed entities in Australia, France, Germany, Spain, and the UK. It collected data from 2005/2006 financial statements from European countries and 2007/2008 financial statements in Australia, considering the following policy options:

1. (a) income statement by function, (b) by nature, or (c) neither;
2. (a) inclusion of a line for EBIT or operating profit, or (b) no such line;
3. (a) equity accounting results included in "operating," (b) immediately after, or (c) after finance;
4. (a) balance sheet shows assets = credits, (b) showing net assets;
5. (a) liquidity decreasing in balance sheet (cash at top), (b) liquidity increasing;
6. (a) statement of changes in equity, including dividends and share issues, (b) SORIE, not including them;
7. (a) direct operating cash flows, (b) indirect;
8. (a) dividends received shown as operating cash flow, (b) as investing;

9. (a) interest paid shown as operating cash flow, (b) as financing;
10. (a) only cost for property, plant, and equipment (PPE), (b) some fair value;
11. (a) investment property at cost, (b) at fair value;
12. (a) some designation of financial assets at fair value, (b) none;
13. (a) capitalization of interest on construction, (b) expensing;
14. (a) first-in first-out (FIFO) for inventory cost, (b) weighted average (WA);
15. (a) actuarial gains and losses to Statement of Recognized Income and Expense (SORIE), (b) to income in full, or (c) corridor; and
16. (a) proportional consolidation of some joint ventures, (b) only equity method.

Following Kvaal and Nobes (2010), the paper of Cole, Branson, and Breesch (2011) examines the patterns of 34 IFRS policy options on European listed entities from Belgium, Germany, the Netherlands, and the UK, in the industries of industrial goods and services or technology as well as Nobes (2013) replicating the research of Kvaal and Nobes (2010) in Australia, France, Germany, Spain, and the UK by extending it to Netherlands, Italy, and Sweden using a new data set from 2008/2009 financial statements and includes Canada to observe the patterns of IFRS policy options using first adoption financial statements of the Canadian listed entities for the year 2011. This trend analysis determines the patterns of the 14 policy options without including the patterns of 2 ((a) inclusion of a line for EBIT or operating profit, or (b) no such line), and 8 ((a) dividends received shown as operating cash flow, (b) as investing) stated above compared to Kvaal and Nobes (2010).

It should be noted that Kvaal and Nobes (2010) and Nobes (2013) analyzed the patterns of IFRS policy options that are frequently observed in listed entities versus KPMG and von Keitz (2006) and Cole et al. (2011) analyzed the patterns of policy options that are frequently and non-frequently observed in listed entities.

Some of the policy options stated above has been removed since KPMG and von Keitz (2006), Kvaal and Nobes (2010), Cole et al. (2011), and Nobes (2013) were issued: 6 (Statement of Changes in Equity, including dividends and shares issues or SORIE, not including them), 13 (capitalization or expense of interest), 15 (actuarial gain to OCI, income in full or corridor method), and 16 (proportionate consolidation or equity method for jointly controlled entities) and new ones were added such as (1) presentation of comprehensive income under (a) one-statement approach or (b) two-statement approach as of the 2007 under IAS 1 [IAS 1.10A] (IASB, 2018e); and (2) the presentation of subsidiaries, associates, and joint ventures on the individual financial statements at cost, at fair value, or using the equity method as of the year 2015 under IAS 27 [IAS 27.10] (IASB, 2018j).

Following the removal of some policy options and addition of new ones, Akdoğan and Öztürk (2015) analyzed the policy options for the year 2008/09 in terms of listed entities from the UK, Germany, France, Italy, Australia, and Turkey. Lourenço, Sarquis, Branco, and Pais (2015) extended the debate on policy options to other European countries, namely Belgium, Denmark, Finland, Norway, Poland, Russia, and Switzerland besides the European countries analyzed in Nobes (2013) and Akdoğan and Öztürk (2015). In addition, Lourenço, Sarquis, Branco, and Magro (2018) extended the debate on the policy options to an additional 20 countries including Australia, Brazil, Canada, Chile, France, Germany, Greece, Israel, Italy, Kuwait, the Netherlands, New Zealand, Oman, Peru, South Africa, South Korea, Spain, Sweden, Turkey, and the UK, besides seven European countries analyzed in Lourenço et al. (2015). Both papers use the 2013 consolidated financial statements of largest publicly listed entities.

In addition, within the literature of accounting policy options, several papers such as Cairns, Massoudi, Taplin, and Tarca (2011) in the context of listed entities in Australia and the UK for the year 2005, Taplin, Verona, and Doni (2011) in the context of listed entities from Germany, France, UK, and Italy for the year 2009, and Christensen and Nikolaev (2013) in the context of listed entities from Germany and the UK for the year 2005/2006, De Souza and Lemes (2016) in the context of listed entities from Brazil, Chile, and Peru for the years 2009–2013 particularly analyzed the patterns of fair value accounting under IAS 16, IAS 38, and IAS 40.

The common denominator of these prior research papers, such as Kvaal and Nobes (2010), Nobes (2013), De Souza and Lemes (2016), Akdoğan and Öztürk (2015), and Lourenço et al. (2015, 2018) indicates that (1) they focus on comparative analysis of IFRS accounting policy options related to listed entities from different countries and (2) diversity in financial reporting is unavoidably expected among the listed IFRS entities operating in different countries at different levels if there is more than one allowable accounting policy option under IFRS. Considering prior research, the objective of this chapter is to focus on whether diversity in financial reporting in the context of the airline industry is replaced by uniformity to some extent in terms of IFRS policy options.

The chapter develops 20 hypotheses of which 18 are based on accounting policy options that are observable in every firm and two are based on accounting policy options that are particularly important for the airline industry. The 18 hypotheses include cosmetic and non-cosmetic policy options. Therefore, it should be noted that cosmetic policy options do not influence comparative analysis of financial information, but it makes sense to observe the preferences given to those options in order to understand the presentation in the global context versus non-cosmetic policy options influence the preparation of financial information, thus leading to comparability of financial information in the airline industry.

1. Balance sheet is entitled as (a) Statement of Financial Position or (b) Balance Sheet [IAS 1.10] (IASB, 2018e).
   Akdoğan and Öztürk (2015) reveal that there is diversity in titling this statement among listed IFRS entities operating in different countries. Therefore, the following hypothesis can be stated:

   H1. There is diversity in titling this statement in the airline industry.

2. Balance sheet (a) shows assets = credits, (b) showing net assets, or (c) neither. Nobes (2013), Akdoğan and Öztürk (2015), and Lourenço et al. (2018) reveal that there is diversity in the presentation of balance sheet among listed IFRS entities operating in different countries. Therefore, the following hypothesis can be stated:

H2. There is diversity in the presentation of balance sheet in the airline industry.

3. Assets are classified (a) liquidity decreasing in balance sheet (cash at top) or (b) liquidity increasing [IAS 1.60].
   Nobes (2013), Akdoğan and Öztürk (2015), and Lourenço et al. (2018) reveal that there is diversity in the presentation of assets among listed IFRS entities operating in different countries. Therefore, the following hypothesis can be stated:

H3. There is diversity in classifying assets on the balance sheet in the airline industry.

4. Traditional income statement (a) by function or (b) by nature [IAS 1.102, IAS 1.103].
   KPMG and von Keitz (2006), Nobes (2013), Akdoğan and Öztürk (2015), and Lourenço et al. (2018) reveal that there is diversity in presenting expenses on the income statement among listed IFRS entities operating in different countries. Therefore, the following hypothesis can be stated:

H4. There is diversity in presenting expenses on the income statement in the airline industry.

5. Comprehensive income is presented under (a) one-statement approach or (b) two-statement approach [IAS 1.10A].
   Akdoğan and Öztürk (2015) and Lourenço et al. (2018) reveal that there is diversity in presenting comprehensive income among listed IFRS entities operating in different countries. Therefore, the following hypothesis can be stated:

H5. There is diversity in presenting comprehensive income in the airline industry.

6. If the comprehensive income is reported under one-statement approach, Öztürk (2011) reveals that there is diversity in titling the statement of comprehensive income (SOCI) among listed IFRS entities operating in different countries [IAS 1.10]. Therefore, the following hypothesis can be stated:

H6. There is a diversity in titling the statement of comprehensive income in the airline industry.

7. If the comprehensive income is reported under two-statement approach, Öztürk (2011) reveals that there is diversity in titling the traditional income statement among listed IFRS entities operating in different countries [IAS 1.10]. Therefore, the following hypothesis can be stated:

H7. There is diversity in titling the traditional income statement in the airline industry.

8. If the comprehensive income is reported under a two-statement approach, Öztürk (2011) reveals that there is diversity in titling the second statement reporting comprehensive income among listed IFRS entities operating in different countries [IAS 1.10]. Therefore, the following hypothesis can be stated:

H8. There is diversity in entitling the second statement reporting comprehensive income in the airline industry.

9. Equity accounting results (a) included in "operating profit" and (b) excluded from operating profit [IAS 1.82c].
Nobes (2013) and Lourenço et al. (2018) reveal that there is diversity in the classification of equity accounting results among listed IFRS entities operating in different countries. Therefore, the following hypothesis can be stated:

H9. There is diversity in the classification of equity accounting results in the airline industry.

10. Statement of cash flows under (a) direct method and (b) indirect method [IAS 7.18] (IASB, 2018g).
KPMG and von Keitz (2006), Cole et al. (2011), Nobes (2013), Akdoğan and Öztürk (2015), and Lourenço et al. (2018) reveal that there is diversity in the method of presenting cash flows from operating activities among listed IFRS entities operating in different countries. Therefore, the following hypothesis can be stated:

H10. There is diversity in the method of presenting cash flows from operating activities in the airline industry.

11. Interest received shown as (a) operating cash flow or (b) as investing [IAS 7.33].
KPMG and von Keitz (2006) and Cole et al. (2011) reveals that there is diversity in the classification of interest received among listed IFRS entities operating in different countries. Therefore, the following hypothesis can be stated:

H11. There is diversity in the classification of interest received in the airline industry.

12. Interest paid shown as (a) operating cash flow or (b) as financing [IAS 7.33].
KPMG and von Keitz (2006), Cole et al. (2011), Nobes (2013), and Lourenço et al. (2018) reveal that there is diversity in the classification of interest payments among listed IFRS entities operating in different countries. Therefore, the following hypothesis can be stated:

H12. There is diversity in the classification of interest payments in the airline industry.

13. Dividend received shown as (a) operating cash flow or (b) as investing [IAS 7.33].
KPMG and von Keitz (2006), Kvaal and Nobes (2010), and Cole et al. (2011) reveal that there is diversity in the classification of dividend received among listed IFRS entities operating in different countries. Therefore, the following hypothesis can be stated:

H13. There is diversity in the classification of dividends received in the airline industry.

14. Dividends paid shown as (a) operating cash flow or (b) as financing [IAS 7.34].
KPMG and von Keitz (2006) reveal that there is diversity in the classification of dividend payments among listed IFRS entities operating in different countries. Therefore, the following hypothesis can be stated:

H14. There is diversity in the classification of dividend payments in the airline industry.

15. Inventory is measured under (a) FIFO, (b) WA, or (c) other [IAS 2.23, IAS 2.25] (IASB, 2018f).
KPMG and von Keitz (2006), Nobes (2013), Akdoğan and Öztürk (2015), and Lourenço et al. (2018) reveal that there is diversity in the valuation of inventory items among listed IFRS entities operating in different countries. Therefore, the following hypothesis can be stated:

H15. There is diversity in the valuation of inventory items in the airline industry.

16. PPE items are measured using the (a) cost model or (b) revaluation model [IAS 16.29] (IASB, 2018i).
KPMG and von Keitz (2006), Cole et al. (2011), Cairns et al. (2011), Christensen and Nikolaev (2013), Nobes (2013), Akdoğan and Öztürk (2015), De Souza and Lemes (2016), and Lourenço et al. (2018) reveal that there is diversity in the measurement of PPE items among listed IFRS entities operating in different countries. Therefore, the following hypothesis can be stated:

H16. There is diversity in the measurement of PPE items in the airline industry.

17. Intangible assets are measured using the (a) cost model or (b) revaluation model [IAS 38.72] (IASB, 2018k).
Taplin et al. (2011) and De Souza and Lemes (2016) reveal that there is diversity in the measurement of intangible assets among listed IFRS entities operating in different countries compared to Cole et al. (2011), Cairns et al. (2011), Christensen and Nikolaev (2013), and Akdoğan and Öztürk (2015). Therefore, the following hypothesis can be stated:

H17. There is diversity in the measurement of intangible assets in the airline industry.

18. Investment property is measured using the (a) cost model or (b) fair value model [IAS 40.30] (IASB, 2018l).
KPMG and von Keitz (2006), Cairns et al. (2011), Christensen and Nikolaev (2013), Nobes (2013), Akdoğan and Öztürk (2015), and De Souza and Lemes (2015) reveal that there is diversity in the measurement of investment properties among listed IFRS entities operating in different countries compared to Cole et al. (2011). Therefore, the following hypothesis can be stated:

H18: There is diversity in the measurement of investment properties in the airline industry.

This chapter has the following structure: Section 2 presents a literature review on accounting policy choice in the airline industry; Section 3 explains the data, accounting period for the research, and the research methodology; Section 4 discusses the findings related to accounting policy choices on IAS 1, IAS 2, IAS 7, IAS 16, IAS 38, and IAS 40 in the airline industry. Finally, Section 5 presents concluding remarks along with main findings.

2. LITERATURE REVIEW ON ACCOUNTING POLICY CHOICE IN THE AIRLINE INDUSTRY

In terms of the accounting policy options in the airline industry, Tan, Tower, Hancock, and Taplin (2002) provides guidance on the diversity of accounting policies in the industry considering the KPMG's and International Air Transport Association (IATA)'s 1992 survey of airlines' annual reports. In addition, Lavi (2016) clarifies another aspect of the diversity of accounting policy options in the airline industry.

One of the areas that diversity in accounting policy options has been observed in prior research is the recognition method of unrealized exchange differences arising from the translation of foreign currency long-term monetary liabilities. In this context, there are two methods that have been used frequently in the airline industry: (1) immediate recognition of unrealized differences in the profit and loss account or (2) the direct-to-equity approach. To prevent this diversity and to provide the basis for comparative financial information, IATA issued the first airline accounting guideline AAG 1: Translation of Long-Term Foreign Currency Borrowings in 1994, leading to immediate recognition of unrealized foreign exchange differences through profit or loss account as the recommended accounting policy that is consistent with IAS 21. In this context, Tan et al. (2002) stated that the immediate recognition approach was adopted by 54% of airlines after the issuance of the guideline. Currently, airlines reporting under IFRS are required to adopt the immediate recognition approach as the only option under IAS 21 leading to uniformity in the preparation of comparative financial information [IAS 21.28] (IASB, 2018m).

A second area that the diversity in accounting policy options has been observed in prior research is the recognition of frequent-flyer liabilities. To prevent diversity in the recognition of frequent-flyer liabilities, IATA issued the second airline accounting guideline AAG 2: Frequent-Flyer Programme Accounting which identified three methods that have been used by airlines: (1) the contingent-liability method; (2) incremental-cost method; and (3) deferred-revenue approach. In this context, Tan et al. (2002) stated that the incremental-cost method has been the recommended method as well as revealing that 93% of airlines recognize frequent-flyer liabilities using the incremental-cost method versus 7% of airlines that use the deferred-revenue approach after the issuance of the guideline. However, IASB issued IFRIC 13 Customer Loyalty Programmes in 2007 by adopting the deferred-revenue approach to establish uniformity for the recognition of frequent-flyer liabilities (Acar & Bayramoğlu, 2020). Therefore, the diversity observed in the recognition of frequent-flyer liabilities under IFRS has been resolved. IFRIC 13 was replaced by IFRS 15 Revenue from Contracts with Customers as of 2018.

A third area that diversity in accounting policy options has been observed in prior research is the recognition of maintenance costs for owned and leased assets. Tan et al. (2002) stated that there have been two methods adopted in recognizing maintenance costs: (1) expensing the cost as a period expense or (2) capitalizing the cost and then amortizing it to the profit and loss account over the period until the next scheduled maintenance. After the former IATA's guidance on maintenance costs was issued, Tan et al. (2002) determined that 89% of airlines recognize it as a period expense versus 11% use the capitalize-and-amortize method. However, the accounting policy for the recognition of maintenance costs is different under IFRS because there is no accounting policy choice. According to IAS 16, maintenance costs for owned aircraft and engines are recorded as expenses during the period when they are incurred as part of regular maintenance. If the maintenance extends the useful life of the asset, maintenance costs on aircraft airframes and engines are capitalized and depreciated over the extended useful life of the aircraft [IAS 16.12, IAS 16.13, and IAS 16.14]. This is consistent with the recent Airline Disclosure Guide: Maintenance Accounting, Aircraft Acquisition Cost and Depreciation as well as IATA Industry Accounting Working Group Guidance IFRS 16, Leases (IATA, 2016b, 2016c, 2020e). On the other hand, this is not the accounting policy for leased aircraft assets, and a provision for major overhauls and inspections is required for leased aircraft assets due to the contractual return condition obligations under IAS 37 (IATA, 2020e). Therefore, it should be noted that the accounting policy under IFRS is uniform in reporting maintenance costs to provide comparative financial information.

Forth area that diversity in accounting policy options has been observed in prior research is the recognition of joint ventures because joint ventures which allow airlines to share risks and capital costs of new aircraft, routes, and facilities are common in airline industry (Lavi, 2016, p. 80). Under IFRS, the former IAS 31 allowed the recognition of jointly controlled entities under two methods: (1) proportionate consolidation or (2) equity method (Akdoğan & Öztürk, 2015). However, IFRS 11 which supersedes IAS 31 removed the option of proportionate consolidation, leading to the preparation of comparable financial information in the airline industry [IFRS 11.24] (IASB, 2018n).

Last area that diversity in accounting policy options has been observed in prior research is the calculation of depreciation. To prevent this diversification, IATA issued the third airline accounting guidance AAG 3: Components of Fleet Acquisition Cost and Associated Depreciation which recommends the use of the straight-line method but there have been two methods commonly used in the airline industry: straight-line method and units of output depreciation (units of activity). After the issuance of AAG 3, Tan et al. (2002) observed that 96% of airlines prefer straight-line method, leading to uniformity to a great extent to provide comparative financial information in the airline industry.

In the context of diversity of airline-specific accounting policy options, it should be noted that several policy options were eliminated through the adoption IATA's guides or through IFRS adoption in preparing and presenting comparable financial statements in the airline industry. Currently, the only airline-specific policy option that exists under IFRS is the three depreciation methods provided by IAS 16: (1) straight-line method, (2) double-declining, and (3) units of production (units of activity) [IAS 16.62] (IASB, 2018i).

19. Depreciation of PPE items using (a) straight-line, (b) diminishing balance, and (c) units of production (units of activity).

Akdoğan and Öztürk (2015) reveal that there is diversity in the depreciation methods used among listed IFRS entities operating in different countries. In addition to Tan et al. (2002), the case prepared by (Bujaki & Durocher, 2014) indicates that the airlines may adopt different depreciation methods such as straight-line or units of activity using 2009 financial statements of three airlines from Canada. Therefore, the following hypothesis can be stated:

H19. There is diversity in the depreciation methods used in the airline industry.

20. Even if depreciation policies of airlines are the same for similar depreciable assets, the estimated useful life of the assets would be different from one airline to another as stated by Mohrman (2009). Therefore, the following hypothesis can be stated:

H20. There is diversity in the expected useful life of airframes in the airline industry considering the component depreciation under IFRS [IAS 16.44].

3. DATA AND RESEARCH METHODOLOGY

3.1 Data

The data have been collected from the IFRS financial statements of the 57 airlines whose annual reporting period ended on December 31, 2018, or its equivalent for the year 2019. The sample has been developed in the regional and global context (Table 1).

3.2 Research Methodology

This research assesses the collected data using the frequency of distribution method regarding the patterns of the IFRS accounting policy choices in terms of presentation and measurement in the airline industry.

4. FINDINGS AND DISCUSSION

4.1 Observations on IAS 1 Presentation of Financial Statements

In terms of IAS 1, this section analyses the trends of the following issues in terms of the airline industry.

(1) Balance sheet is entitled as (a) Statement of Financial Position (benchmark) or (b) Balance Sheet.
    Findings reveal that the preparers of financial information prefer the title of statement of financial position in preparing and presenting this statement, consisting of 77% of the airlines (Fig. 1).
(2) Balance sheet format is based on (a) Assets = Liabilities + Equity (total assets), (b) Assets – Liabilities = Equity (net assets), or (c) Equity + Long-term Liabilities = Total Assets – Current Liabilities (capital employed).

Table 1. List of Airlines.

Americas	Turkish Airlines
GOL Linhas Aereas	Pegasus Airlines
Azul Brazilian Airlines	Norwegian Air
Air Transat	*Africa – Middle East*
WestJet	Royal Jordanian
Air Canada	Kenya Airways
Cargojet Airways	Jazeera Airways
LATAM Airlines Group	Air Mauritius
Aeromexico	Qatar Airways
Volaris	Comair
COPA Airlines	Emirates
Europe	Air Arabia
Croatia Airlines	Abu Dhabi Aviation
Finnair – Finnair Group	*Asia-Pacific*
Air France – KLM Group	Regional Express
Lufthansa Group	Alliance Airlines
Aegean Group	Qantas
Aer Lingus	Virgin Australia
Ryanair	Korean Air
Wizz Air	Asiana Airlines
TAP Group	Air Asia X
SAS – SAS Group	Air New Zealand
International Airlines Group	Cebu Pacific Air
Virgin Atlantic Group	Singapore Airlines
Air Partner	Sri Lankan Airlines
Easy Jet	*China and North Asia*
British Airways	Cathay Pacific Airlines
Fast Jet	Air China Group
Icelandair	China Southern Airlines
Norwegian Air	China Eastern Airlines
El Al	China Airlines
Aeroflot	

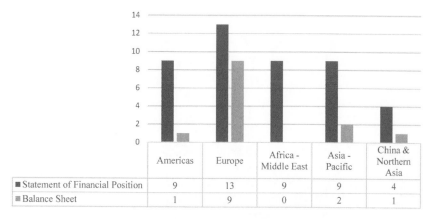

	Americas	Europe	Africa - Middle East	Asia - Pacific	China & Northern Asia
■ Statement of Financial Position	9	13	9	9	4
■ Balance Sheet	1	9	0	2	1

Fig. 1. Title of the Balance Sheet.

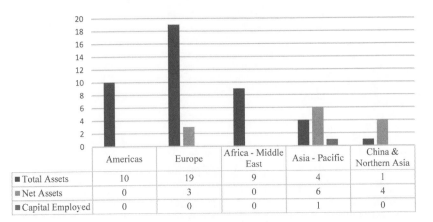

	Americas	Europe	Africa - Middle East	Asia - Pacific	China & Northern Asia
■ Total Assets	10	19	9	4	1
■ Net Assets	0	3	0	6	4
■ Capital Employed	0	0	0	1	0

Fig. 2.   Format of the Balance Sheet.

Findings reveal that preparers of financial information prefer the format of "total assets" in presenting this statement, referring to 75% of the airlines (Fig. 2). On the other hand, 23% of airlines have this statement in the format of "net assets." In addition, the format of the balance sheet of Singapore Airlines is not like any of these formats because the airline's balance sheet is in the format of "capital employed."

(3) Balance sheet shows assets (a) liquidity increasing order (from non-current to current) or (b) liquidity decreasing order (from current to non-current). Findings reveal that 58% of the airlines declare a classified balance sheet (assets with increasing liquidity) versus 42% of the airlines declare a classified balance sheet (assets with decreasing liquidity) (Fig. 3).

When 2nd and 3rd policy choices are considered together, this research reveals that there are six formats of the balance sheet in the airline industry

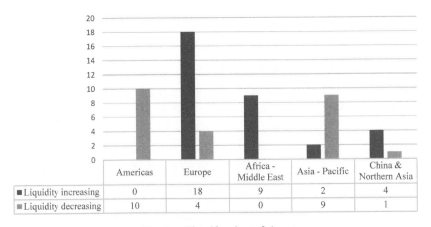

	Americas	Europe	Africa - Middle East	Asia - Pacific	China & Northern Asia
■ Liquidity increasing	0	18	9	2	4
■ Liquidity decreasing	10	4	0	9	1

Fig. 3.   Classification of Assets.

leading to diversity. The first three of them indicate a country-specific structure but the last three of them show an industry-specific nature.

Formats 1 and 2 are based on the concept of "total assets" as shown in Figs. 4 and 5 versus format 3 depends on the concept of "net assets" as shown in Fig. 6. The common denominator of these formats is to show totals of assets, liabilities, and equity items in addition to classified totals of assets and liabilities. No other metric is presented in these formats. Therefore, they could be considered as country-specific in nature.

Format 1 is used by the airlines from Northern and Southern American countries, as well as airlines from some European, Asia-pacific, and Northern Asian countries, namely from Brazil, Canada, Chile, Chinese Taipei, Israel, Mexico, Panama, Philippines, Russia, South Korea, Sri Lanka, and Turkey (Fig. 4).

Format 2 is used by the airlines from European countries including members of the European Union, and European Economic Area, as well as from African and Middle Eastern countries, namely from Croatia, Finland, France, Germany, Greece, Ireland, Iceland, Jersey, Jordan, Kenya, Kuwait, Mauritius, Norway, Portugal, Qatar, South Africa, Spain, Sweden, UAE, and the UK[1] (Fig. 5). On the other hand, different from others, Ryanair from the UK classifies its liabilities from current to non-current.

Format 3 is used by the airlines from Australia and New Zealand (Fig. 6).

Format 4 is used by the airlines from China, Malaysia, and some airlines from the UK[2] (Fig. 7). It is like format 3, except for the manner of asset classification. In addition to conventional totals reported on the balance sheet, Air Partner, Easy Jet, and Air Asia X report net current assets (liabilities) versus Virgin Atlantic, Air China, China Southern Airlines and China Eastern Airlines report not only net current assets (liabilities) but also total assets minus current liabilities. These two metrics are presented right after the current liabilities and provide the financial analysts the opportunity to analyze net working capital and capital employed. Due to the additional metrics, this balance sheet could be considered as an industry-specific statement, but priority was given to the asset presentation at the top in a traditional manner.

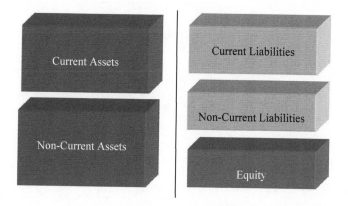

Fig. 4. Format 1 "Total Assets" Balance Sheet (Assets with Decreasing Liquidity).

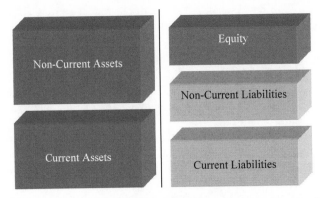

Fig. 5. Format 2 "Total Assets" Balance Sheet (Assets with Increasing Liquidity).

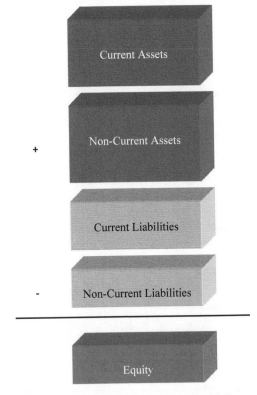

Fig. 6. Format 3 "Net Assets" Balance Sheet (Assets with Decreasing Liquidity).

Format 5 is used by an airline only from Singapore (Singapore Airlines) (Fig. 8). In addition to conventional totals, what is different from prior balance sheets is the fact that equity + non-current liabilities are presented at the top

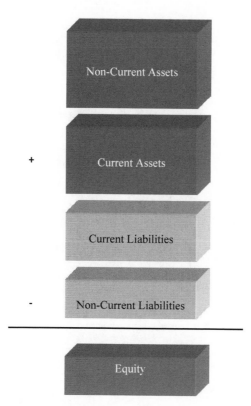

Fig. 7. Format 4 "Net Assets" Balance Sheet (Assets with Increasing Liquidity).

of the balance sheet to emphasize capital employed that is used to finance non-current assets. In a capital-intensive industry, preference given to reporting of capital employed at the top is reasonable to provide information on the financial soundness of the airline. In addition, the airline reports net current assets (liabilities) right after the current liabilities to measure net working capital.

Format 6 is used by one airline from Hong Kong (Cathay Pacific Airlines) (Fig. 9). In addition to conventional totals reported on the balance sheet, this format reports three additional metrics: net current assets (liabilities), net non-current assets (liabilities), and total assets minus current liabilities. The airline reports non-current assets and non-current liabilities at the top of the balance sheet to provide financial information about whether the airline can finance its non-current assets with its non-current liabilities. This type of reporting is reasonable for a capital-intensive firm. In addition, it reports net current assets (liabilities) and the amount of capital employed after the current liabilities. Therefore, this format makes it possible to directly observe and analyze the airline's ability to meet its current liabilities with its current assets, the airline's ability to finance its non-current assets with its non-current liabilities, and its capital employed. This balance sheet format provides the opportunity to have a complete and clear financial picture of the airline in terms of its presentation format and its metrics.

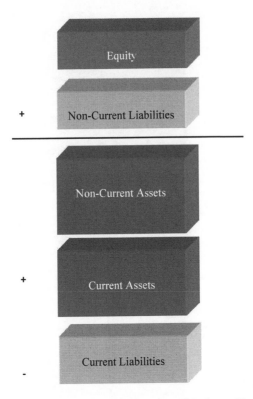

Fig. 8.   Format 5 "Capital Employed" Balance Sheet
(Assets with Increasing Liquidity).

Reporting assets at the top of the balance sheet is a traditional form. However, preparing and presenting a balance sheet specific to the airline industry could be reasonable considering the relevance and materiality concepts of accounting. Instead of presenting assets at the top, items that are expected to provide relevant financial information should be provided at the top of the balance sheet to underline strategic items from an airline perspective. In this context, it should be noted that format 6 has an important role to analyze the size of leased aircrafts within non-current assets versus their effect over the short-term and long-term lease liabilities to evaluate the financial position of the airline (Fig. 9).

(4) Traditional income statement is presented (a) by function, or (b) by nature.

In line with the prior research of Baker, Ding, and Stolowy (2005), findings reveal that an income statement by nature is the dominant practice in airline financial reporting, indicating that 75% of the airlines report their expenses by nature versus 25% of the airlines that report their expenses by function (Fig. 10).

When the determinants of presenting this statement by function or by nature are observed in terms of the airline industry, it should be noted that (a) presenting an income statement by function or by nature could be the only option under

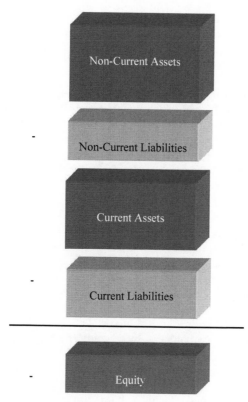

Fig. 9. Format 6 "Net Assets" Balance Sheet (Assets with Increasing Liquidity).

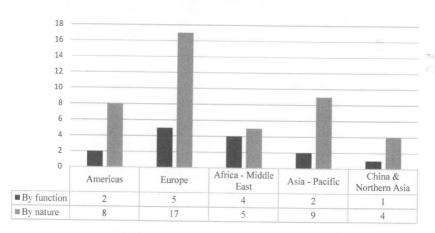

	Americas	Europe	Africa - Middle East	Asia - Pacific	China & Northern Asia
■ By function	2	5	4	2	1
■ By nature	8	17	5	9	4

Fig. 10. Presentation of Expenses on the Income Statement.

the national accounting practice of any airline's country as a reflection over IFRS consistent with Kvaal and Nobes (2010) and Akdoğan and Öztürk (2015), and (b) presenting an income statement by nature could be a mimetic practice in order to follow foreign competitors in the airline industry even if income statement by nature is not allowed under national accounting practice (Baker et al., 2005).

Considering the determinants mentioned above, the following examples were detected from the analysis of airlines:

(a) Lourenço et al. (2018) indicates that 80% of listed entities in Kuwait, 83% of listed entities in Chile, 88% of listed entities in Russia, 90% of listed entities in Sweden, 98% of listed entities in South Korea, and all the listed entities in Brazil, Greece, Israel, and Turkey prepare their income statements by function considering their 2013 IFRS financial statements. This dominant practice of income statement by function may be clarified by Kvaal and Nobes (2010) and Nobes (2013), which show evidence that the pre-IFRS policies is the most powerful single explanatory variable for a company's IFRS policy choices. In this context, findings reveal that Gol Linhas Aereas, El Al, Latam Airlines, Korean Air, Asiana Airlines, Turkish Airlines, and Pegasus Airlines continue to prepare their 2018 IFRS income statements by function as a reflection of pre-IFRS national accounting practice over IFRS. However, Azul Brazilian Airlines, Aegean, Aeroflot, Jazeera Airways, and SAS reveal a mimetic practice by presenting their 2018 IFRS income statements by nature rather than by function.

(b) In France, an income statement by nature is required under local accounting practice for non-consolidated financial statements but an IFRS income statement could be by nature or by function (Le Manh, 2017). When Kvaal and Nobes (2010) and Lourenço et al. (2015) are comparatively examined, it should be noted that there is an increasing trend from 54.8% to 73% in France on the adoption of IFRS income statement by function. Therefore, the adoption of income statement by nature could be considered as a mimetic practice for Air France – KLM.

(c) In China, an income statement by function is required under Accounting Standards for Business Enterprises of China (Riccardi, 2016, p. 234). However, Air China, China Southern Airlines, and China Eastern Airlines are listed in stock exchanges outside of China (please see Chapter 1). Therefore, they prefer preparing their IFRS income statement by nature. This situation could also be a mimetic practice.

(d) In the UK, this research points out that British Airways prepared an income statement by function up until 2005 (British Airways, 2005, 2006). In 2006, the airline switched from by function to by nature as a mimetic practice at the first-time adoption of IFRS.

(e) In Ireland, this research determines that Aer Lingus also prepared an income statement by function up until 2005 (Aer Lingus, 2005, 2006). In 2006, the airline moved from by function to by nature as a mimetic practice at the first-time adoption of IFRS.

(5) Comprehensive income is reported (a) under one-statement approach or (b) under two-statement approach.

Findings reveal that 68% of the airlines declare their comprehensive income under two-statement approach versus 32% of them declare their comprehensive income under one-statement approach (Fig. 11).

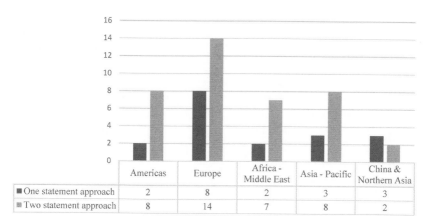

	Americas	Europe	Africa - Middle East	Asia - Pacific	China & Northern Asia
One statement approach	2	8	2	3	3
Two statement approach	8	14	7	8	2

Fig. 11. Presentation of Comprehensive Income.

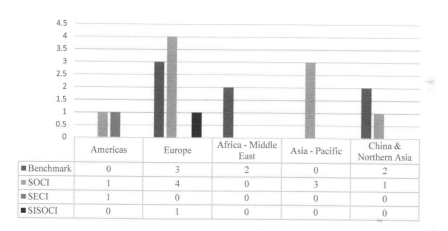

	Americas	Europe	Africa - Middle East	Asia - Pacific	China & Northern Asia
Benchmark	0	3	2	0	2
SOCI	1	4	0	3	1
SECI	1	0	0	0	0
SISOCI	0	1	0	0	0

Fig. 12. Titling SOCI Under One-statement Approach.

(6) If the comprehensive income is reported under one-statement approach, this statement is titled as (a) statement of profit or loss and other comprehensive income (SOPLOCI) (benchmark); (b) SOCI; (c) statement of earnings and comprehensive income; and (d) statement of income including statement of other comprehensive income, given the flexibility provided by the standard.

In terms of the 18 airlines reporting under one-statement approach, findings reveal that the primary and secondary title selection of the preparers of financial information is the title of SOCI, consisting of 50% of airlines versus the benchmark title consisting of 39% of airlines (Fig. 12).

(7) If the comprehensive income is reported under two-statement approach, the traditional income statement is titled as (a) statement of profit or loss (benchmark); (b) statement of operations; (c) statement of earnings; (d) statement

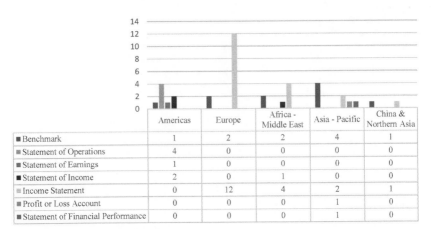

	Americas	Europe	Africa - Middle East	Asia - Pacific	China & Northern Asia
■ Benchmark	1	2	2	4	1
■ Statement of Operations	4	0	0	0	0
■ Statement of Earnings	1	0	0	0	0
■ Statement of Income	2	0	1	0	0
■ Income Statement	0	12	4	2	1
■ Profit or Loss Account	0	0	0	1	0
■ Statement of Financial Performance	0	0	0	1	0

Fig. 13.   Titling Traditional Income Statement under Two-statement Approach.

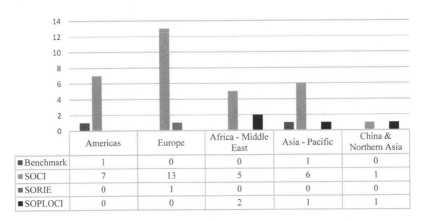

	Americas	Europe	Africa - Middle East	Asia - Pacific	China & Northern Asia
■ Benchmark	1	0	0	1	0
■ SOCI	7	13	5	6	1
■ SORIE	0	1	0	0	0
■ SOPLOCI	0	0	2	1	1

Fig. 14.   Titling SOCI Under Two-statement Approach.

of income; (e) income statement; (f) profit or loss account; and (g) statement of financial performance, given the flexibility provided by the standard.

Considering 39 airlines reporting under two-statement approach, findings reveal that 49% of airlines use the title of income statement, and 26% of them use the benchmark title (Fig. 13).

(8) If the comprehensive income is reported under two-statement approach, the second statement reporting comprehensive income is entitled as (a) statement of other comprehensive income (benchmark), (b) SOCI, (c) SORIE, and (d) SOPLOCI, given the flexibility provided by the standard.

Findings reveal that 82% of airlines use the title of SOCI (Fig. 14).

(9) Equity accounting results are (a) excluded from operating profit or (b) included in operating profit.

Findings reveal that (1) 36 airlines report this information and (2) 83% of these airlines report their equity accounting results excluded from operating

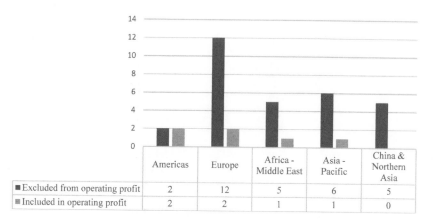

Fig. 15. Reporting Equity Accounting Results.

	Americas	Europe	Africa - Middle East	Asia - Pacific	China & Northern Asia
■ Excluded from operating profit	2	12	5	6	5
■ Included in operating profit	2	2	1	1	0

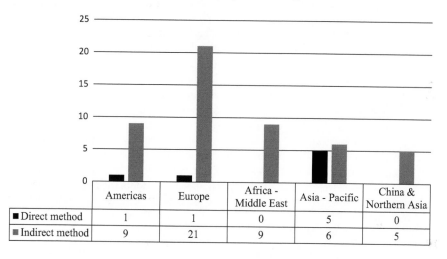

	Americas	Europe	Africa - Middle East	Asia - Pacific	China & Northern Asia
■ Direct method	1	1	0	5	0
■ Indirect method	9	21	9	6	5

Fig. 16. Reporting Cash Flows from Operating Activities.

profit versus 17% report their equity accounting results included in operating profit (Fig. 15).

4.2 Observations on IAS 7 Statement of Cash Flows

In terms of IAS 7, this section analyses the trends of the following issues in terms of the airline industry.

(1) Cash flows from operating activities are presented (a) by direct method or (b) by indirect method.

Findings indicate that (1) all airlines declare their statement of cash flows under IFRS; (2) 88% of airlines prepare their statement of cash flows under indirect method versus 12% prepare their statement of cash flows under the direct method (Fig. 16).

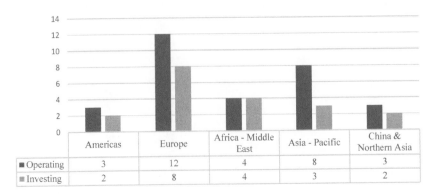

	Americas	Europe	Africa - Middle East	Asia - Pacific	China & Northern Asia
■ Operating	3	12	4	8	3
■ Investing	2	8	4	3	2

Fig. 17.   Classification of Interest Received.

(2) Interest received is presented (a) as operating cash flows or (b) as investing cash flows.

Findings show that (1) 49 airlines report this information on the statement of cash flows; (2) 61% of these airlines report their interest received within the operating section versus 39% report this cash inflow within the investing section (Fig. 17).

(3) Interest paid is presented (a) as operating cash flows, (b) as financing cash flows, (c) interest paid allocated to operating and financing cash flows, or (d) interest paid allocated to operating and investing cash flows due to interest paid and capitalized on qualifying assets.

Findings show that (1) 54 airlines report this information on the statement of cash flows; (2) 61% of airlines declare their interest paid within the operating section versus 35% declare their interest paid within the investing section; and (3) there are two airlines that particularly considers the allocation of this cash outflow into different business activities of the airline in the Asia-Pacific region (Fig. 18).

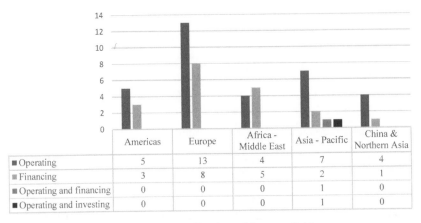

	Americas	Europe	Africa - Middle East	Asia - Pacific	China & Northern Asia
■ Operating	5	13	4	7	4
■ Financing	3	8	5	2	1
■ Operating and financing	0	0	0	1	0
■ Operating and investing	0	0	0	1	0

Fig. 18.   Classification of Interest Paid.

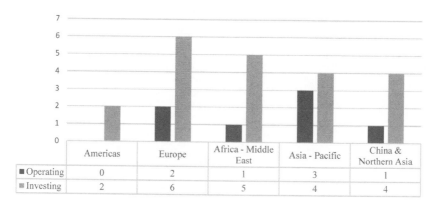

Fig. 19. Classification of Dividend Received.

(4) Dividend received is presented (a) as operating cash flows or (b) as investing. Findings show that (1) 28 airlines report this information on the statement of cash flows and (2) 75% of these airlines declare their dividend received within the investing section versus 25% of declare this cash inflow within the operating section (Fig. 19).

(5) Dividend paid is presented (a) as operating cash flows or (b) as financing cash flows.

Findings point out that (1) 37 airlines declare this information on the statement of cash flows of which 6 from Americas, 13 from Europe, 6 from Middle East – Africa, 7 from Asia-Pacific, and 5 from China and Northern Asia; and (2) all airlines report their dividend payments within the cash flows from financing activities.

4.3 Observations on IAS 2 Inventory, IAS 16 PPE, IAS 38 Intangible Assets, and IAS 40 Investment Property

This section analyses the patterns of the following policy options in terms of the airline industry:

(1) Inventory items are measured at (a) FIFO, (b) WA, (c) a mixture of both, (d) specific identification (SI), and (e) a mixture of FIFO, WA, and specific identification.

Findings show that (1) 47 airlines disclosed this accounting policy and (2) around 64% of airlines measure their inventory under WA method versus around 28% prefer FIFO. In this context, two airlines, namely Asiana Airlines and Cebu Pacific Air prefer the moving WA method (Fig. 20).

In addition, three airlines prefer using more than one method as seen on (Table 2) as follows.

(2) PPE items are measured using (a) the cost model, (b) revaluation model, or (c) a mixture of both.

Findings indicate that (1) 57 airlines declared this accounting policy; (2) around 95% of airlines measure their PPE items using the cost model;

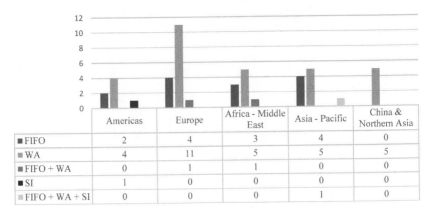

	Americas	Europe	Africa - Middle East	Asia - Pacific	China & Northern Asia
■ FIFO	2	4	3	4	0
▨ WA	4	11	5	5	5
■ FIFO + WA	0	1	1	0	0
■ SI	1	0	0	0	0
▨ FIFO + WA + SI	0	0	0	1	0

Fig. 20.   Methods of Inventory Valuation.

Table 2.   Airlines Using Multiple Inventory Valuation Methods.

Airlines	Description	Method
Croatia Airlines	Office supplies, catering, and uniforms	WA
(Croatia Airlines, 2018)	Spare parts	FIFO
Qatar Airways	Spare parts, catering materials	FIFO
(Qatar Airways, 2019)	Food and beverages, and goods for resale	WA
Korean Air (Korean Air, 2018)	Merchandise, raw materials, supplies (In-flight meals)	FIFO
	Goods	Total average
	Raw materials (Air transport/Aerospace)	Moving average
	Materials in transit	Specific identification

and (3) the remaining 5% that refers to three airlines measure some portion of PPE items using cost model and some portion of PPE items using revaluation model (Fig. 21). In this context, (1) Croatia Airlines revalues its aircrafts and engines but use the cost model for other PPE items; (2) Kenya Airlines revalues its land and buildings but use the cost model for other PPE items; and (3) Sri Lankan Airlines revalues its land, buildings, and flight kitchens but use the cost model for other PPE items.

(3) Intangible asset items are measured using (a) the cost model or (b) revaluation model.

Findings indicate that (1) 51 airlines that have these assets declare their accounting policy and (2) all of them measure their intangible assets using cost model.

(4) Investment properties are measured using (a) the cost model or (b) the fair value model.

Findings show that (1) 12 airlines have investment properties; (2) around 67% of these airlines prefer the cost model in investment property valuation versus 33% prefer the fair value model; and (3) airlines from the Americas do not have investment properties (Fig. 22).

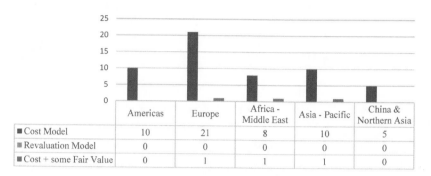

	Americas	Europe	Africa - Middle East	Asia - Pacific	China & Northern Asia
■ Cost Model	10	21	8	10	5
▨ Revaluation Model	0	0	0	0	0
■ Cost + some Fair Value	0	1	1	1	0

Fig. 21. Valuation of PPE Items.

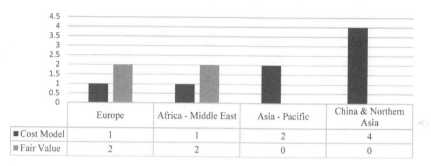

	Europe	Africa - Middle East	Asia - Pacific	China & Northern Asia
■ Cost Model	1	1	2	4
▨ Fair Value	2	2	0	0

Fig. 22. Valuation of Investment Properties.

4.4. Analysis of Accounting Policy Options Related to the Airline Industry

There are two accounting policy options related to IAS 16 that are important for the airline industry as follows.

(1) PPE items are depreciated using (a) the straight-line method or (b) others. Findings show that (1) 57 airlines report PPE items and (2) all of them depreciate their PPE items under straight-line method. This is the consistent with the findings for the year 2014 provided by Airline Disclosure Guide (IATA, 2016c, p. 12).

(2) Useful life of the PPE items.
IAS 16 does not state the useful life of the PPE items in terms of number of years. Therefore, the preparers of financial information are not informed for how long they will depreciate each specific PPE item. Instead, IAS 16 states that the useful life the PPE items are determined by the preparers of financial information, depending on the discretion of the entity where they consider for how long the entity expects to use the entity's PPE items [IAS 16.57].

In terms of the airline industry, this research determines the following regional patterns considering the expected useful life of the airframes regarding component depreciation.

Table 3.　Expected Useful Lives in the Airlines of Americas.

	5–10 Years	5–20 Years	5–30 Years	6–12 Years	7–10 Years	12 Years	15–20 Years	25 Years	27 Years	35–45 Years
Americas	1	1	1	1	1	1	1	1	1	1

Table 4.　Expected Useful Lives in the Airlines of Asia-Pacific.

	2.5–20 Years	4–22 Years	5–12 Years	5–25 Years	6–15 Years	15 Years	15–20 Years	18 Years	25 Years	15.000– 60,000 h	Non-declared
Asia-Pacific	1	1	1	1	1	1	1	1	1	1	1

In the Americas and Asia-Pacific, data gathered reveals that the useful lives adopted by North American, South American, and Asia-Pacific airlines are quite variable, and the interval of useful lives is quite large (Tables 3 and 4).

In Europe, the useful lives adopted by the airlines focus on 20, 20–25, 23, and 25 years of depreciation (Fig. 23). They are more balanced than useful lives declared by the airlines operating in the Americas and Asia-Pacific.

In the Middle East – Africa, the useful lives adopted by the airlines focus usually on 15 and 20 years (Fig. 24). They are more balanced than useful lives declared by the airlines operating in the Americas and Asia-Pacific.

In China and Northern Asia, the useful lives adopted by the two airlines focus on 15–20 years but the interval of useful lives is quite large for the other three airlines (Fig. 25).

The regional analysis reveals that the expected useful lives adopted by airlines are diverse, consistent with the findings for the year 2014 provided by Airline Disclosure Guide (IATA, 2016c, p. 12). Therefore, it should be noted that (1) only 54% of airlines can establish an approximate common denominator in terms of the useful lives in the global context; (2) 42% of airlines report quite variable useful lives; and (3) 4% of airlines do not declare their useful lives (Fig. 26).

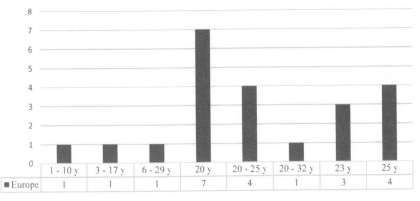

	1 - 10 y	3 - 17 y	6 - 29 y	20 y	20 - 25 y	20 - 32 y	23 y	25 y
■ Europe	1	1	1	7	4	1	3	4

Fig. 23.　Expected Useful Lives in European Airlines.

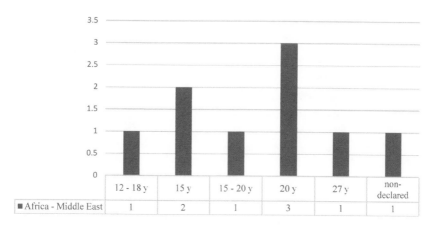

Fig. 24. Expected Useful Lives in Airlines of Middle East – Africa.

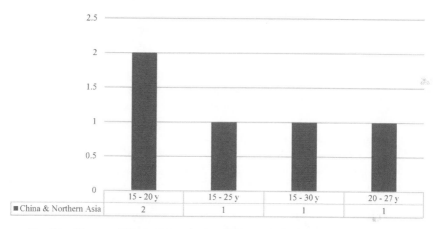

Fig. 25. Expected Useful Lives in the Airlines of China and Northern Asia.

4.5. Overall Analysis of the Findings

Within the framework of the 20 hypotheses developed by this chapter, the following observations can be stated as follows:

1. *H1* is accepted by findings because airlines still prefer the title of balance sheet even if **IASB** is in favor of the title of statement of financial position.
2. *H2* is accepted by findings because airlines report their financial position using different formats: total assets, net assets, or capital employed.
3. *H3* is accepted by findings because airlines report their assets using either liquidity decreasing order or liquidity increasing order.
4. *H4* is accepted by findings because most airlines report their expenses by nature as a tradition of their country or as a mimetic practice versus some airlines report their expenses by function due to their country's pre-IFRS practice.

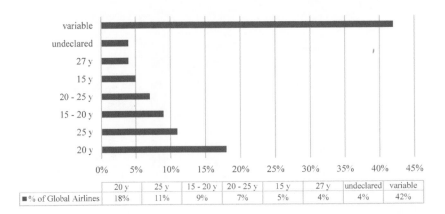

	20 y	25 y	15 - 20 y	20 - 25 y	15 y	27 y	undeclared	variable
■% of Global Airlines	18%	11%	9%	7%	5%	4%	4%	42%

Fig. 26. Percentage of Airlines in the Global Context in Terms of Useful Lives.

5. *H5* is accepted by findings because most airlines prefer reporting comprehensive income under two-statement approach versus some airlines prefer the one-statement approach.
6. *H6–H8* are accepted by findings because preparers of financial information in airlines use the flexibility provided by the standard IAS 1 in titling SOCI under one-statement approach, and income statement and statement of other comprehensive income under two-statement approach.
7. *H9* is accepted by findings because most airlines exclude equity accounting results from operating profit leading to uniformity in financial reporting for the purpose of comparative financial information versus some airlines include equity accounting results into operating profit.
8. *H10* is accepted by findings because most airlines report their operating cash flows using the indirect method versus there are some airlines that prefer the direct method. Diversity of the method of reporting operating cash flows does not influence the comparability of financial information in the context of "net cash flows from operating activities" but the diversity in the classification of interest received, interest paid, dividend received, and dividend paid does.
9. *H11* is accepted by findings because most airlines reporting interest received reports these amounts in the operating section of statements cash flows leading to uniformity in financial reporting for the purpose of comparative financial information versus some airlines report interest received in the investing section.
10. *H12* is accepted by findings because most airlines reporting interest paid reports these amounts in the operating section of statements cash flows leading to uniformity in financial reporting for the purpose of comparative financial information versus some airlines report interest paid in the financing section.
11. *H13* is accepted by findings because most airlines reporting dividend received reports this amount in the investing section of the statement of cash flows leading to uniformity in financial reporting for the purpose of comparative financial information versus some airlines report dividend received in the operating section.

12. *H14* is rejected by findings because airlines reporting dividend payments report their dividend payments in the financing section of the statement of cash flows, thus leading to reporting comparable financial information.

13. *H15* is accepted by findings because several methods in inventory valuation were adopted by airlines, leading to diversity in financial reporting. Airlines adopt WA method and subsequently FIFO. Thus, this case weakens the comparability of financial information. Since airlines are one of the types of service businesses, these results are consistent with the results of Jaafar and McLeay (2007) whose paper detects the patterns of inventory valuation methods in the non-IFRS but European context.

14. *H16* is accepted by findings because there are three airlines that revalue some of their PPE items, referring to diversity in the valuation of PPE items. However, most airlines use the cost model, leading to uniformity in financial reporting and comparative financial information in the airline industry.

15. *H17* is rejected by findings because intangible assets are valued using the cost model leading to uniformity in financial reporting and comparative financial information in the airline industry.

16. *H18* is accepted by findings because both cost model and fair value model are observed in the airline industry leading to diversity in financial reporting and this weakens the comparability of financial information in context of investment properties.

17. *H19* is rejected by findings because airlines prefer the straight-line method rather than units of activity in reporting depreciation on the balance sheet and income statement leading to methodological uniformity in the calculation of depreciation. This result is consistent with the IATA's airline accounting guide. This helps in the preparation of comparable financial information.

18. *H20* is accepted by findings because airlines prefer different useful lives for the similar depreciable assets such as airframes. In terms of depreciation, even if the straight-line method creates common denominator in financial reporting, the expected useful lives adopted by airlines weaken the comparability of financial information. This research observes that 54% airlines declare more balanced useful lives than the 42% of airlines, leading to comparative financial information to a reasonable extent. Within the 42%, there are some airlines whose declared useful life interval is quite large.

5. CONCLUSION

This chapter focuses on 20 hypotheses on IFRS accounting policy options in the context of the airline industry. Some of the policy options are cosmetic and therefore are related to presentation versus some of them are non-cosmetic and thus are related to measurement. Diversity observed in cosmetic accounting policy options does not influence the comparability of financial information. However, diversity observed in non-cosmetic accounting policy options influence the comparability of financial information. Even though diversity exists (1) on the reporting of expenses and equity accounting results on the income statement;

(2) on the dividend received, interest received, and interest paid on the statement of cash flows; and (3) on the valuation of inventory and PPE items, findings reveal that airlines are inclined to uniformity in financial reporting in such contexts. The most diverse area in airline financial reporting involves expected useful lives that are thoroughly based on the judgmental determination of the preparers of financial information in the airline industry and the airlines' management due to principle-based IFRSs. The expected useful life should be regulated so that similar depreciable assets are depreciated within a similar period in the industry. For instance, IATA should provide a guide to minimize the inconsistency experienced in airframes' depreciation.

NOTES

1. British Airways and Fast Jet.
2. Virgin Atlantic, Air Partner and Easy Jet.

CHAPTER 3

SOME OBSERVATIONS ON IFRS 15 AND IFRS 16 IN THE AIRLINE INDUSTRY: THE CASE OF AIR FRANCE – KLM

ABSTRACT

This chapter focuses on the IFRS 15 Revenue from Contracts with Customers and IFRS 16 Leases in the airline industry considering the case of Air France – KLM (AF-KLM). This airline timely adopted IFRS 15 and early adopted IFRS 16 for the year 2018 and restated its 2017 financial statements using the full retrospective method so that the 2018 financial statements of the airline provide comparative financial information during the transition phase from IAS 18 to IFRS 15 as well as from IAS 17 to IFRS 16. In the first part of the chapter, liquidity, solvency, and profitability ratios along with cash flow ratios were used to analyze the cumulative effect of IFRS 15 and IFRS 16 using 2017 and restated 2017 financial statements. In this context, results indicate that the liquidity ratios decreased, and the solvency ratios increased in general. In addition, the cumulative effect of IFRS 15 and IFRS 16 created an upward change in general on profitability ratios based on the several performance parameters that should be considered during the transition from IAS 18 to IFRS 15 and from IAS 17 to IFRS 16. Overall, IFRS 15 has minor effect and IFRS 16 has major effect on the financial statements of AF-KLM. In the second part of the chapter, the compliance level of the mandatory disclosures requirements of the airline was examined from the lessee

Perspectives on International Financial Reporting and Auditing in the Airline Industry
Studies in Managerial and Financial Accounting, Volume 35, 51–80
Copyright © 2022 by Emerald Publishing Limited
All rights of reproduction in any form reserved
ISSN: 1479-3512/doi:10.1108/S1479-351220220000035003

standpoint and the research pointed out that the airline fully complied with these disclosures at its first adoption of IFRS 16 and provided some voluntary disclosures as well.

Keywords: Airline Industry; IFRS 15; revenue; IFRS 16; Leases; disclosures; ratios

1. INTRODUCTION

This chapter focuses on IFRS 15 Revenue from Contracts with Customers and IFRS 16 Leases at their first-time adoption in the airline industry because these two standards issued by the International Accounting Standards Board (IASB) improve the true and fair financial reporting in financial statements, include the topics that have had been debated in the airline accounting since the 1992 survey of airlines' annual reports prepared by KPMG & International Air Transport Association (IATA) (Tan, Tower, Hancock, & Taplin, 2002).

1.1 IFRS 15 Revenue from Contracts with Customers

While the former standard IAS 18 Revenue (predecessor of IFRS 15) recognized revenues when the risks and rewards of ownership of goods were substantially transferred from the seller to the buyer, IATA issued the guide AAG 4: Recognition of Revenue in 1996 (Tan et al., 2002) and adopted the accrual basis of accounting for recognition of revenue consistent with IAS 18. Therefore, revenue which includes the transportation of passengers, and cargo, has been recognized when transportation is provided, thus leading to a "deferred revenue" in the current liabilities until transportation is provided. However, the treatment of commissions, discounts, and the recognition of unredeemed tickets have been different between airlines.

IASB issued IFRS 15 in 2014 as a standard that replaces IAS 18 and IAS 11 Construction Contracts, and the related Interpretations on revenue recognition: IFRIC 13 Customer Loyalty Programmes, IFRIC 15 Agreements for the Construction of Real Estate, IFRIC 18 Transfers of Assets from Customers and SIC-31 Revenue – Barter Transactions Involving Advertising Services, to eliminate the significant diversity in revenue recognition practices, limited guidance on topics such as accounting for arrangements with multiple elements, and complex transactions (IASB, 2014).

Since the objective is to eliminate inconsistencies and weaknesses experienced in previous revenue standards and the deficiencies in terms of recognition, measurement, and disclosure of revenue (IASB, 2014), IFRS 15 is expected (1) to improve the comparability of revenue from contracts with customers; (2) to reduce the need for interpretive guidance to be developed on a case-by-case basis to address emerging revenue recognition issues; and (3) to provide more useful information through improved disclosure requirements.

Compared to IAS 18, IFRS 15 has adopted a "performance obligation" approach (Napier & Stadler, 2020, p. 475). Therefore, the company that adopts IFRS 15 must consider the following five steps for revenue recognition (Kieso, Weygandt, & Warfield, 2020; Özerhan, Marşap, & Yanık, 2015): (1) identify the contract with the customer; (2) identify the performance obligations in the contract; (3) determine the transaction price; (4) allocate the transaction price to the performance obligations in the contract; and (5) recognize revenue when the company satisfies a performance obligation.

To better understand the five steps of revenue recognition, the following example that considers the revenue recognition between the Air France – KLM (AF-KLM) and airline passenger (ticket buyer) is illustrated (Table 1).

Under the IFRS 15, the deferred revenue approach continues in the recognition of revenue for passenger tickets and freight at the issuance date but the timing of recognizing the value of tickets that have been issued but never been used, has changed. Under IAS 18, the value of such tickets was recognized at the date of issuance, but IFRS 15 deferred such recognition until the transportation date initially foreseen (Air France – KLM, 2017, 2018). Therefore, no revenue will be recognized prior to the flight being performed.

In addition, the recognition of ancillary services is also important under IFRS 15 in the context of whether they are distinct from the travel component of the transaction or not. This is a significant determinant of a single contract or separate contracts for the airlines (Lavi, 2016). To promote comparability and consistency in reporting, the IATA Industry Accounting Working Group issued Guidance on IFRS 15 (IATA, 2020d). In this regard, the timing of revenue associated with non-distinct ancillary services that generally occur in conjunction with the flight such as checking of baggage and excess baggage, seat assignment

Table 1. Steps of Revenue Recognition: The Case of AF-KLM.

Five Steps of Revenue Recognition	The Case of AF-KLM & Airline Passenger
(1) Identify the contract with the airline passenger	AF-KLM has signed a contract to provide flight service to an airline passenger
(2) Identify the performance obligations in the contract	AF-KLM has only one performance obligation which is to provide flight service to the airline passenger
(3) Determine the transaction price	The transaction price is the amount of consideration that a company expects to receive from a customer in exchange for providing the flight service. In this case, the transaction price is €100
(4) Allocate the transaction price to the performance obligations in the contract	AF-KLM has only one performance obligation which is to provide flight service to the airline passenger
(5) Recognize revenue when the airline satisfies a performance obligation	The transaction price is received in advance at the issuance date and recorded as deferred revenue. AF-KLM recognizes revenue of €100 for the sale of flight ticket to the airline passenger when the performance obligation is satisfied, that is, to provide the flight service

fees, and priority boarding fees that were recognized at the transaction date under IAS 18, have been deferred to the flight date under IFRS 15. On the other hand, distinct ancillary services such as fees to access an airline's airport lounges which are not specifically associated with the travel component of the transaction, may be recognized on a systematic basis that reflects the fulfillment of the related performance obligation.

Overall, this chapter expects that transition from IAS 18 to IFRS 15 will have minor effect on the revenue recognition of the airlines because the deferred revenue approach is still in effect, there are some timing changes, and most ancillary services are non-distinct as shown by the IATA's guidance.

1.2 IFRS 16 Leases

While the former IAS 17 Leases (predecessor of IFRS 16) required classification of leases as operating leases or finance leases and permitted operating leases to be off-balance sheet, leading to the lack of transparency of information about lease obligations, unrecorded lease assets, and lease liabilities were substantial (IASB, 2016u). This effect has been verified by (Beattie, Edwards, & Goodacre, 1998; Duke, Hsieh, & Su, 2009; Imhoff, Lipe, & Wright, 1991, 1997).

Toward the objective of faithful representation and greater transparency of leases on the financial statements, IASB issued IFRS 16 Leases in 2016 leading to the capitalization of operating leases as if they are finance leases in order to provide faithful representation of lease commitments to investors and creditors to have a complete picture of the financial position of a company (IASB, 2016t, 2016u).

As observed in the industries of telecommunication, retail, energy, media, health care, information technology, fast-food, and transport (Akbulut, 2018; Akdoğan & Erhan, 2020; Duke, Franz, & Hsieh, 2012; IASB, 2016t; Özdoğan & Uygun, 2020; Sarı, Altıntaş, & Taş, 2016; Tai, 2013), the airline industry is one of the industries where leases are mostly pertinent for fleet assets. In this context, Tan et al. (2002) declares that IATA regulated the accounting for leases by issuing AAG 6: Accounting for Leases of Aircraft Fleet Assets which recommended that finance leases be brought onto the balance sheet and treated as acquired assets versus operating leases where lease rentals are charged to the statement of profit or loss over the lease term. This approach was consistent with IAS 17. Following the adoption of IFRS 16, IATA issued a new guide entitled as Industry Accounting Working Group Guidance IFRS 16, Leases to regulate accounting for leases in the airline industry (IATA, 2020e).

Following the adoption of IFRS 16, airlines report all their lease assets except for their short-term leases and lease assets with low value and their related liabilities on their statement of financial position (IASB, 2018q). Therefore, the transition from IAS 17 to IFRS 16 is expected to have major effect on the financial statements of the airlines.

This chapter has the following structure: Section 2 presents the literature review pertaining to the effect of the adoption of IFRS 15 and IFRS 16; Section 3 explains the data, accounting period for the data, constraints of the research and the research methodology; Section 4 discusses (1) the effect of the adoption of IFRS 15 on the net sales of 57 airlines; (2) the cumulative effect of the adoption of IFRS 15 and IFRS 16 on the financial statements of AF-KLM; and (3) the analysis of the disclosures reported by the financial statements of AF-KLM from the lessee standpoint at the first-time adoption of IFRS 16. Finally, Section 5 presents concluding remarks along with main findings.

2. LITERATURE REVIEW ON THE ADOPTION OF IFRS 15 AND IFRS 16 IN THE AIRLINE INDUSTRY

This section is divided into three sub-sections. The section analyses (1) the literature review pertaining to IFRS 15; (2) the literature review pertaining to IFRS 16; and (3) the literature review on cumulative effect of IFRS 15 and IFRS 16.

2.1 Literature Review on the Effect of IFRS 15

The study by Napier and Stadler (2020) discusses the effects of IFRS 15 on a sample of the largest 48 European companies from Belgium, Switzerland, Germany, Denmark, Spain, France, UK, Italy, and the Netherlands, and operate in 14 different industries of which neither the transportation industry nor the airline industry are included in the sample. To develop this research, authors benefited from 2018 annual reports, comment letters, and interviews. This study classifies the effects of the IFRS 15 under five headings: (a) accounting effects, (b) information effects, (c) real affects, (d) indirect effects, and (e) other findings.

In the context of the accounting effects of IFRS 15 related to recognition and measurement changes, Napier and Stadler (2020) adopted three parameters: the effect on the opening balance of retained earnings, the difference in revenue under IFRS 15 and IAS 18, and the difference in profit under IFRS 15 and IAS 18. Considering these parameters, findings reveal that the accounting effects of IFRS 15 are minor for most companies.

Within the framework of the accounting effects of IFRS 15 related to recognition and measurement changes analyzed by Napier and Stadler (2020), this chapter analyses the accounting effect of IFRS 15 for 57 airlines by extending the research in one aspect of transportation industry. For this purpose, this chapter adopts the pure "change in revenue" parameter, because retained earnings and profit also include the effect of other standards that were simultaneously adopted by the airlines such as IFRS 9 (first-time adoption) and IFRS 16 (early adoption).

2.2 Literature Review on the Effect of IFRS 16

In designing the literature review section on IFRS 16, this chapter primarily considers the expected effects of IFRS 16 declared by IASB on financial metrics for a company in general (IASB, 2016t, pp. 53–54). The current ratio and asset turnover ratio decrease while the leverage ratio, EBIT/operating profit ratio, Earnings Before Interest, Tax, Depreciation, Amortization (EBITDA), and operating cash flow, increase because of IFRS 16 (Table 2). On the other hand, the direction of some profitability ratios depends on the characteristics of the lease portfolio. In other words, lease intensity, either operating or financial, is a determinant of the direction of the profitability metrics (IASB, 2016t, p. 64).

In line with the declaration of IASB, research papers that reveal the possible effects of IFRS 16 in the context of the airline industry were issued by several authors.

Öztürk (2016) studied the possible effects of IFRS 16 on the statement of financial position of Turkish Airlines, Pegasus Airlines, and Lufthansa Airlines. This research observes the weight of aircraft fleet owned and leased (operational lease or finance lease) over a five-year accounting period and states that if the weight of operational leases within the aircraft fleet is greater than the weight of financial leases, the effect of IFRS 16 on the liquidity and financial structure

Table 2.   Key Financial Metrics Influenced by IFRS 16.

Metric	What it Measures	Common Method of Calculation	Expected Effect of IFRS 16
Current ratio	Liquidity	Current assets/current liabilities	Decrease
Leverage	Long-term solvency	Liabilities/equity	Increase
Interest coverage	Long-term solvency	EBITDA/interest expense	Depends
Asset turnover	Profitability	Sales/total assets	Decrease
EBIT/Operating profit	Profitability	Various methods – profit that does not consider earnings from investments and the effects of interest and taxes	Increase
EBITDA	Profitability	Profit before interest, tax, depreciation, and amortization	Increase
Earnings Before Interest, Tax, Depreciation, Amortization and Rent (EBITDAR)	Profitability	Profit before interest, tax, depreciation, amortization, and rent	No change
Profit or loss	Profitability	As reported applying IFRS	Depends
EPS	Profitability	Profit or loss/number of shares in issue	Depends
ROCE	Profitability	EBIT/equity plus financial liabilities	Depends
ROE	Profitability	Profit or loss/equity	Depends
Operating cash flow	Profitability	Various methods – cash flow from operating activities does not include cash related to equity and borrowings	Increase
Net cash flow	Profitability and liquidity	Difference between cash inflows and cash outflows	No change

of an airline is expected to be severe. To take the financial picture of each airline between 2010 and September 2015, this research focuses on the following ratios: current ratio, total liabilities/equity, current liabilities/equity, non-current liabilities/equity, total liabilities/total assets, non-current assets/equity, and non-current assets/continuous capital. In this regard, the results indicate that the current ratio is expected to decrease, and debt ratios are expected to increase. However, the expected change over the liquidity and financial structure of airlines is expected to be low for Lufthansa Airlines, moderate for Turkish Airlines, and high for Pegasus Airlines when the operational lease intensity of the aircraft fleet is considered.

Öztürk (2016) stated above considers only the lease intensity of the aircraft fleet structure of airlines. However, the following research (Alabood, Abuaddous, & Bataineh, 2019; Gouveia, 2019; Maali, 2018; Öztürk & Serçemeli, 2016; Veverková, 2019) focuses on both the aircraft fleet structure of airlines and the method of constructive capitalization developed by Imhoff et al. (1993, 1997). In addition, they consider not only liquidity and solvency ratios but also profitability ratios. It should be noted that the effect of IFRS 16 over the profitability ratios should be analyzed on a case-by-case basis, considering the positive and negative income impact stated by Duke et al. (2009) in the context of adjusting net income.

Öztürk and Serçemeli (2016) examined the possible effects of IFRS 16 on the statement of financial position and statement of income of Pegasus Airlines for the year 2015 and considered the following ratios: total liabilities/equity, total liabilities/total assets, Return on Assets (ROA), and Return on Equity (ROE). This paper states that leverage ratios are expected to increase. In terms of profitability, the airline's ROA is expected to go down versus its ROE is expected to go up without adjusting net income in the numerator as a constraint of this research. On the other hand, Aktaş, Karğın, and Arıcı (2017) states that Pegasus Airlines' ROA is expected to go up after the restatement of net income for the year 2015.

Joubert, Garvie, and Parle (2017) examined the effects of IFRS 16 on the statement of financial position and statement of income of two Australian airlines for 2015 and 2016: Qantas Airlines and Virgin Australia. This research takes the following ratios into account: total liabilities/equity and ROA. It reveals that the leverage ratio is expected to go up. In terms of profitability, Virgin Australia's ROA is expected to go up versus Qantas Airlines' ROA is expected to go down from 2015 to 2016. However, this study calculates ROA without adjusting earnings before interest and tax in the numerator as a constraint of this research. When the operating lease intensity is taken into account, Virgin Australia is affected more compared to Qantas Airlines.

Maali (2018) examined the possible effects of IFRS 16 on the statement of financial position and statement of income for the year 2016 in terms of major airline companies operating in the Middle East. The sample includes Emirates Airlines, Air Arabia, Royal Jordanian, Oman Air, Turkish Airlines, and Qatar Airways. This study focuses on total liabilities/total assets, ROA, and ROE, and reveals that the leverage ratios are expected to go up for each airline. In terms of profitability, this research calculates ROA and ROE considering adjusted net income. Airlines with a positive income effect (Royal Jordanian Airlines, Oman Air, and Turkish Airlines) show an upward trend on ROA versus airlines with negative income effect (Qatar Airways, Emirates Airlines, and Air Arabia) reveal a downward trend on ROA. This varies from one airline to another depending on the operational lease intensity of the aircraft fleet. The same trend applies for ROE as well, except for Oman Air whose data are not applicable. When the operating lease intensity is under consideration, Royal Jordanian Airlines and Emirates Airlines are the mostly effected airlines.

Morales-Díaz and Zamora-Ramírez (2018) examined the possible effects of IFRS 16 on the statement of financial position and statement of income of all European quoted companies for the year 2015 with a subsection of transportation. Therefore, the sample consists of 29 transportation companies including AF-KLM, IAG, Lufthansa, Ryanair, and Aegean Airlines. By making significant changes to Imhoff et al. (1991), the authors adopt a discount rate that is better adapted to the credit risk inherent in the financial operations by obtaining the Bloomberg Euro interest rate curves per sector and rating. This paper uses the following ratios: liabilities/equity, liabilities/assets, ROA, and EBITDA/interest expense. It states that leverage ratios are expected to increase, but interest coverage ratio and ROA are expected to decrease.

Veverková (2019) examined the possible effects of IFRS 16 on the statement of financial position and statement of income of the 15 European airlines headquartered in the European Union, Switzerland, and Norway considering the accounting period of 2010–2016. This research takes the following ratios into account: current ratio, total liabilities/total assets, total liabilities/equity, ROA, and ROE, and states that the liquidity ratio is expected to decrease versus leverage ratios which are expected to increase. In terms of profitability, ROA is expected to decrease versus ROE which is expected to increase on average, and they were calculated by considering adjusted EBIT. However, no consideration was given to the positive or negative income effects of Duke et al. (2009). When the operating lease intensity is considered, the most affected airlines were the European airlines with 95.7%, 96.42%, and 97.8% operating leases.

In addition, depreciation costs and interest expenses are important determinants of the profitability under IFRS 16, but Veverková (2019) reveals that huge operational lease intensity does not always mean that the airline has both high depreciation costs and interest expenses at the same time. Even if depreciation costs are on a straight-line basis, interest expense decreases from year to year.

Gouveia (2019) examined the possible effects of IFRS 16 on the statement of financial position and statement of income from the perspective of TAP Portugal for the year 2017. This research was designed following Imhoff et al. (1991). It considers the following ratios: liabilities/equity, total liabilities/total assets, sales/total assets, EBITDA/interest expense, net income/assets, and net income/equity. The results reveal that leverage ratios are expected to go up, and interest coverage ratio is expected to go down. In terms of profitability, asset turnover is expected to decrease versus ROA which is expected to increase. On the other hand, ROE is expected to go down due to negative shareholders' equity.

Yu (2019) examined the possible effects of IFRS 16 on the statement of financial position and statement of income from the perspective of Air China for the year 2017. This research focused on total liabilities/total assets and asset turnover. The results reveal that the leverage ratio is expected to go up versus the profitability ratio is expected to go down.

Alabood et al. (2019) examined the possible effects of IFRS 16 on the statement of financial position and statement of income from the perspective of three airline companies which are operating in the Middle East (The Royal Jordanian Airlines Company (RJ), Saudi Airlines Catering (SAC), and Qatar Airways Company (QAC) for the year 2016). Each airline adopted different operating lease strategies which showed high 77%, moderate 21%, and low 0% reliance on operating leases. Total liabilities/total assets and total liabilities/total equity increased in all airlines consistent with prior research. While ROA decreased in the three airlines, ROE increased in the SAC and QAC, but decreased in the RJ.

Najar, da Costa Marques, da Silva Carvalho, and Mello (2019) analyzed Gol Linhas and Latam and obtained similar results on the possible effects of IFRS 16 for the period 2014–2016.

As stated by Alabood et al. (2019), Joubert et al. (2017), Maali (2018), Morales-Díaz and Zamora-Ramírez (2018), Najar et al. (2019), Öztürk (2016), and Veverková (2019), it should be noted that airlines with major off-balance sheet leases are expected to be influenced by IFRS 16 seriously in terms of liquidity and leverage ratios. However, there is no consistent result regarding the effect of IFRS 16 on profitability ratios like ROE and ROA, depending on the financial performance of the airlines at the time of IFRS 16 adoption.

As observed, prior research shows the expected effects of IFRS 16 on the financial statements in terms of liquidity, solvency, and profitability. However, this chapter contributes to the accounting literature by comparing the values reported on the 2017 financial statements of AF-KLM with restated 2017 values on the 2018 financial statements, thus leading to the observation of the change on the financial statements of the airline following early adoption of IFRS 16 in terms of liquidity, solvency, and profitability, complemented by some cash flow ratios stated by (Güleç & Bektaş, 2019). This chapter also analyses the financial position, financial performance, and cash flows for the year 2018.

2.3 Literature Review on the Cumulative Effect of IFRS 15 and IFRS 16

Belesis, Sorros, Karagiorgos, and Kousounadis (2021) discuss the cumulative effect of adopting IFRS 15 and IFRS 16 on a hypothetical case of maritime company financial statements. It analyses EBITDA, net working capital, current ratio, acid test ratio, loans to assets ratio, debt to equity ratio, gross profit margin, net profit margin, and ROE and ROA before and after the simultaneous adoption of these standards. The study shows that the effect of IFRS 15 is minor but the effect of IFRS 16 is major on maritime company that charter-in vessels.

Within the framework of Belesis et al. (2021), this chapter analyses the cumulative effect of IFRS 15 and IFRS 16 on "AF-KLM" financial statements by extending the research on the airline industry.

2.4. Literature Review on the Compliance Level of Disclosures of
IFRS 15 and IFRS 16

Compared to the non-compliance that means that companies fail to fully provide the information required by pertinent reporting standards in their financial statements (Glaum, Schmidt, Street, & Vogel, 2013), compliance means that companies fully provide the information required by the related financial reporting standards in the disclosures of the financial statements. In such context, there is a limited amount of research dealing with specific IFRS standards.

Glaum et al. (2013) analyzed the compliance level of mandatory disclosures on IFRS 3 Business Combinations and IAS 36 Impairment of Assets through a sample of 357 entities from manufacturing, financial, and non-financial service industries whose shares are publicly traded and whose financial statements are subject to IFRS. This was done in the context of 17 European countries including Austria, Belgium, Czech Republic, Denmark, Finland, France, Germany, Hungary, Ireland, Italy, Luxembourg, the Netherlands, Poland, Spain, Sweden, Switzerland, and the UK. This research analyzed the disclosures for the year 2005 which was the first-time adoption of IFRS in Europe and identified substantial non-compliance due to the accounting traditions and other country- and company-specific factors.

Similar to the research of Glaum et al. (2013), Tsalavoutas, André, and Dionysiou (2014) analyses the compliance level of mandatory disclosures on IFRS 3, IAS 36, and IAS 38 Intangible Assets at the first year of adoption of IFRS 3 (financial year 2010/11) by establishing a sample of non-financial entities including Australia, Austria, Belgium, Denmark, Finland, France, Germany, Greece, Ireland, Italy, the Netherlands, Norway, Portugal, Spain, Sweden, Switzerland, and the UK. This paper points out that there is usually significant non-compliance regarding the disclosures of IFRS 3, IAS 36, and IAS 38.

Another study on the level of compliance with the disclosure requirements is based on IFRS 8 Operating Segments. Kobbi-Fakhfakh, Shabou, and Pigé (2018) analyzed the disclosures of IFRS 8 by establishing a sample of 440 entities from EU countries and the UK considering the industries of manufacturing, services, retail trade, construction, and utilities. This research found significant disparity in the disclosures of IFRS 8.

Regarding the mandatory disclosure requirements, there are two standards that have been recently adopted: IFRS 15 and IFRS 16. In this context, IFRS 15 has been researched by Boujelben and Kobbi-Fakhfakh (2020) and Coetsee, Mohammadali-Haji, and van Wyk (2021).

Boujelben and Kobbi-Fakhfakh (2020) analyzed the compliance level of mandatory disclosures for IFRS 15 through a sample of 22 entities whose shares are publicly traded and thus subject to IFRS and operating in the telecommunication and construction sectors. The sample covers entities from EU countries including France, Germany, Netherlands, Sweden, Belgium, Spain, Italy, Austria, and Finland. This research analyses the disclosures of the 2018 financial statements for the first-time adoption of IFRS 15. It found that there is a lack of full compliance with the disclosure requirements of IFRS 15; however, improvement toward the compliance with mandatory disclosures is expected in the upcoming years.

Coetsee et al. (2021) analyses the compliance level of mandatory disclosures for IFRS 15 through a sample of 60 entities operating in the industries of basic materials, consumer goods, consumer, financial, healthcare services, oil and gas, technology, and telecommunications, and whose shares are traded on the Johannesburg Stock Exchange. This paper provides observations related to disclosures of the IFRS financial statements for the first-time adoption of IFRS 15 in South Africa in 2018 or in the middle of 2019. It states that disclosures related to revenue usually appeared orderly, concise, coherent, and appropriately cross-referenced for the first-time adoption of IFRS 15 but there are some disclosures that require improvement.

The results of both research papers complement each other to some extent stating that mandatory disclosure requirements of IFRS 15 should be improved. Through this way, the compliance level of entities' financial statements is expected to increase.

On the other hand, Tsalavoutas, Tsoligkas, and Evans (2020) states that "in-depth and single topic" studies on the compliance level of mandatory disclosures such as leasing in the context of IFRS 16 is absent. In this context, Ali (2021) is the first attempt on mandatory disclosure requirements of IFRS 16. By preparing a sample of all 42 companies whose shares are publicly listed on the Bahraini stock market in 2019, this research tested the level of mandatory presentation and disclosure requirements at the first-time adoption of IFRS 16 in terms of transition, presentation, lessee, and lessor and finds that the level of compliance is average with a grade of 58.72% with a maximum of 83% and minimum of 15%.

Considering prior research of Ali (2021), this chapter extends the prior research on the airline industry from the lessee standpoint and provides the starting point for the compliance level research on mandatory disclosure requirements of IFRS 16 in the airline industry for the first-time through early adoption of IFRS 16 by AF-KLM.

3. DATA AND RESEARCH METHODOLOGY

3.1 Data

The starting point of this chapter is based on the IFRS income statements of 57 airlines in order to determine the effect of IFRS 15 in the airline industry (Table 3). In addition, AF-KLM is the only airline timely adopted IFRS 15 and early adopted IFRS 16 for the year 2018, using the full retrospective method (FRM). Therefore, data from the financial statements and disclosures of AF-KLM was used to determine the cumulative effect of IFRS 15 and IFRS 16.

3.2 Accounting Period for the Data

To analyze the financial statements of airlines, annual reports for the accounting period ended on December 31, 2017 and December 31, 2018, were considered to observe values reported under IAS 17 in year 2017 and under IFRS 16 in years restated 2017 and 2018.

Table 3.   List of Airlines.

Americas	Turkish Airlines
GOL Linhas Aereas	Pegasus Airlines
Azul Brazilian Airlines	Norwegian Air
Air Transat	*Africa – Middle East*
WestJet	Royal Jordanian
Air Canada	Kenya Airways
Cargojet Airways	Jazeera Airways
LATAM Airlines Group	Air Mauritius
Aeromexico	Qatar Airways
Volaris	Comair
COPA Airlines	Emirates
Europe	Air Arabia
Croatia Airlines	Abu Dhabi Aviation
Finnair – Finnair Group	*Asia-Pacific*
AF-KLM Group	Regional Express
Lufthansa Group	Alliance Airlines
Aegean Group	Qantas
Aer Lingus	Virgin Australia
Ryanair	Korean Air
Wizz Air	Asiana Airlines
TAP Group	Air Asia X
SAS – SAS Group	Air New Zealand
International Airlines Group	Cebu Pacific Air
Virgin Atlantic Group	Singapore Airlines
Air Partner	Sri Lankan Airlines
Easy Jet	*China and North Asia*
British Airways	Cathay Pacific Airlines
Fast Jet	Air China Group
Icelandair	China Southern Airlines
Norwegian Air	China Eastern Airlines
El Al	China Airlines
Aeroflot	

3.3. Constraint of the Research

This chapter provides insights about one airline that simultaneously adopted IFRS 15 and IFRS 16 and thus the results cannot be generalized for the entire airline industry.

3.4 Research Methodology

This chapter adopts the method "change in revenue" to observe the effect of IFRS 15 in the airline industry. In addition, the chapter uses liquidity, solvency, and profitability ratios complemented by cash flow ratios for the year 2017, restated 2017, and 2018 to analyze the cumulative effect of IFRS 15 and IFRS 16 on AF-KLM. In addition, compliance level analysis for the disclosures of leases from the lessee standpoint is based on the method of content analysis.

4. FINDINGS AND DISCUSSION

4.1 First-time Adoption of IFRS 15 and IFRS 16

First-time adoption of IFRS 15 and IFRS 16 provides the preparers of financial statements the opportunity to adopt these standards under two options [IFRS 15.C3, IFRS 16.C5] either (a) they are applied retrospectively to each prior reporting period presented applying IAS 8 Accounting Policies, Changes in Accounting Estimates and Errors (FRM); or (b) they applied retrospectively with the cumulative effect of initially applying these standards recognized at the date of initial application (modified retrospective method (MRM) – cumulative catch-up method) (IASB, 2018p, 2018q).

In the first-time adoption of IFRS 15, 33% of the airlines from the region of the Americas, Europe, and Asia-Pacific preferred "FRM" versus 67% of the airlines from all regions applied the "MRM" (Table 4).

In addition to IFRS 15, IFRS 16 was simultaneously early adopted by two airlines. In this context, AF-KLM adopted IFRS 16 by applying the "FRM" versus Easy Jet adopted IFRS 16 by using the "MRM." Due to the availability of the information on lease composition, the cumulative effect of IFRS 15 and IFRS 16 focuses on AF-KLM.

4.2 Effect of the Adoption of IFRS 15 in the Airline Industry

Compared to the study by Napier and Stadler (2020), this chapter considers "change in revenue" as the only parameter to observe the effect of IFRS 15 in the airline industry in order to observe the pure change in revenue.

4.2.1 The Case of the Airlines from Americas

Airlines from Americas experience the change in revenue from IAS 18 to IFRS 15 between –4.80% and 0.09% (Table 5). The average change in revenue in the region is approximately –0.93%. Comparative data was provided by 90% of airlines in the disclosures of financial statements except for Cargojet Airways that made a declaration of "no material effect."

4.2.2 The Case of the Airlines from Europe

Airlines from Europe experience the change in revenue from IAS 18 to IFRS 15 between –5.03% and 30.47% including Air Partner which deviates from the general pattern of the change in revenue in the region (Table 6). Consistent with Napier and Stadler (2020), the change in revenue in the airlines that did not provide comparative

Table 4. Adoption Methodology of IFRS 15 in the Airline Industry.

	Full Retrospective Method	%	Modified Retrospective Method	%
Americas	8	42	2	5
Europe	8	42	14	37
Middle East and Africa	–	–	9	24
Asia-Pacific	3	16	8	21
China and Northern Asia	–	–	5	13
Total	19	100	38	100

Table 5. Change in Revenue in the Airlines of the Americas.

	Method Adopted		Change in Revenue %	Restated Data IFRS 15 Versus IAS 18
	FRM	MRM		
Gol Linhas Aereas	√		−2.1872	√
Azul Brazilian Airlines		√	−1.0278	√
Air Transat	√		−4.7994	√
WestJet	√		0.0963	√
Air Canada	√		0	√
Cargojet Airways	√		0	No data – declaration of no material effect
LATAM Airlines		√	−0.8026	√
Aeromexico	√		−0.1628	√
Volaris	√		−0.1739	√
COPA Airlines	√		−0.2283	√

Table 6. Change in Revenue in the Airlines of the Europe.

	Method Adopted		Change in Revenue %	Restated Data IFRS 15 versus IAS 18
	FRM	MRM		
Croatia Airlines		√	0	No data – declaration of no material effect
Finnair		√	0	No data – declaration of no material effect
AF-KLM	√		0.3219	√
Lufthansa Group		√	−5.0289	√
Aegean Group		√	0	No data – declaration of no material effect
Aer Lingus	√		−0.0830	√
Ryanair		√	−0.4912	√
Wizz Air		√	−0.1808	√
TAP Group	√		0.0293	√
SAS Group		√	0	No data – declaration of no material effect
International Airlines	√		−0.4005	√
Virgin Atlantic Group	√		−1.2914	√
Air Partner	√		30.47	√
Easy Jet		√	−0.3589	√
British Airways	√		0.3681	√
Fast Jet		√	0	No data – declaration of no material effect
Icelandair	√		−0.1086	√
Norwegian Air		√	−1.1836	√
El Al		√	−0.2468	√
Aeroflot		√	0	No data – declaration of no material effect
Turkish Airlines		√	−0.0731	√
Pegasus Airlines		√	0.2907	√

data and declared "no material effect" was assumed to be 0. In this context, the average change in revenue in the region is –0.40% without Air Partner effect versus 1% with Air Partner effect. Comparative data was provided by around 73% of airlines.

4.2.3 The Case of the Airlines from Middle East and Africa

Airlines from Middle East and Africa experience the change in revenue from IAS 18 to IFRS 15 between 0% and 1.95% (Table 7). Consistent with Napier and Stadler (2020), the change in revenue in the airlines that did not provide comparative data and declared "no material effect" was assumed to be 0. In this context, the average change in revenue in the region is approximately 0.22%. Comparative data was not provided by almost 90% of airlines except for Qatar Airways.

4.2.4 The Case of the Airlines from Asia-Pacific

Airlines from Asia-Pacific experience the change in revenue from IAS 18 to IFRS 15 between –0.26% and 2.08% (Table 8). Consistent with Napier and Stadler (2020), the change in revenue in the airlines that did not provide comparative data and declared "no material effect" was assumed to be 0. The same policy was adopted for the airlines that did not provide comparative data and did not make any materiality declaration. In this context, the average change in revenue in the region is approximately 0.30%. Comparative data was provided by almost 64% of airlines.

4.2.5 The Case of the Airlines from China and Northern Asia

Airlines from China and Northern Asia experience the change in revenue from IAS 18 to IFRS 15 between 0% and 1.75% (Table 9). Consistent with Napier and Stadler (2020), the change in revenue in the airlines that did not provide comparative data and did not make any materiality declaration was assumed to be 0. In this context, the average change in revenue in the region is approximately 0.42%. Comparative data was provided by 80% of airlines.

Table 7. Change in Revenue in the Airlines of the Middle East and Africa.

| | Method Adopted | | | |
	FRM	MRM	Change in Revenue %	Restated Data IFRS 15 versus IAS 18
Royal Jordanian		√	0	No data – declaration of no material effect
Kenya Airways		√	0	No data – declaration of no material effect
Jazeera Airways		√	0	No data – declaration of no material effect
Air Mauritius		√	0	No data – declaration of no material effect
Qatar Airways		√	1.9511	√
Comair		√	0	No data – declaration of no material effect
Emirates		√	0	No data – declaration of no material effect
Air Arabia		√	0	No data – declaration of no material effect
Abu Dhabi Aviation		√	0	No data – declaration of no material effect

Table 8.   Change in Revenue in the Airlines of the Asia-Pacific.

| | Method Adopted | | | |
	FRM	MRM	Change in Revenue %	Restated Data IFRS 15 versus IAS 18
Regional Express		√	−0.0063	√
Alliance Airlines		√	0	No data – declaration of no material effect
Qantas	√		0.3986	√
Virgin Australia		√	−0.2572	√
Korean Air		√	0	No data – assumed to be immaterial
Asiana Airlines		√	0.9807	√
Air Asia X		√	0	No data – assumed to be immaterial
Air New Zealand	√		0.1890	√
Cebu Pacific Air		√	2.0831	√
Singapore Airlines		√	0	No data – assumed to be immaterial
Sri Lankan Airlines	√		−0.1338	√

Table 9.   Change in Revenue in the Airlines of the China and Northern Asia.

| | Method Adopted | | | |
	FRM	MRM	Change in Revenue %	Restated Revenue Data IFRS 15 versus IAS 18
Cathey Pacific Airlines		√	1.7499	√
Air China Group		√	0.0346	√
China Southern Airlines		√	0.0885	√
China Eastern Airlines		√	0.2417	√
China Airlines		√	0	No data – assumed to be immaterial

4.2.6 Overall Analysis of the Airlines

The change in revenue from IAS 18 to IFRS 15 in the global context refers to approximately −0.19% on average without Air Partner effect versus 0.35% with Air Partner effect. Air Partner is the only airline that experienced major change in the determination of revenue during the transformation process from IAS 18 to IFRS 15. Therefore, it is like a noise in the general pattern of the change in airlines' revenue. In this regard, the global analysis reveals that the transition from IAS 18 to IFRS 15 had minimal effect on airlines except for exceptional cases.

In addition, around 65% of airlines provided comparative data based on IAS 18 and IFRS 15 versus 26% of airlines did not provide comparative data but declared "no material effect" and 9% of airlines did not provide comparative data as well as did not make any materiality declaration.

4.3 Effects of IFRS 15 and IFRS 16 on the Statement of Financial Position

After the adoption of IFRS 15 and IFRS 16, total assets and liabilities of AF-KLM increased by around 23% and 29%, respectively, versus the total equity which decreased by around 20% when the statement of financial position of the year 2017 and the restated the statement of financial position of the year 2017 were analyzed in the general context.

In particular, the difference between 2017 total current assets and the restated 2017 total current assets refers to 0.07% versus the difference between 2017 total non-current assets and the restated 2017 total non-current assets is 36%. On the other hand, the difference between 2017 total current liabilities and the restated 2017 total current liabilities is 9% versus the difference between 2017 total non-current liabilities and restated 2017 total non-current liabilities refers to almost 50%. As observed, major changes took place in the long-term assets and liabilities, but the effect of both standards was not at the same level.

Considering all these changes, the effects of IFRS 15 and IFRS 16 on the items of statement of financial position are discussed below.

4.3.1 Perspectives on IFRS 15

There are three major balance sheet items which were affected by the adoption of IFRS 15 (Air France – KLM, 2017, 2018): (1) trade receivables; (2) other provisions; and (3) deferred revenue on ticket sales.

Increase in "trade receivables": Before the adoption of IFRS 15, the revenue recognition on ticket issuing and change fee had been done at the date of change or issuance. However, the revenue recognition on ticket issuing and change fees has changed and is now done at the transport date after the adoption of IFRS 15, because these ticket issuing and change fees are not considered to be a separate service providing a benefit to the passenger in the absence of transportation. In connection with sales revenue account, therefore, the "trade receivables" account also increased by around 1% during the transition from IAS 18 to IFRS 15. This change in policy has a minor effect on the total current assets.

Decrease in "other provisions": Before the adoption of IFRS 15, the recognition on the power-by-the hour contracts (overhaul of aircraft equipment and engines) had been based on the invoicing schedule, that is, according to flight hours and thus a provision had been made for the expected costs. This amount had been reported in "other provisions." However, recognition on the power-by-the hour contracts has changed and is based on the costs incurred after the adoption of IFRS 15. Therefore, "other provisions" account decreased by around 5% during the transition from IAS 18 to IFRS 15.

Increase in "deferred revenue on ticket sales": Before the adoption of IFRS 15, revenue related to unused tickets had been recognized at the date the ticket was issued. However, revenue recognition of unused ticket has changed and is based on a historical statistical rate for unused tickets which is regularly updated, at the theoretical date of the transport after the adoption of IFRS 15. Therefore, "deferred revenue on ticket sales" account increased by around 4.50% during the transition from IAS 18 to IFRS 15.

As analyzed above, the adoption of IFRS 15 does not lead to a major change on the statement of financial position of AF-KLM before and after the restatement for the year 2017.

4.3.2 Perspectives on IFRS 16

Under IFRS 16, the preparers of financial information must present the leased assets and the lease liabilities on the statement of financial position regardless of the types of the lease. There are two options to present leased assets that also called the right-of-use assets and lease liabilities under IFRS 16.

Right-of-use assets and lease liabilities are presented in the statement of financial position or disclosed in the notes [IFRS 16.47] (IASB, 2018r). If they are presented on the face of the statement of financial position, they should be separately presented from other assets and other liabilities. However, if they are not presented separately, the preparers of financial statements should include right-of-use assets within the same line item as that within which the corresponding underlying assets would be presented if they were owned; and disclose which items in the statement of financial position include those right-of-use assets and lease liabilities.

In the context of AF-KLM, observations reveal that the company presents its right-of-use assets as a separate item from other non-current assets on the face of the statement of financial position because the amount of right-of-use assets is material. Consisting of around 27% of non-current assets and 19% of total assets in restated 2017, and 25% of non-current assets and 18% of total assets in 2018, these assets are the second biggest item reported on the assets of the statement of financial position right after the flight equipment which reports owned aircraft after the adoption of IFRS 16 involving 37% of the fleet in 2017 and 39% of the fleet in 2018.

When the composition of right-of-use assets is examined, the airline's capitalized lease contracts include aircraft lease contracts, real estate lease contracts, and other assets lease contracts such as company cars, spare parts, and engines. Being the major item, aircraft consist of around 66% and 60% of the right-of-use assets in restated 2017 and 2018 (Fig. 1). In this context, data reveals that leased aircraft consists of 63% of the fleet in 2017 and 61% in 2018, as evidence that AF-KLM is a lease intensive airline.

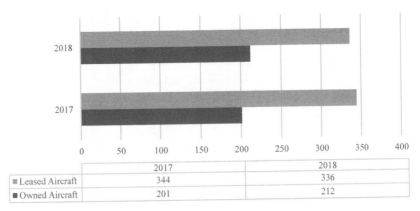

	2017	2018
■ Leased Aircraft	344	336
■ Owned Aircraft	201	212

Fig. 1.   Composition of Aircraft Fleet of AF-KLM.

When the lease composition of AF-KLM is examined, finance-leased aircraft consists of 20%, and operating leased aircraft consists of 43% of the fleet in 2017 versus the number of finance-leased aircraft involves around 17%, and operating leased aircraft involves 44% of the fleet in 2018 (Fig. 2). Before the adoption of IFRS 16, the statement of financial position for the year 2017 reflected the effect of only 31% of leased aircraft but the restated statement financial position for the year 2017 reflects the effects of an additional 69% of leased aircraft, except for the two capitalization exemptions proposed by the standard for lease contracts with a duration equal or less than 12 months and lease contracts for which the underlying asset has a low value which has been defined by the airline as below US$5,000 (Air France – KLM, 2018). Therefore, observations reveal that right-of-use assets are the item which has a major change in the total non-current assets.

On the other hand, the company presents its lease liabilities as a separate item from other current liabilities and other non-current liabilities. However, it reports its lease related liabilities in two ways. The airline reports its debts on financial leases with bargain options in the "financial debt" account on the statement of financial position. In this context, analysis reveals that there is almost a 4% decrease between the 2017 and restated 2017 financial lease debt considering both its short-term and long-term structure because the airline benefited from the two capitalization exemptions mentioned above. This debt has been existed since the former standard IAS 17 came into force as a standard requiring the capitalization of financial leases. Therefore, its effect on total liabilities has been already reflected.

The airline reports its lease liabilities other than "debts on financial lease with bargain option" in the "lease debt" account. This account is a new one reported on the statement of financial position considering the effect of IFRS 16. As it is in the case of "financial debt" account, the company presents its short-term lease debt as a separate item within the current liabilities consisting of 8% of current liabilities and around 4% of total liabilities in restated 2017 and 2018. However, the amount of long-term lease debt is material. Consisting of around 25% non-current liabilities and 14% of total liabilities in restated 2017, and 24%

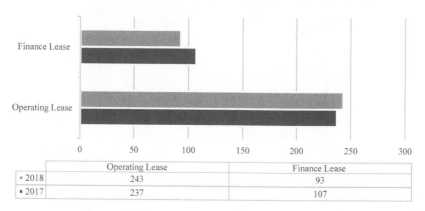

Fig. 2.   Lease Composition of Aircraft Fleet of AF-KLM.

of long-term liabilities and 13% of total liabilities in 2018, long-term lease debt is the second largest item reported in the liabilities section of the statement of financial position right after the long-term financial debt.

When the composition of lease liabilities other than "debts on financial leases with bargain options" is examined, around 20% of lease debt is current versus around 80% of lease debt which is non-current in restated 2017 as well as around 22% of lease debt is current versus around 78% of lease debt which is non-current in 2018. This indicates that most leases are long-term in nature.

In addition, the content of these lease debts includes lease debt – aircraft, lease debt – real estate, and lease debt – other. Consisting of the major lease debt item, lease debt – aircraft consists of around 81% of total lease debt in restated 2017 and around 77% of total lease debt in 2018.

In addition, the airline recognizes return obligation liability in respect of the required maintenance obligations within the framework of the lease of aircraft to lessors under IFRS 16. Therefore, this amount increased current and non-current liabilities of the airline.

Therefore, observations reveal that the reflection of all lease liabilities through the "lease debt" account in addition to the existing "financial debt" account as well as the return obligation liability have major effect on the 2017 and restated 2017 current and non-current liabilities.

As analyzed above, the adoption of IFRS 16 leads to a major change on the statement of financial position of AF-KLM before and after the restatement for the year 2017.

4.4 Effects of IFRS 15 and IFRS 16 on the Income Statement

4.4.1 Perspectives on IFRS 15

There are two items affected by the adoption of IFRS 15 in terms of the income statement: (1) sales revenue and (2) external expenses such as the commissions paid to agents, booking fees, and credit card commissions. In this context, research reveals that sales revenue of the airline increased by 0.32% and external expenses increased by 3.16%. IFRS 15 has minor effect on the income statement of AF-KLM before and after the restatement for the year 2017.

4.4.2 Perspectives on IFRS 16

The airline prepares its traditional income statement by nature (Air France – KLM, 2017, 2018). In this context, three issues should be considered: (1) the airline was reporting EBITDAR and EBITDA on the face of the income statement due to the operating lease costs under IAS 17; (2) because operating leases are presented as if they are finance leases under IFRS 16, the reporting of the aircraft operating lease costs were removed at the 2017 restatement, and thus EBITDA became the only performance measure, and an increase in EBITDA was realized, consistent with the expectations of IFRS 16 (IASB, 2016t); thus EBITDA increased by around 46%; and (3) while aircraft operating lease costs were removed, depreciation expenses and interest expenses are recorded on the income statement (Marşap & Yanık, 2018). Thus, aircraft operating lease costs were replaced by additional lease-based depreciation expenses and interest expenses on the income statement. Therefore, the airline's depreciation expenses increased by around 60% and interest expenses increased by around 150% at the 2017 restatement due to the lease effect.

IFRS 16 has major effect on the income statement of AF-KLM before and after the restatement for the year 2017.

4.5 Effects of IFRS 15 and IFRS 16 on the Statement of Cash Flows

4.5.1 Perspectives on IFRS 15
The airline prepares its statement of cash flows using the indirect approach in the operating section. In this context, IFRS 15 has very minor effect on the restated statement of cash flows in terms of net income and change in working capital requirement.

4.5.2 Perspectives on IFRS 16
Considering the indirect approach, preparers of financial information use restated net income for the period and restated depreciation expenses to calculate restated net cash flows from operating activities to reflect the effects of IFRS 16. Therefore, net income increased by 159% and the amount of net cash flows from operations increased by around 41% after the restatement.

As a reflection of IFRS 16 due to the maintenance of leased aircraft, net cash flows from investing activities increased by around 10%.

The airline classifies cash paid from lease liabilities in the financing section of the statement of cash flows in line with [IFRS 16.50]. But interest paid including leases is classified in the operating section. The amount of interest paid increased by 140% at the 2017 restatement.

In addition, the airline presented "payment of debt resulting from finance lease liabilities" in the financing section before the restatement but started to represent its cash payments on all lease debts in this account after the restatement, leading to an increase in cash outflows from lease debts of around 38%.

4.6 Effect of IFRS 15 and IFRS 16 on the Ratios

This section of the chapter considers the financial analysis of the airline's financial statements for the year 2017, 2017(restated), and 2018 by observing the effects of IFRS 15 and IFRS 16 during the transition process in terms of liquidity, solvency, and profitability of the airline.

4.6.1 Liquidity Ratios
Considering liquidity ratios, this chapter focuses on net working capital, current ratio, and its cash basis counterpart. Before the analysis of these metrics, it should be noted that the composition and reported 2017 and restated 2017 values of current assets are the same after the adoption of IFRS 15 and IFRS 16 except for the slight increase in the amount of trade receivables but the composition and values 2017 and restated 2017 of current liabilities changed because "other provisions"

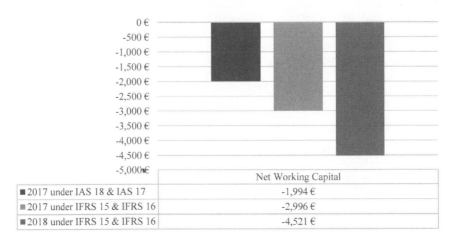

	Net Working Capital
■ 2017 under IAS 18 & IAS 17	-1,994 €
■ 2017 under IFRS 15 & IFRS 16	-2,996 €
■ 2018 under IFRS 15 & IFRS 16	-4,521 €

Fig. 3. Net Working Capital for AF-KLM in Millions.

and "deferred revenue" increased due to the adoption of IFRS 15 and IFRS 16. The preparers of financial information included all the lease liabilities except for short-term leases and leases of low-value assets into the statement of financial position, and thus a separate liability item reports short-term portion of all lease liabilities as well as return obligation liabilities in respect of the required mainte-nance obligations within the framework of the lease of aircraft to lessors.

In this context, net working capital is negative before and after the restatement (Fig. 3). The weakness of the net working capital increases as a reflection of the lease related current liability items, following IFRS 15 and IFRS 16. Net working capital decreased by 50% after the restatement.

Consistent with the decreasing trend in net working capital, the current ratio reveals the same decreasing trend of 9% from 2017 to restated 2017 (Fig. 4). In addition, the cash basis counterpart of the current ratio also confirms this fact. However, the slight increase of this ratio should not be misleading because the cash basis counterpart of the current ratio is based on restated net cash flows from operations under the indirect method which led to a 41% increase in the operating cash flows due to the restated net income through restated sales rev-enue, and restated depreciation expenses, following the adoption of IFRS 15 and IFRS 16. Both the current ratio and its cash basis counterpart verify the decrease in liquidity from 2017 to restated 2017.

In addition, the downward trend of net working capital from restated 2017 to 2018 continued. In this regard, the total of current assets went down by 14% versus the total of current liabilities which went up by 2% from restated 2017 to 2018. The tightening of current assets is greater than the expansion of current lia-bilities due to the payment of the current portion of financial debt and lease debt that was due in 2018. Therefore, the current ratio declined below the level of the restated 2017. Consistent with the 2018 current ratio, the airline's net cash flows from operations decreased by around 9.50% in 2018 versus its current liabilities which decreased by 2%, leading to a lower cash flow ratio.

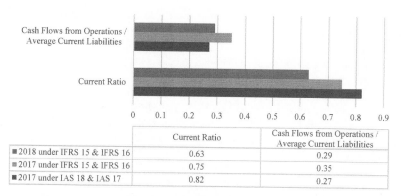

	Current Ratio	Cash Flows from Operations / Average Current Liabilities
■2018 under IFRS 15 & IFRS 16	0.63	0.29
■2017 under IFRS 15 & IFRS 16	0.75	0.35
■2017 under IAS 18 & IAS 17	0.82	0.27

Fig. 4. Current Ratio and its Cash Basis Counterpart for AF-KLM.

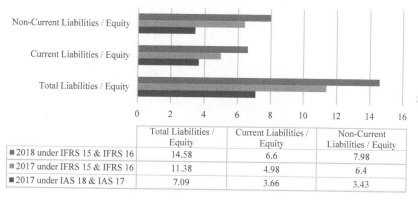

	Total Liabilities / Equity	Current Liabilities / Equity	Non-Current Liabilities / Equity
■2018 under IFRS 15 & IFRS 16	14.58	6.6	7.98
■2017 under IFRS 15 & IFRS 16	11.38	4.98	6.4
■2017 under IAS 18 & IAS 17	7.09	3.66	3.43

Fig. 5. Leverage Ratios on Equity for AF-KLM.

4.6.2 Solvency Ratios

In terms of solvency ratios, this chapter considers the leverage on equity ratios (total liabilities/equity, current liabilities/equity, and non-current liabilities/ equity), leverage on asset ratio (total liabilities/total assets), interest coverage ratio, and its cash basis counterpart.

Due to the decrease in other provisions (current and non-current) and increase in deferred revenue (current only) in terms of IFRS 15, and the inclusion of lease liabilities (current and non-current) to the statement of financial position except for the lease liabilities on short-term leases and leases of low-value assets, as well as return obligation liability (current and non-current) in terms of IFRS 16, the composition of current liabilities and non-current liabilities was changed (Fig. 5). Therefore, leverage on equity ratios revealed an upward trend from 2017 to restated 2017. Total liabilities/equity went up by 61%, current liabilities/equity increased by 36%, and non-current liabilities/equity increased by 87% after the restatement. When the change in total liabilities/equity ratio is examined in the current and non-current context, it should be noted that the increase in non-current liabilities/equity ratio is greater than current liabilities/equity ratio due to the long-term nature of leases. In addition, total liabilities/equity increased by 28% from restated 2017 to 2018 due to the increase in trade payables, deferred revenue, and additional long-term leases in 2018.

Consistent with leverage on equity ratios, leverage on asset ratio also decreased due to the decrease in other provisions (current and non-current) and increase in deferred revenue (current only) and the increase in lease liabilities following the adoption of IFRS 15 and IFRS 16 (Fig. 6). In this context, debt financing of total assets increased by 6% from 2017 to restated 2017, and 2% from restated 2017 to 2018.

Consistent with the leverage ratios on equity, the cash basis counterpart of these leverage ratios also confirm that the debt payment ability of the airline decreases from 2017 to restated 2017 following the adoption of IFRS 15 and IFRS 16 and in 2018 as well (Fig. 7).

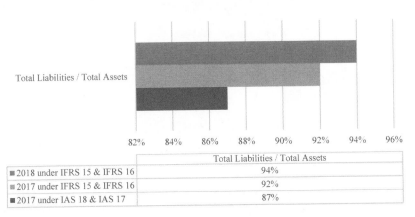

	Total Liabilities / Total Assets
▪ 2018 under IFRS 15 & IFRS 16	94%
▪ 2017 under IFRS 15 & IFRS 16	92%
▪ 2017 under IAS 18 & IAS 17	87%

Fig. 6. Leverage Ratio on Assets for AF-KLM.

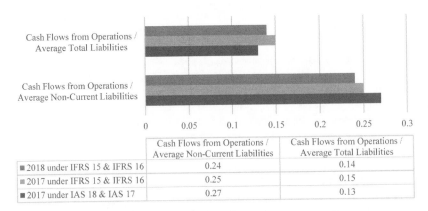

	Cash Flows from Operations / Average Non-Current Liabilities	Cash Flows from Operations / Average Total Liabilities
▪ 2018 under IFRS 15 & IFRS 16	0.24	0.14
▪ 2017 under IFRS 15 & IFRS 16	0.25	0.15
▪ 2017 under IAS 18 & IAS 17	0.27	0.13

Fig. 7. Cash Basis Leverage Ratios for AF-KLM.

In addition, the airline's interest coverage ability decreased from 2017 to restated 2017 following **IFRS 15** and **IFRS 16** (Fig. 8). Even if the airline's sales revenue increased by 0.32% and selling expenses increased by 3.16% after the restatement under **IFRS 15** versus **EBITDA** which increased by around 30% due to the removal adjustment of aircraft operating lease costs under **IFRS 16**, the airline's cost of financial debt reported on the face of the income statement increased by 129% due to the inclusion of operating lease interest expenses into the cost of financial debt. Therefore, this situation created a 42% decrease in the interest coverage ratio. In line with this finding, the cash basis counter part of the interest coverage ratio also confirms that the airline's interest payment ability decreased by around 39%. In 2018, both ratios did not make a considerable upward shift because **EBITDA** decreased by 11% versus interest expense decreased by 17% as well as (cash flows from operations + interest paid) decreased by 10% versus interest paid which decreased by 15% in 2018. This change kept the upward shift limited.

4.6.3 Profitability Ratios

In terms of profitability, this chapter takes the following metrics into consideration: asset turnover ratio, EBITDA/Net Sales, EBIT/Net Sales, Net Income/Net Sales, ROA, and ROE.

(1) The asset turnover ratio decreased around 18% from 2017 to restated 2017 due to the increase in trade receivables under **IFRS 15** and the reflection of right-of-use assets in total assets following the adoption of **IFRS 16** while sales revenue increased by 0.32% under **IFRS 15** (Fig. 9). In 2018, the increase in sales revenue of 2.50% and the decrease in total assets of 3% created an upward shift over the asset turnover ratio.

(2) To analyze the change in EBITDA/Net Sales ratio from 2017 to restated 2017, two parameters are considered on the face of income statement: (1) sales revenue increased by 0.32% under **IFRS 15** and (2) EBITDA increased by around 46% due to the removal of aircraft operating lease costs reported between EBITDAR and EBITDA on the income statement, following the adoption

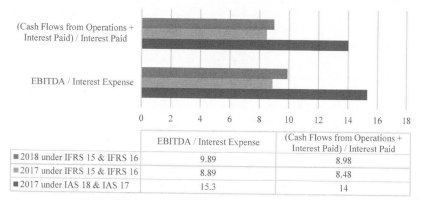

	EBITDA / Interest Expense	(Cash Flows from Operations + Interest Paid) / Interest Paid
■ 2018 under IFRS 15 & IFRS 16	9.89	8.98
■ 2017 under IFRS 15 & IFRS 16	8.89	8.48
■ 2017 under IAS 18 & IAS 17	15.3	14

Fig. 8. Interest Coverage and Payment for AF-KLM.

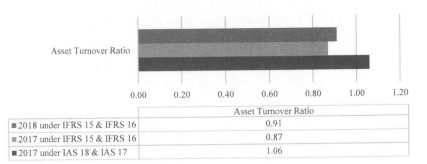

	Asset Turnover Ratio
■ 2018 under IFRS 15 & IFRS 16	0.91
■ 2017 under IFRS 15 & IFRS 16	0.87
■ 2017 under IAS 18 & IAS 17	1.06

Fig. 9.   Asset Turnover Ratio for AF-KLM.

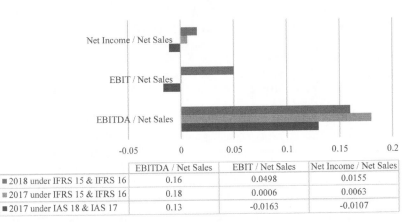

	EBITDA / Net Sales	EBIT / Net Sales	Net Income / Net Sales
■ 2018 under IFRS 15 & IFRS 16	0.16	0.0498	0.0155
■ 2017 under IFRS 15 & IFRS 16	0.18	0.0006	0.0063
■ 2017 under IAS 18 & IAS 17	0.13	-0.0163	-0.0107

Fig. 10.   Profitability Ratios Related to Net Sales for AF-KLM.

of IFRS 16 (Fig. 10). Therefore, this ratio improved after the restatement. In addition, the ratio slightly decreased in 2018 due to the increase in airline's expenses, leading to a decrease in EBITDA.

(3) To observe the change in EBIT/Net Sales ratio from 2017 to restated 2017, the items reported between EBITDA and EBIT are considered: (a) amortization, depreciation, and provisions; and (b) sales of aircraft equipment, and other non-current income and expenses. These items carried EBITDA to EBIT that refers to income from operating activities (operating profit or loss) of the airline. In 2017, EBIT/Net Sales ratio is negative because the airline experienced an operating loss (Fig. 10). However, this operating loss turned out to be an operating profit due to the domino effect of the removal of the aircraft operating lease costs from the income statement under IFRS 16. Therefore, the negative EBIT/Net Sales ratio turned out to be a positive ratio after the restatement. In 2018, the airline improved its EBIT as well as its sales revenue, and thus leading to a considerable increase in the ratio.

(4) To determine the change in Net Income/Net Sales from 2017 and restated 2017, the change in the value of items reported right after the EBIT is

important in addition to considering the domino effect of the items reported above the EBIT line. In 2017, the airline experienced a loss at the level of net income (Fig. 10). After the restatement, this loss turned out to be a profit. In this context, the 459% positive increase in other net financial income and expenses that offset the 150% increase in net cost of financial debt particularly due to the adoption of IFRS 16 provided the airline the opportunity to declare profit after the restatement. In 2018, the airline improved its net income by 152% through increasing its sales revenue, its EBIT, and decreasing its net cost of financial debt.

(5) In 2017, ROA and ROE were negative due to the loss at the level of net income (Fig. 11). After the restatement, both ratios turned out to be positive. In 2018, both ratios improved due to the increase in net income.

4.6.4 Summary of Ratio Analysis
This is the summary of the ratio analysis that is based on the simultaneous adoption of IFRS 15 and IFRS 16. Therefore, it reveals the cumulative effect of IFRS 15 and IFRS 16 on the ratios of the AF-KLM (Table 10).

4.7 Analysis of Disclosures under IFRS 16

Due to the major effect of IFRS 16 on the financial statements compared to IFRS 15, this section analyses the compliance level of mandatory disclosures under IFRS 16 in addition to voluntary disclosures.

4.7.1 Perspectives on Mandatory Disclosures
In the first year of adoption, the research reveals that the airline met the mandatory disclosures from the lessee perspective in both restated 2017 and 2018. The airline's IFRS 16 related disclosures show full compliance for the mandatory disclosure requirements. The disclosures provided by the airline (Air France – KLM, 2018) are shown below (Table 11).

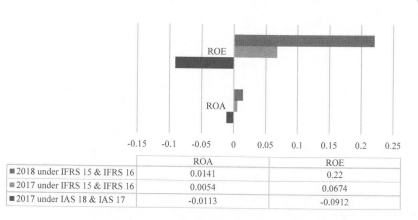

	ROA	ROE
■ 2018 under IFRS 15 & IFRS 16	0.0141	0.22
■ 2017 under IFRS 15 & IFRS 16	0.0054	0.0674
■ 2017 under IAS 18 & IAS 17	-0.0113	-0.0912

Fig. 11. ROA and ROE for AF-KLM.

Table 10.   Effect on the Ratios after the Restatement.

	Effect after the Restatement
Liquidity ratios	
Net working capital	Decrease
Current ratio	Decrease
Cash flows from operations/average current liabilities	Slight increase
Solvency ratios	
Total liabilities/equity	Increase
Total current liabilities/equity	Increase
Total non-current liabilities/equity	Increase
Total liabilities/total assets	Increase
Cash flows from operations/average non-current liabilities	Decrease
Cash flows from operations/average total liabilities	Slight increase
EBITDA/interest expense	Decrease
(Cash flows from operations + interest paid)/ interest paid	Decrease
Profitability	
Asset turnover ratio	Decrease
EBITDA/net sales	Increase
EBIT/net sales	Increase
Net income/net sales	Increase
ROA	Increase
ROE	Increase

4.7.2 Perspectives on the Voluntary Disclosures

In addition to the mandatory disclosures, the standard regulates additional voluntary qualitative and quantitative information about the lessee's leasing activities to help the users of financial information to assess the effect of leases over the financial position, performance, and cash flows [IFRS 16.59]. Among the voluntary disclosures, this research points out that the disclosure related to the lessee's leasing activities is the only voluntary disclosure adopted the airline. Disclosure provided by the airline (Air France – KLM, 2018) is shown below (Table 12).

5. CONCLUSION

This chapter reveals that the reflection of the simultaneous adoption of IFRS 15 and IFRS 16 is variable over the financial statements. In the general context, the effect of IFRS 15 is minor over the financial statements of the airlines except for Air Partner versus the effect of IFRS 16 is major over the financial statements due to the inclusion of all leased assets and lease liabilities except for short-term leased assets and leased assets with low value. In particular, the minor effect of IFRS 15 and major effect of IFRS 16 also holds for the case of AF-KLM as well. Therefore, the shift of liquidity and solvency ratios that was experienced in AF-KLM is expected to be almost the same for other airlines. However, this is not expected to be the case for profitability ratios because there are several parameters

Table 11. Mandatory Disclosures of the AF-KLM.

Required Disclosure	Declaration by AF-KLM
Depreciation charge for right-of-use assets by class of underlying asset [IFRS 16.53a]	The airline's capitalized lease contracts are aircraft lease contracts, real estate lease contracts, and other assets lease contracts such as company cars, spare parts, and engines. Their depreciation expenses were reported in the disclosure of the right-of-use assets
Interest expense on lease liabilities [IFRS 16.53b]	The interest expense was reported in the "net cost of financial debt and other financial income and expenses" disclosure of the airline
A lessee that benefits from exemptions provided by the IFRS 16.6 for its short-term leases and leases of low-value assets, does not capitalize them. Therefore, that lessee that accounts for short-term leases or leases of low-value assets discloses that fact [IFRS 16.60] and must satisfy the following three disclosures [IFRS 16.53c, 16.53d, 16.53e]	The airline declared that it benefited from this exemption and declared as follows in the disclosure of "restatement of 2017 financial statements": The two capitalization exemptions proposed by the standard – lease contracts with a duration equal or less than 12 months and lease contracts for which the underlying asset has a low value when new which has which has been defined by the airline as below US$5,000
The expense relating to short-term leases accounted for applying IFRS 16.6. This expense need not include the expense relating to leases with a lease term of one month or less [IFRS 16.53c]	The airline declared its short-term rent which is not capitalized in the disclosure of the right-of-use assets
The expense relating to leases of low-value assets accounted for applying IFRS 16.6. This expense shall not include the expense relating to short-term leases of low-value assets included in IFRS 16.53c [IFRS 16.53d]	The airline declared its leases of low-value assets which are not capitalized in the disclosure of the right-of-use assets
The expense relating to variable lease payments not included in the measurement of lease liabilities [IFRS 16.53e]	The airline declared its variable rent payments which are not capitalized in the disclosure of the right-of-use assets
Income from subleasing right-of-use assets [IFRS 16.53f]	No observation in terms of subleasing
Total cash outflow for leases [IFRS 16.53g]	Total cash flow for leases was reported in the disclosure of "lease debt" as reimbursement as well as it was declared in the investing section of the statement of cash flows
Additions to right-of-use assets [IFRS 16.53h]	The airline reported its additions in the disclosure of the right-of-use assets as a new contract
Gains or losses arising from sale and leaseback transactions [IFRS 16.53i]	No observation in terms of sales and leaseback transactions
The carrying amount of right-of-use assets at the end of the reporting period by class of underlying asset [IFRS 16.53j]	The carrying amount of right-of-use assets by class of aircraft, maintenance, land and real estate, and other was reported in the disclosure of the right-of-use assets as of December 31, 2017 and December 31, 2018
Maturity analysis of lease liabilities [IFRS 16.58]	The airline reported the maturity analysis of lease liabilities in the disclosure of "lease debt" as the lease debt maturity breakdown

Table 12. Voluntary Disclosures of AF-KLM.

Voluntary Disclosure	Declaration by AF-KLM
The nature of the lessee's leasing activities [IFRS 16.59a]	Leasing activities were stated in the accounting policy section of the airline's annual report under subtitle of lease contracts *Types of capitalized lease contracts* *Aircraft lease contracts* include leased aircraft *Real estate lease contracts* include surface areas rented in hubs, lease contracts on building dedicated to the maintenance business, customized lounges in airports other than hubs and lease contracts on office buildings *Other assets lease contracts* correspond to company cars, pools of spare parts and engines. *Types of non-capitalized lease contracts* The group uses the two exemptions foreseen by the standard allowing for non-recognition in the balance sheet: short-term lease contracts and lease contracts for which the underlying assets have a low value *Short duration lease contracts* are the contracts whose duration is equal to or less than 12 months. They mainly relate to leases of (a) surface areas in our hubs with a reciprocal notice period equal to or less than 12 months; (b) accommodations for expatriates with a notice period equal to or less than 12 months; and (c) spare engines for a duration equal to or less than 12 months *Low-value lease contracts* concern assets with a value equal to or less than US$5,000. They include, notably, lease contracts on printers, tablets, laptops, and mobile phones

that should be considered in terms of change in profitability such as upward or downward change in sales revenue, external expenses, EBITDAR, aircraft operating lease costs, EBITDA, amortization, depreciation and provisions, EBIT, net cost of financial debt, and other financial income and expenses at the transition process from IAS 18 to IFRS 15 and from IAS 17 to IFRS 16.

In addition, the mandatory disclosures requirements of the AF-KLM are in full compliance with the standard at its first adoption. The airline provides some voluntary disclosure as well.

In this context, further research would be to measure the change in ratios under the simultaneous effect of IFRS 15 and IFRS 16 considering the airlines whose aircraft fleet is based on operating lease almost in full, and to observe compliance level of mandatory disclosure requirements of the entire IFRS adopting airline industry.

CHAPTER 4

SOME OBSERVATIONS ON IFRS 8 OPERATING SEGMENTS: THE CASE OF THE AIRLINE INDUSTRY

ABSTRACT

This chapter focuses on the application of segment reporting under IFRS 8 in the context of the airline industry. It analyses the airlines' disclosures related to segment reporting considering 11 aspects of segment reporting in the regional and global context. Observations reveal that reporting of segmental disclosures in the airline industry is diverse at different levels. In this regard, the following conclusions were drawn: (1) the nature of segments reported by the airlines is diverse due to methods adopted in preparation of operating segments; (2) factors such as internal reporting system, and nature of business used to identify the airline's reportable segments were stated by most airlines; (3) types of products and services from which each reportable segment derives its revenues were stated by all airlines; (4) proportion of total revenues represented by separately reportable segments exceeds 75% of the revenue rule of IFRS 8; (5) most segmental performance measures are non-IFRS and diverse; (6) a limited number of airlines use dual reporting currency in segment reporting; (7) most airlines reported segment assets and liabilities for each reportable segment; (8) most airlines reported between 6 and 10 income and expense items in segment reporting; (9) segmental cash flow information is reported by one airline; (10) in terms of entity-wide disclosures, most airlines reported their revenue from major products and services in the revenue disclosures, most airlines reported their revenues on a geographical basis but few airlines reported

Perspectives on International Financial Reporting and Auditing in the Airline Industry
Studies in Managerial and Financial Accounting, Volume 35, 81–123
ISSN: 1479-3512/doi:10.1108/S1479-351220220000035004

their non-current assets on a geographical basis; and (11) more than half of the airlines did not declare the identity of the Chief Operating Decision Maker.

Keywords: IFRS 8; operating segments; airline industry; segment reporting; disclosures; diversity

1. INTRODUCTION

Segment information provides users of the financial statements with the information needed to evaluate an entity's different types of business activities and the different economic environments in which it operates (IATA, 2016d; Kieso, Weygandt, & Warfield, 2020). The objective of segment reporting is to help the users of financial information to better understand an entity's financial performance, to better assess its prospects for future net cash flows, and to make more informed judgments about the entity because traditional financial statements do not provide information related to different sectors and different geographic activities of the entity (Kieso et al., 2020; Marşap, 2001).

In the context of segment related disclosures, entities experience hesitations to disclose segmented data for various reasons (Kieso et al., 2020): (1) competitors, labor unions, suppliers, and certain government regulatory authorities may find additional disclosure helpful but this may harm the reporting company due to increased transparency; (2) the entity's management may be reluctant to take intelligent business risks due to the additional disclosure because shareholders may be dissatisfied with management due to segment reporting losses or unsatisfactory earnings; and (3) the usefulness of segmented information is limited due to the diversity in the choice of segments, and cost allocation among companies.

On the other hand, investors support the declaration of segment related disclosures for several reasons (Kieso et al., 2020): (1) segmented information is needed by potential and existing investors for the purpose of intelligent investment decision-making regarding a diversified company; and (2) investors can evaluate the differences between segments in terms of growth rate, risk, and profitability through sales and earnings of individual segments.

Considering International Financial Reporting Standards (IFRS), segment reporting has been regulated by IFRS 8 Operating Segments since 2009 which superseded IAS 14R Segment Reporting. IFRS 8 [IFRS 8.5] defines an operating segment as a component of an entity (a) that engages in business activities from which it may earn revenues and incur expenses; (b) whose operating results are regularly reviewed by the entity's Chief Operating Decision Maker (CODM) to make decisions about resources to be allocated to the segment and assess its performance; and (c) for which discrete financial information is available (IASB, 2018o).

In this context, Lucchese and Di Carlo (2016) compare the requirements of IAS 14R and IFRS 8 and state that the disclosures that were required or just encouraged from (a) to (n) under IAS 14R, except total assets and reconciliations, were transformed to be subordinated disclosures where they will be disclosed if the data is included in the segment results and regularly reviewed by the CODM (Table 1).

Table 1. Items of Disclosures Required by IAS 14 and IFRS 8.

	IAS 14R	IFRS 8
a) Revenues	Yes	Subordinated
b) Revenues from transactions with other operating segments of the same entity	Yes	Subordinated
c) Material items of income and expenses disclosed in accordance with IAS 1 Presentation Financial Statements	Just encouraged	Subordinated
d) Depreciation and amortization	Yes	Subordinated
e) Material non-cash items other than depreciation and amortization	Yes	Subordinated
f) Interest revenue and interest expense	Just encouraged	Subordinated
g) The entity's interest in the profit or loss of associates and joint ventures accounted for by the equity method	Yes	Subordinated
h) Income tax expense or income	Yes	Subordinated
i) Segment result	Yes	Subordinated
j) Total assets	Yes	Yes
k) The amount of investment in associates and joint ventures accounted for by the equity method	Yes	Subordinated
l) The amounts of additions to non-current assets other than financial instruments, deferred tax assets, post-employment, benefit assets (see IAS 19) and rights arising under insurance contracts	Yes	Subordinated
m) Liabilities	Yes	Subordinated
n) Reconciliations	Yes	Yes
Capital additions	Just encouraged	Not indicated
Other profitability measures	Just encouraged	Not indicated
Cash flow	Just encouraged	Not indicated
Entity-wide disclosure – Information about products and services	Not indicated	Yes
Entity-wide disclosure – Information about geographic areas	Not indicated	Yes
Entity-wide disclosure – Information about major customers	Not indicated	Yes

Due to the global nature of the airline industry, two research studies were considered in the design of this chapter: (1) the research of Nichols, Street, and Cereola (2012) which analyses the disclosures of IFRS 8 for the year 2009 in the European context considering 335 European blue-chip companies listed in 14 European stock exchanges; and (2) the Airline Disclosure Guide on Segment Reporting prepared by International Air Transport Association (IATA) in association with KPMG which focuses on a sample of 17 airlines in order to illustrate segment reporting under IFRS 8 for the year 2014 (IATA, 2016d). The purpose of these research studies is to promote comparability and consistency in the application of IFRS 8 Operating Segments.

This chapter analyses 11 sections related to segment reporting in the context of Nichols et al. (2012) and IATA (2016d) by revisiting the application of IFRS 8 in the airline industry in order to analyze the current status of segment reporting in the regional and global context with a sample of 52 airlines rather than 17 to observe the diversity and comparability in segment reporting in the IFRS context.

1.1. The Nature and Number of Segments Reported by the Airlines

Nichols et al. (2012) define the types of reportable segments under IFRS 8 as *single segment, pure line of business, matrix line of business, mixed line of business, pure geographic, matrix geographic*, and *mixed geographic*. In this context, the matrix approach focuses on two perspectives: (1) segments are primarily based on the lines of business and one or more lines of business may be disaggregated into geographic regions; or (2) segments are primarily based on geographic regions and one or more geographic regions may be disaggregated into lines of business. On the other hand, the mixed approach focuses on a combination of line of business and geographic segments: (1) segments primarily include lines of business in addition to geographic region(s); or (2) segments primarily include geographic regions in addition to lines of business.

In the same context, IATA (2016d) focuses on the four main types of segmental information: (1) *Business units* are related to the nature of the services provided and the revenue earned and most typically include revenue from passenger, cargo, and maintenance services; (2) *Operating entities* represent individually run and operated brands or businesses; (3) *Combination* represents the reportable segments that are a mixture of business units and operating entities; and (4) *Whole business* is where the whole operation is considered to be one segment reporting to the CODM where the business is performed based on resource allocation for benefit of a group network.

Within the framework of the types of reportable segments indicated by Nichols et al. (2012) and IATA (2016d), it should be noted that (1) "single segment" of Nichols et al. (2012) refers to the "whole business" of IATA (2016d) with or without the segment type of "others"; (2) "pure line of business" of Nichols et al. (2012) refers to the "business units" of IATA (2016d); and (3) "mixed line of business" and "mixed geographic" of Nichols et al. (2012) is similar to the "combination" of IATA (2016d) but there is a slight difference due to the concept of operating entities in the airline industry.

In this context, this chapter analyses the trends of the composition of the different types of reportable segments in the airline industry in the regional and global context. In addition, this chapter observes the number of segments reported by airlines except for the segment type "others."

1.2. Factors Used to Identify the Airline's Reportable Segments

The disclosures section of IFRS 8 (IFRS 8.22) states that factors used to identify the entity's reportable segments must be disclosed. In this context, this chapter analyses whether these factors were disclosed, and which factors were generally displayed for the reporting period in the regional and global context.

1.3. Types of Products and Services from which Each Reportable Segment Derives its Revenues

The disclosures section of IFRS 8 (IFRS 8.22) requires the declaration of types of products and services from which each reportable segment derives its revenues. In this context, this chapter analyses whether these products and services were disclosed, and which products and services were displayed by the sampled airlines for the reporting period in the regional and global context.

1.4. Proportion of Total Revenues Represented by Separately Reportable Segments

IFRS 8 (IFRS 8.15) requires that total external revenue reported by operating segments must represent at least 75% of the entity's revenue. In this context, this chapter analyses the airlines with one or more reportable operating segments excluding segment type of "others" to observe the pattern of percentage representation of revenue over the reportable segments for the reporting period in the regional and global context.

1.5. Segmental Performance Measures

IFRS 8 states that an entity must report a measure of profit or loss for each reportable segment [IFRS 8.23] and the CODM can use one or more performance measures of an operating segment's profit or loss for the allocation of resources to the segment and the assessment of its performance [IFRS 8.25].

Nichols et al. (2012) indicate that European companies report one, two, or three segment profitability metrics and most of the segment profitability metrics disclosed are non-IFRS. Operating profit (segment result or operating income), earnings before interest and tax (EBIT), earnings before tax, and earnings before interest, tax, depreciation, and amortization (EBITDA) are the most common. On the other hand, they indicate "net income" or "profit or loss" as another preferred segment profitability metric in the European context. It has been defined by IAS 1 [IAS 1.7] (IASB, 2018e) and therefore it is an IFRS metric.

Based on the research of Nichols et al. (2012), this chapter analyses the trends of segmental performance measures in terms of the number of reported segment profitability metrics per airline, and in the context of the adoption of the IFRS and non-IFRS metrics because IFRS 8 does not define a specific segmental performance metric.

1.6. Reporting Currency in Segment Reporting

IATA (2016d) reveals that Korean Air is one of the airlines which prefers dual reporting currency in segment reporting. Considering prior research, this chapter analyses whether there is any other airline which prefers dual reporting currency in segment reporting.

1.7. Total Assets, Total Liabilities, and Other Asset Items for Each Reportable Segment

IFRS 8 states that an entity must report a measure of total assets and liabilities for each reportable segment if such amounts are regularly provided to the CODM [IFRS 8.23]. In addition, IFRS 8 states that an entity must disclose (a) the amount of investment in associates and joint ventures accounted for by the equity method, and (b) the amounts of additions to non-current assets other than financial instruments, deferred tax assets, net defined benefit assets and rights arising under insurance contracts, if the specified amounts are included in the measure of segment assets reviewed by the CODM or are otherwise regularly provided to the CODM, even if not included in the measure of segment assets [IFRS 8. 24].

Nichols et al. (2012) report that items of information that are disclosed for reportable segments under IFRS 8 such as segment assets, segment liabilities, equity method investment, and additions to non-current assets vary in the European context.

Considering prior research, this chapter analyses whether there is diversity in the reporting of items of balance sheet that are disclosed for reportable segments in the airline industry.

1.8. Income and Expense Items Disclosed

IFRS 8 states that an entity must disclose (a) revenues from external customers; (b) revenues from transactions with other operating segments of the same entity; (c) interest revenue; (d) interest expense; (e) depreciation and amortization; (f) material items of income and expense disclosed in accordance with IAS 1 Presentation of Financial Statements; (g) the entity's interest in the profit or loss of associates and joint ventures accounted for by the equity method; (h) income tax expense or income; and (i) material non-cash items other than depreciation and amortization about each reportable segment if the specified amounts are included in the measure of segment profit or loss reviewed by the CODM, or are otherwise regularly provided to the CODM, even if not included in that measure of segment profit or loss [IFRS 8.23].

Nichols et al. (2012) informs that items that are disclosed for segment profitability vary in the European context. IATA (2016d) states that 18% of airlines having one or more reportable segment except the segment of "others" report

"5 or less" income and expense items, 46% of these airlines report "between 7 and 9" items, and 36% of these airlines report "15 or more" items. Considering prior research, this chapter analyses whether there is diversity in the reporting of items of segment profitability under IFRS 8 in the airline industry and the number of income and expense items reported on the airlines' segment related disclosures for the reporting period in the regional and global context.

In addition, the chapter focuses on whether there is any airline that reports segment interest revenue net of its interest expense which indicates that CODM relies primarily on net interest revenue for the purpose of resource allocation decisions and assessment of the performance of the segment if the most segment's revenue is not from interest [IFRS 8.23].

1.9. Segmental Cash Flow Information

IFRS 8 does not regulate the reporting of segmental cash flow information. However, IAS 7 [IAS 7.50(d)], as a voluntary disclosure, encourages the reporting of segmental cash flow information to understand the financial position and liquidity of an entity having one or more reportable segment except for the segment type of "others" (IASB, 2018g). In this context, Nichols et al. (2012) emphasize that segmental cash flow information is relevant to understanding the entity's overall financial position, liquidity, and cash flows. This fact is also supported by the paper of Street and Stanga (1989).

Nichols et al. (2012) states that 29% of the European entities reported segmental cash flow information as a voluntary disclosure in the initial adoption of IFRS 8. In this regard, this chapter analyses whether segmental cash flow information is disclosed in the airline industry.

1.10. Entity-wide Disclosures

There are four types of entity-wide disclosures under IFRS 8. This chapter analyses the reporting pattern of the following issues: (1) revenue from external customers for products and services; (2) revenue by geographical areas; (3) geographical allocation of assets; and (4) information about major customers.

Revenue from external customers for products and services: Unless the necessary information is not available and the cost to develop would be excessive, IFRS 8 states that an entity must report the revenues from external customers for each product and service, or each group of similar products and services [IFRS 8.32].

This chapter analyses the pattern of the airlines reporting revenues from external customers for each product and service and where they report this information in the context of (a) revenue disclosure, (b) the face of the income statement, or (c) segmental disclosure.

Revenue by geographical areas: Unless the necessary information is not available and the cost to develop would be excessive, IFRS 8 states that an entity must report revenues from external customers (i) attributed to the entity's country of domicile and (ii) attributed to all foreign countries in total from which the entity derives revenues [IFRS 8.33]. If revenues from external customers attributed to an individual foreign country are material, those revenues must also be disclosed.

In this context, IATA (2016d) declares that there are four methods that are typically used by airlines to define geographic sectors: (1) *Origin method* refers to the country or region where the sales originated; (2) *Departure method* refers to the country or region where the flight departed; (3) *Destination method* refers to the country or region of the ticket destination; and (4) *Network approach* takes into account both departure and arrival location (such as Europe – North America and North America – Europe sectors as part of the same "Atlantic" area).

Considering these methods, this chapter analyses the pattern of airlines reporting revenue by geographical areas and the methods adopted by airlines in reporting this information.

Geographical allocation of assets: Unless the necessary information is not available and the cost to develop would be excessive, IFRS 8 states that an entity must report non-current assets other than financial instruments, deferred tax assets, post-employment benefit assets, and rights arising under insurance contracts (i) located in the entity's country of domicile and (ii) located in all foreign countries in total in which the entity holds assets [IFRS 8.33]. If assets in an individual foreign country are material, those assets must be separately disclosed.

In this regard, IATA (2016d) declares that there are several methods adopted by airlines: (1) *Location method* refers to location of entities assets; (2) *Deployment approach* is valid if assets and associated costs are limited to certain routes (such as specific fleet types owned by the airline are deployed on an "Atlantic" area only); (3) *No disclosure* method is adopted when airlines state that a disclosure of assets on a geographic basis in an accurate manner is not possible as a result of aircraft moving flexibly around the world.

Considering these methods, this chapter analyses the pattern of airlines reporting geographical allocation of assets and the methods adopted by airlines in reporting this information.

Information about major customers: IFRS 8 states that the entity must disclose revenues from transactions with a single external customer amount to 10% or more of an entity's revenues, the total amount of revenues from each such customer, and the identity of the segment or segments reporting the revenues [IFRS 8.34].

In this context, this chapter analyses whether there is such a case of customer in the airline industry.

1.11. Identity of the CODM

IFRS 8 identifies the CODM as a function that regularly reviews the operating results of the entity to make decisions about resources to be allocated to the segment and assess its performance [IFRS 8.7] such as a Chief Executive Officer (CEO), Chief Operating Officer, or a group of executive directors or others. The standard does not explicitly state that the identity of CODM must be disclosed.

In this context, Nichols et al. (2012) state that 36% of European entities disclosed the identity of the CODM in the segment disclosures such as (a) the Board of Directors (BoD); (b) a high level of management group such as executive committee, management board, executive board, and executive management team; and (c) an individual such as CEO, president, and general manager.

Considering Nichols et al. (2012), this chapter analyses the number of airlines declaring the identity of the CODM, and the composition of its identity in the airline industry.

This chapter has the following structure: Section 2 presents a literature review on IFRS based segment reporting in the airline industry; Section 3 explains the data, accounting period for the data, and the research methodology; Section 4 discusses the regional and global findings of the segment reporting based on IFRS 8 in the airline industry. Finally, Section 5 presents concluding remarks along with main findings.

2. LITERATURE REVIEW ON IFRS 8 SEGMENT REPORTING IN THE AIRLINE INDUSTRY

The Airline Disclosure Guide on Segment Reporting prepared by IATA & KPMG (2016d) is the only academic research to observe the patterns of segment reporting in the airline industry under IFRS 8. It considers the financial statements and disclosures of the year 2014 to promote the comparability and consistency of segment reporting in the airline industry. However, the sample of this prior research includes 17 airlines, only. Therefore, it does not fully represent the IFRS based financial reporting of the airline industry in the regional and global context due to limited number of airlines from Asia-Pacific, Europe, Americas, China and Northern Asia, and Middle East and Africa.

Instead, this chapter extends the sample from 17 to 52 airlines to take a comprehensive IFRS based segmental picture of the airline industry in the regional and global context.

3. DATA AND RESEARCH METHODOLOGY

3.1 Data

The sample is based on 52 airlines whose financial reporting is based on IFRS. The data has been collected from their annual financial statements whose reporting period ends on December 31, 2018 or its equivalent for the year 2019. The sample has been developed in the regional and global context as follows (Table 2).

3.2 Research Methodology

This research assesses collected data using the frequency of distribution and the content analysis methods followed by Nichols et al. (2012) and IATA (2016d).

Table 2.   List of Airlines.

Americas	*Africa – Middle East*
GOL Linhas Aereas	Royal Jordanian
Azul Brazilian Airlines	Kenya Airways
Air Transat	Jazeera Airways
Air Canada	Air Mauritius
LATAM Airlines Group	Comair
Aeromexico	Emirates
Volaris	Air Arabia
COPA Airlines	Abu Dhabi Aviation
Europe	*Asia-Pacific*
Croatia Airlines	Regional Express
Finnair – Finnair Group	Alliance Airlines
Air France – KLM Group	Qantas
Lufthansa Group	Virgin Australia
Aegean Group	Korean Air
Ryanair	Air Asia X
Wizz Air	Air New Zealand
TAP Group	Cebu Pacific Air
SAS – SAS Group	Singapore Airlines
International Airlines Group	Sri Lankan Airlines
Virgin Atlantic Group	*China and North Asia*
Air Partner	Cathay Pacific Airlines
Easy Jet	Air China Group
British Airways	China Southern Airlines
Fast Jet	China Eastern Airlines
Icelandair	China Airlines
Norwegian Air	
El Al	
Aeroflot	
Turkish Airlines	
Pegasus Airlines	

4. FINDINGS

4.1. Observations on Segment Reporting in the Americas

4.1.1 The Nature and Number of Segments Reported by the American Airlines

The sample of airlines from this region reveals that methods of deriving segments are based on "whole business," "business units," and "matrix line of business" (Table 3). Matrix line of business of Aero Mexico focuses on single reportable segment titled "air transportation" and disaggregated into three geographic regions: (1) Mexico; (2) Northern, Central, and Southern America; and (3) Europe and Asia. In this sample, all segments are reportable and there is no segment type of "others."

4.1.2 Factors Used to Identify the Airline's Reportable Segments

The number of the airlines declaring the factors used to identify their reportable segments is stated below (Table 4). It includes the following airlines: Copa Airlines, Air Canada, Azul Brazilian, and Gol Linhas. Factors refer to resource allocation and business management, internal reporting system, and nature of business.

Table 3. Segmental Reporting Categories by Airlines from Americas.

# of Segments	Airline	Whole Business	Business Units	Matrix Line of Business	Total
1	Copa Airlines	√			
	Volaris	√			
	Air Canada	√			
	Air Transat	√			
	Azul Brazilian	√			5
1	Aero Mexico			√	1
2	Gol Linhas		√		2
	Latam		√		

Table 4. Declaration of Segmental Factors by Airlines from Americas.

N = 8	Yes	No
Airlines declared the factors	4 (50%)	4 (50%)

4.1.3 Types of Products and Services from which Each Reportable Segment Derives its Revenues

Information related to the types of products and services from which each reportable segment derives its revenue was stated by all airlines. Products and services constituting the segments are provided below (Fig. 1). In this context, the composition of some of the products and services should be noted to provide a clear picture: (1) combined airlines activities, generally, refer to passenger and cargo services; and (2) holiday travel comprises vacation packages, hotel stays, and air travel.

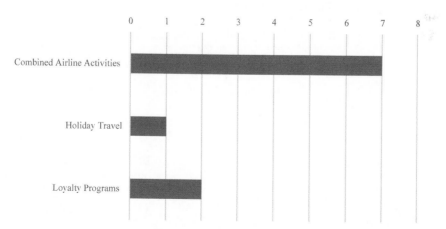

Fig. 1. Types of Products and Services by Airlines from Americas.

4.1.4 Proportion of Total Revenues Represented by Separately Reportable Segments
In the Americas region, the total external revenue of identified reportable segments of the sampled airlines with one or more reportable segments represents 100% of the airlines' total revenues because none of their airlines declared the segment type "others."

4.1.5 Segmental Performance Measures
In the Americas region, most airlines use one measure of segmental performance (Table 5). Two airlines (Latam and Aero Mexico) use non-IFRS performance measures as the following: "segment profit" and "profit before flight equipment rental expense, depreciation and amortization, financial income and expenses and income taxes (EBITDAR)" (Table 5). On the other hand, one airline (Gol Linhas) declares "gross profit," "operating result before financial result, net and income taxes," "income before income taxes" as the non-IFRS performance measure as well as "net income for the year" as the IFRS performance measure.

4.1.6 Reporting Currency
The sampled airlines reported their segment related disclosures using a single currency in the Americas region, including US Dollars, Pesos, Canadian Dollars, and Brazilian Reals.

4.1.7 Total Assets, Total Liabilities, and Other Asset Items for Each Reportable Segment
Since two airlines (Gol Linhas and Latam) have more than one reportable segment, they declared their total segment assets and total segment liabilities as follows (Table 6). In addition, one airline (Gol Linhas) classified its segment assets and liabilities as current and non-current as well as one airline (Latam) reported the amounts of additions to non-current assets.

Table 5. Analysis of Profitability Measures.

$N = 3$	1 Measure	4 Measures
Number of airlines	2 (67%)	1 (33%)
	Non-IFRS measure	Non-IFRS + IFRS measure
Number of airlines	2 (67%)	1 (33%)

Table 6. Composition of the Balance Sheet Items Disclosed by Airlines of the Americas.

Items Required Under IFRS 8 If Certain Conditions are Met	Number of Airlines Disclosing	Percentage of Airlines $N = 2$
Segment assets	2	100%
Segment liabilities	2	100%
Equity method investment	0	0%
Additions to non-current assets	1	50%

4.1.8 Income and Expense Items Disclosed

As in the previous case, Gol Linhas and Latam are the only airlines that declared their income and expense items for multiple reportable operating segments as follows (Table 7). Both reported 11 or more income and expense items including required and non-required items under IFRS 8. In this context, both disclosed almost all required items for each reportable segment as seen below (Table 8).

As an additional observation, depreciation and amortization is included in the accounts of "cost of services provided" and "administrative expenses" in the segment reporting of Gol Linhas, due to the segmental income statement by function. In addition, Latam's material non-cash items include disposal of fixed assets, inventory losses, doubtful accounts, and exchange differences.

4.1.9 Segmental Cash Flow Information

In the Americas region, Latam is the only airline that declared its net cash flows from operating, investing, and financing activities related to its two reportable segments. The airline also stated its cash outflows due to the purchases of PPE items and intangible asset items on a segmental basis.

4.1.10 Entity-wide Disclosures

Revenue from external customers for products and services: Except for Air Transat, seven airlines declared their revenues from external customers for each product

Table 7. Number of Income/Expense Items Reported by Airlines of the Americas.

Income and Expense Items Disclosed	Number of Airlines Disclosing	Percentage of Airlines $N = 2$
5 or less	0	0%
Between 6 and 10	0	0%
11 or more	2	100%

Table 8. Items of Profit/Loss Disclosures Reported by Airlines of the Americas.

Items Required Under IFRS 8 If Certain Conditions are Met	Number of Airlines Disclosing	Percentage of Airlines $N = 2$
Revenues from external customers	2	100%
Intersegment revenues	1	50%
Interest revenue	2	100%
Interest expense	2	100%
Depreciation and amortization	2	100%
Equity method income	2	100%
Income tax expense/benefit	2	100%
Material non-cash items other than depreciation and amortization (impairment)	1	50%

and service by classifying as passenger revenue, cargo and mail revenue, and mileage revenue. Most airlines reported this information in the disclosures of revenue prepared following IFRS 15 (Table 9).

Revenue by geographical areas: Airlines provided revenue related information by geographical areas at different levels (Fig. 2). Five airlines (Copa Airlines, Volaris, Aero Mexico, Air Canada, and Latam) declared the amount of the revenue and the method used to allocate revenue by geographical areas but one airline (Gol Linhas) did not declare the method used to allocate revenue by geographic areas even if it declared the amount of revenue as seen below.

On the other hand, there are some special cases in the segmental reporting of the revenue by geographic areas in the Americas region: two airlines did not report revenue by geographical areas in monetary terms because (1) Air Transat stated that it generates revenue mainly in the Americas and its revenues are not material outside the Americas and (2) Azul Brazilian stated that it generates revenue mainly in Brazil. Therefore, revenue stated on the face of the income statement can also be considered as a geographical representation of the revenue.

As an additional observation, one airline (Volaris) stated its major revenue generating region in the segmental disclosures as a percentage such as 30% of operating revenue from the United States.

Table 9. Reporting of the Revenue from External Customers by Airlines from Americas.

	Number of Airlines Disclosing	Percentage of Airlines $N = 8$
On the face of the income statement	2	25%
Disclosure of revenue	5	63%
Disclosure of segment reporting	0	–
No disclosure	1	12%

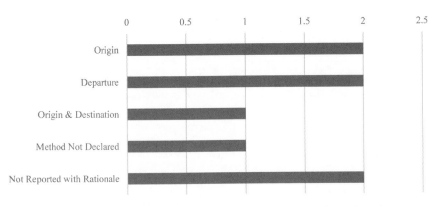

Fig. 2.   Geographical Allocation of Revenue by Airlines from Americas.

Geographical allocation of assets: Four airlines (Aero Mexico, Air Canada, Gol Linhas, and Latam) did not report the geographical allocation of their non-current assets without rationale. On the other hand, four other airlines declared their rationales on why there is no suitable basis to allocate those assets geographically in the disclosures as follows: (1) Copa Airlines stated that its aircraft fleet is mobile across geographic markets; (2) Volaris declared that its non-current assets are not material in foreign countries; (3) Air Transat expressed that its non-current assets are not material outside the Americas; and (4) Azul Brazilian Airlines stated that its non-current assets are mainly located in Brazil.

Information About Major Customers: None of the airlines disclosed information about the major customers. But Latam also stated that there was no revenue from transactions with a single customer amounting to 10% or more of total revenue.

4.1.11 Identity of the CODM
The identity of the CODM was declared by two airlines in the disclosures of segment reporting (Table 10). More than half the airlines did not declare the identity of the CODM.

4.2. Observations on Segment Reporting in the Europe

4.2.1 The Nature and Number of Segments Reported by the Airlines
The sample of airlines from this region reveals that methods of deriving segments are based on "whole business," "business units," and "combination" (Table 11). Some airlines (Aeroflot, Fast Jet, Tap Portugal, IA Group, and Air France – KLM) that have two or more reportable segments, also have segment type of "others."

4.2.2 Factors Used to Identify the Airline's Reportable Segments
The number of the airlines declaring the factors used to identify the airlines' reportable segments is stated below (Table 12). This includes all airlines except for Virgin Atlantic. Factors refer to the following issues: maximization of overall profitability, consideration of entire route network, internal reporting system, resource allocation decisions, as well as nature of operations and services such as different aircraft and airline services.

Table 10. Identity of CODM by Airlines from Americas.

Airlines	$N = 8$	%	CODM
Aero Mexico, Air Canada	2	25	An individual: CEO
Non-declared	6	75	–
Total	8	100	

Table 11.   Segmental Reporting Categories by Airlines from Europe.

# of Segments	Airline	Whole Business	Business Units	Operating Entities	Combination	Total
1	Pegasus	√				
	El Al	√				
	Norwegian	√				
	British Airways	√				
	Easy Jet	√				
	Virgin Atlantic UK	√				12
	SAS	√				
	Wizz Air	√				
	Ryanair	√				
	Aegean	√				
	Finnair	√				
	Croatia	√				
2	Turkish Airlines		√			2
	Aeroflot		√			
3	Icelandair		√			1
4	TAP		√			
	Air Partner		√			
	Air France – KLM				√	4
	Fast Jet				√	
5	Lufthansa				√	2
	IA Group			√		

Table 12.   Declaration of Segmental Factors by Airlines from Europe.

N = 21	Yes	No
Airlines declared the factors	20 (95%)	1 (5%)

4.2.3 Types of Products and Services from which Each Reportable Segment Derives its Revenues

Information related to the types of products and services from which each reportable segment derives its revenue was stated by all airlines in the region. Products and services constituting the segments are provided below (Fig. 3). In this context, the composition of some of the products and services should be noted to provide a clear picture: (1) regular public transport includes passenger services; and (2) non-airline business covers leasing, consulting, training, and hotel services.

4.2.4 Proportion of Total Revenues Represented by Separately Reportable Segments

In the European region, the total external revenue of identified reportable segments of the airlines with two or more reportable segments (excluding segment type "others") represents more than 75% of the airlines' total revenues (Fig. 4).

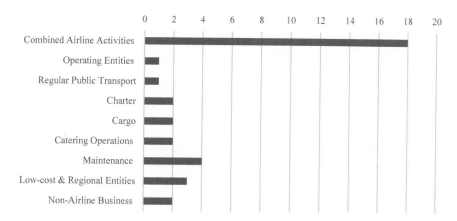

Fig. 3. Types of Products and Services by Airlines from Americas.

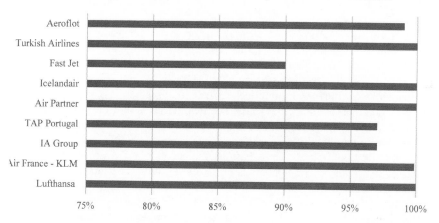

Fig. 4. Proportion of Revenues from Reportable Segments by Airlines from Europe.

4.2.5 Segmental Performance Measures

In the European region, more than half of the airlines use two measures of segmental performance (Table 13). Some airlines (Aeroflot, IA Group, Icelandair, Air Partner, Turkish Airlines, and Lufthansa) use non-IFRS performance measures including the following: "segment gross profit," "segment operating profit," "segment profit before tax from continuing operations," "segment EBIT," "adjusted EBIT," "segment EBITDA," "segment EBITDAR," "operating profit," "operating profit before exceptional items," "operating profit after exceptional items," "segmental gross profit," "operating profit before exceptional and other items," and "segment result" (Table 13). On the other hand, some airlines use a combination of non-IFRS and IFRS performance measures: (1) Fast Jet: EBITDA, "loss before tax," and "net loss"; (2) Air France/KLM: EBITDA, and "net income from continuing operations"; (3) TAP Portugal: "net operating income" and "net income from continuing operations."

Table 13.   Analysis of Profitability Measures from European Airlines.

$N = 9$	1 Measure	2 Measures	3 Measures
Number of airlines	1 (11%) Non-IFRS Measure	5 (56%) IFRS Measure	3 (33%) Non-IFRS + IFRS Measure
Number of airlines	6 (67%)	0	3 (33%)

4.2.6 Reporting Currency

Most airlines reported their segment related disclosures using a single currency in the region, including Euro, Pound, US Dollars, Norwegian Krone, and Turkish Lira. Croatian Airlines is the only airline whose segment reporting is based on Euro and Croatian Kuna.

4.2.7 Total Assets, Total Liabilities, and Other Asset Items for Each Reportable Segment

In the European region, some airlines having more than one reportable segment (Lufthansa, Air France – KLM, IA Group, Icelandair, Turkish Airlines, and Aeroflot) declared their total segment assets (Table 14). Five of them except for Lufthansa declared total segment liabilities as well. On the other hand, TAP Portugal and Air Partner did not declare their total segment assets and liabilities but provided their rationales: (1) TAP Portugal declared that they were not presented to the CEO; and (2) Air Partner stated that there was no suitable basis to allocate assets and liabilities on a segment basis.

As an additional observation, Fast Jet reported total segmental non-current assets rather than total segment assets. Four airlines (Lufthansa, Icelandair, Turkish Airlines, and Aeroflot) declared the amount of investment in associates accounted for by the equity method and five airlines (Lufthansa, Air France – KLM, Icelandair, Turkish Airlines, and Aeroflot) reported the amounts of additions to non-current assets.

4.2.8 Income and Expense Items Disclosed

Most airlines with multiple reportable operating segments reported "between 6 and 10" income and expense items including required and non-required items under IFRS 8 (Table 15).

Table 14.   Composition of the Balance Sheet Items Disclosed by European Airlines.

Items Required Under IFRS 8 If Certain Conditions are Met	Number of Airlines Disclosing	Percentage of Airlines $N = 9$
Segment assets	6	67%
Segment liabilities	5	56%
Equity method investment	4	44%
Additions to non-current assets	5	56%

Table 15. Number of Income/Expense Items Reported by European Airlines.

Number of Income and Expense Items Disclosed	Number of Airlines Disclosing	Percentage of Airlines $N = 9$
5 or less	2	22%
Between 6 and 10	5	56%
11 or more	2	22%

As an additional observation, the reporting of material non-cash items such as impairment losses (IA Group, Icelandair, and Turkish Airlines) is not frequently observed as seen below (Table 16), as well as two airlines (Air France – KLM, and IA Group) declared interest revenue and interest expense as net finance charges which would indicate that the CODM relies primarily on net interest revenue to assess the performance of the segment.

4.2.9 Segmental Cash Flow Information
None of the airlines reported segmental cash flows from operating, investing, and financing activities.

4.2.10 Entity-wide Disclosures
Revenue from external customers for products and services: Most airlines declared this revenue in the disclosures related to revenue under IFRS 15 (Table 17).

Table 16. Items of Profit/Loss Disclosures Reported by European Airlines.

Items Required Under IFRS 8 If Certain Conditions are Met	Number of Airlines Disclosing	Percentage of Airlines $N = 9$
Revenues from external customers	9	86%
Intersegment revenues	8	71%
Interest revenue	7	43%
Interest expense	7	57%
Depreciation and amortization	7	71%
Equity method income	6	43%
Income tax expense/benefit	6	29%
Material non-cash items other than depreciation and amortization (impairment)	3	29%

Table 17. Reporting of the Revenue from External Customers by European Airlines.

	Number of Airlines Disclosing	Percentage of Airlines $N = 21$
On the face of the income statement	5	24%
Disclosure of revenue	12	57%
Disclosure of segment reporting	4	19%

Revenue by geographical areas: All the airlines provided revenue related information by geographical areas. However, 17 airlines (except for Pegasus, El Al, Aegean, and Turkish Airlines) declared the methods that they used to declare geographic areas as seen below (Fig. 5). In addition, Ryanair declared its revenue by geographical areas considering revenue generated from countries in excess of 10% of total revenue.

Geographical allocation of assets: Seven airlines (British Airways, Easy Jet, SAS, Lufthansa, IA Group, Air Partner, and Fast Jet) reported their geographical allocation of their non-current assets, but one of them (Fast Jet) did not declare its method of reporting those assets (Fig. 6).

On the other hand, eight airlines did not report any information in this context without rationale versus six airlines which declared the rationale behind why they were not able to allocate those assets. In this context, (1) Pegasus Airlines declared that it has single reportable segment; (2) other airlines (Norwegian Air, Virgin Atlantic, Ryanair, and Finnair) stated that their major revenue earning

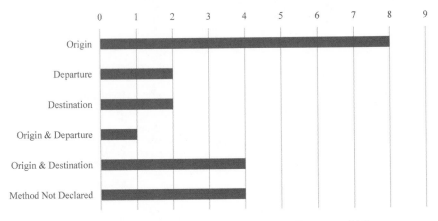

Fig. 5. Geographical Allocation of Revenue by European Airlines.

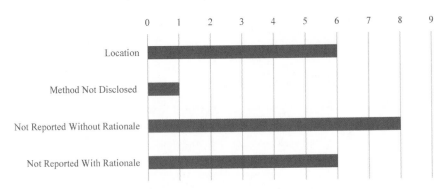

Fig. 6. Geographical Allocation of Assets by European Airlines.

assets (aircraft fleet) are employed across their worldwide route network, therefore there was no suitable basis to allocate those assets in the geographical context; and (3) one airline (SAS) declared that it allocated most of its non-current assets other than their aircraft assets by location method but there was no suitable basis for its aircraft fleet.

Information About Major Customers: Twenty-one airlines did not disclose any information about the major customers. But three of them (Finnair, Air Partner, and SAS) stated that there was no revenue from transactions with a single customer amounting to 10% or more of total revenue for the reporting period.

4.2.11 Identity of the CODM
Fifteen airlines declared the identity of the CODM in the disclosures of segment reporting as seen below (Table 18). More than half of the airlines did not report the identity of the CODM.

4.3. Observations on Segment Reporting in the Middle East and Africa

4.3.1 The Nature and Number of Segments Reported by the Airlines
The sample of airlines from this region reveals that methods of deriving segments are based on "whole business" and "business units" (Table 19). In this context, some airlines that have one or more than one reportable segment (Kenya Airways, Comair, Emirates, Air Arabia, and Abu Dhabi), also have the segment type of "others." On the other hand, Jazeera Airways did not report any other segmental information other than its reportable segments.

Table 18. Identity of CODM by European Airlines.

Airlines	$N = 21$	%	CODM
Pegasus, Easy Jet, Aegean, Air Partner, and Fast Jet	5	24	BoDs
El Al, Ryanair, and Aeroflot	3	14	An Individual: CEO and General Director
Norwegian, Air France/ KLM, IAG, Wizzair, Finnair, SAS, and British Airways	7	33	Executive management (similar terminology: Executive Committee, Management Committee, Senior Management Team, Group Executive Board, Executive Directors and other key management personnel, and Group Management)
Non-declared	16	29	–
Total	21	100	

Table 19.   Segmental Reporting Categories by Airlines from Middle East and Africa.

# of Segments	Airline	Whole Business	Business Units	Total
1	Air Arabia	√		2
	Royal Jordon	√		
2	Emirates		√	
	Air Mauritius		√	
	Jazeera Airways		√	6
3	Comair		√	
4	Abu Dhabi		√	
	Kenya Airways		√	

4.3.2 Factors Used to Identify the Airline's Reportable Segments
Factors used to identify the airlines' reportable segments were stated by six airlines except for Jazeera and Royal Jordon in the region as seen below (Table 20). Factors generally refer to internal reporting system, strategic business units operating at different sectors, internal management risks and earning structure, as well as strategic decisions.

4.3.3 Types of Products and Services from which Each Reportable Segment Derives its Revenues
Information related to the types of products and services from which each reportable segment derives its revenue was stated by all airlines in the region. Products and services constituting the segments are provided below (Fig. 7). In this context,

Table 20.   Declaration of Segmental Factors by Airlines from Middle East and Africa.

N = 8	Yes	No
Airlines declared the factors	6 (75%)	2 (25%)

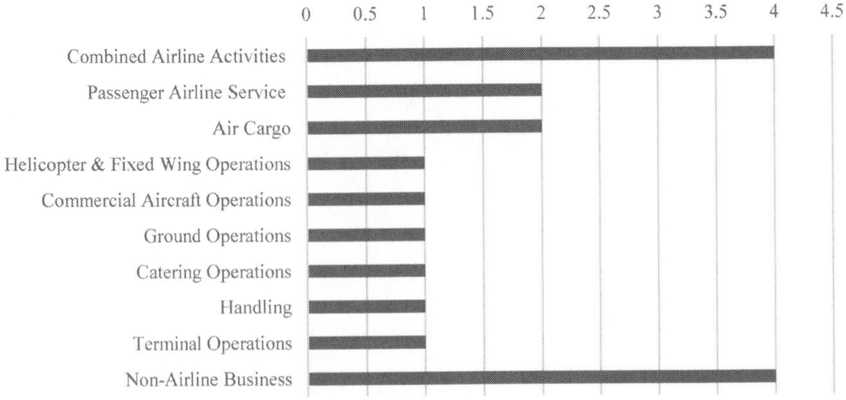

Fig. 7.   Types of Products and Services by Airlines from Middle East and Africa.

the composition of some of the products and services should be noted to provide a clear picture: (1) helicopter and fixed wing operations include charter flights and third-party maintenance; (2) commercial aircraft operations cover commercial air transportation and aircraft management; and (3) non-airline business includes the management of airline's investment portfolio, tourism and hospitality, property investment and training businesses, as well as lease rental income.

4.3.4 Proportion of Total Revenues Represented by Separately Reportable Segments

In the region, the total external revenue of identified reportable segments of the airlines having one or more than one reportable segment (excluding segment type "others") represents more than 75% of the airlines' total revenues (Fig. 8).

4.3.5 Segmental Performance Measures

In the region, most airlines use one measure of segmental performance (Table 21). Airlines having one or more reportable segments (excluding segment type "others") (Kenya Airways, Air Mauritius, Comair, Emirates, and Air Arabia) reported their profit or loss for each reportable segment using non-IFRS performance measures as the following: "segment result," "segment profit," "operating profit," "segment result before administrative expenses including impairment losses, impairment in an associate, other operating income, fair value gain on investment property, financial income and financial expense," and "segmental operating profit before depreciation, amortization, property rental income, unrealized translation loss on dollar denominated loan, impairments and profit on sale of assets" (Table 21). On the other hand, Abu Dhabi Aviation reports "profit for the year" (net income) as IFRS performance measure. Jazeera has no disclosure in this context.

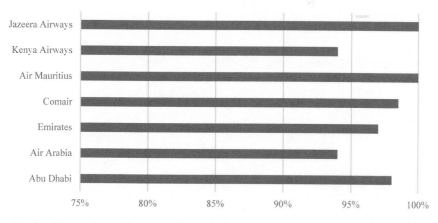

Fig. 8. Proportion of Revenues from Reportable Segments by Airlines from Middle East and Africa.

Table 21. Analysis of Profitability Measures by Airlines from Middle East and Africa.

$N = 7$	1 Measure	%	2 Measures	%
Number of airlines	5	71	1	14
	Non-IFRS Measure		IFRS Measure	
Number of airlines	5	71	1	14

4.3.6 Reporting Currency
The sampled airlines reported their segment related disclosures using a single currency in the region, including Emirati Dirham, Kuwaiti Dinars, Rand, Euro, US Dollars, and Shilling.

4.3.7 Total Assets, Total Liabilities, and Other Asset Items for Each Reportable Segment
Among the airlines having one or more reportable segments (excluding segment type "others"), five airlines (Abu Dhabi, Air Arabia, Emirates, Comair, and Air Mauritius) declared their total segment assets while four of these five airlines (except for Emirates) declared total segment liabilities as well (Table 22). On the other hand, one airline (Kenya Airways) was not able to declare its total segment assets and liabilities, stating that there was no suitable basis to allocate assets and liabilities on a segment basis as well as one airline (Jazeera Airways) which did not declare its segment assets and liabilities without any rationale.

As an additional observation, two airlines provided a brief description of segment assets: (1) Air Arabia stated the composition of assets that are not included within the segment assets such as investment properties, investment in joint ventures and associates as well as short-term investment, and (2) Emirates declared that segment assets include intersegment receivables.

In addition, one airline (Emirates) declared the amount of investment in associates accounted for by the equity method and four airlines (Air Arabia, Emirates, Comair, and Air Mauritius) reported the amounts of additions to non-current assets.

4.3.8 Income and Expense Items Disclosed
Most airlines with multiple reportable operating segments reported "between 5 or less" income and expense items including required and non-required items under IFRS 8 (Table 23).

Table 22. Composition of the Balance Sheet Items Disclosed by Airlines from Middle East and Africa.

Items Required Under IFRS 8 If Certain Conditions are Met	Number of Airlines Disclosing	Percentage of Airlines $N = 7$
Segment assets	5	71%
Segment liabilities	4	57%
Equity method investment	1	14%
Additions to non-current assets	4	57%

Table 23. Number of Income/Expense Items Reported by Airlines from Middle East and Africa.

Number of Income and Expense Items Disclosed	Number of Airlines Disclosing	Percentage of Airlines $N = 7$
0	1	14%
5 or less	3	43%
Between 6 and 10	1	14%
11 or more	2	29%

As an additional observation, the reporting of income tax expense (Emirates and Air Mauritius) and material non-cash items such as impairment losses (Comair and Air Mauritius) is not frequently observed as seen below (Table 24).

4.3.9 Segmental Cash Flow Information
None of the airlines reported segmental cash flows from operating, investing, and financing activities.

4.3.10 Entity-wide Disclosures
Revenue from external customers for products and services: All airlines provided this information, but most airlines reported it in the disclosures of revenue under IFRS 15 (Table 25).

Table 24. Items of Profit/Loss Disclosures Reported by Airlines from Middle East and Africa.

Items Required Under IFRS 8 If Certain Conditions are Met	Number of Airlines Disclosing	Percentage of Airlines $N = 7$
Revenues from external customers	6	86%
Intersegment revenues	5	71%
Interest revenue	3	43%
Interest expense	4	57%
Depreciation and amortization	5	71%
Equity method income	3	43%
Income tax expense/benefit	2	29%
Material non-cash items other than depreciation and amortization (impairment)	2	29%

Table 25. Reporting of the Revenue from External Customers by Airlines from Middle East and Africa.

	Number of Airlines Disclosing	Percentage of Airlines $N = 8$
On the face of the income statement	0	–
Disclosure of revenue	7	88%
Disclosure of segment reporting	1	12%

Revenue by geographical areas: Two airlines (Emirates and Air Mauritius) provided revenue related information by geographical areas under origin method and destination method (Fig. 9). However, two airlines (Kenya Airways and Royal Jordan) did not state the methods that they used to declare geographic areas as seen below. In addition, revenue information by geographical areas was not declared by two airlines (Air Arabia and Jazeera Airways) without rationale versus two airlines (Abu Dhabi and Comair) did not provide revenue information by geographical areas with rationale: (1) Abu Dhabi stated that it primarily operates within United Arab Emirates and (2) Comair declared that it primarily operates within South Africa.

Geographical allocation of assets: None of eight airlines reported their non-current assets by geographic areas. Excluding the following four airlines: Air Arabia, Jazeera Airways, Air Mauritius, and Royal Jordan, other four airlines (Abu Dhabi, Emirates, Comair, and Kenya Airways) stated their rationales. In this context, (1) two airlines (Emirates and Kenya Airways) stated that there was no suitable basis to allocate aircraft assets in the geographical context because they are employed across their worldwide route network; and (2) other two airlines (Abu Dhabi and Comair) stated that they operate within their bases.

Information about major customers: None of the airlines disclosed any information about the major customers versus two airlines (Emirates and Kenya Airways) stated that there was no revenue from transactions with a single customer amounting to 10% or more of total revenue for the reporting period.

4.3.11 Disclosure of Identity of the CODM

Two airlines declared the identity of the CODM in the disclosures of segment reporting as seen below (Table 26). More than half of the airlines did not declare the identity of CODM.

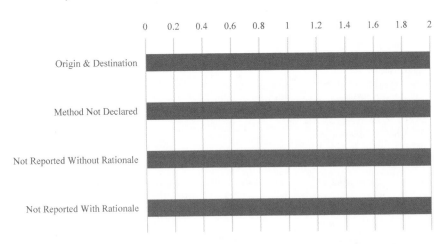

Fig. 9.   Geographical Allocation of Revenue by Airlines from Middle East and Africa.

Table 26. Identity of CODM by Airlines from Middle East and Africa.

Airlines	$N = 8$	%	CODM
Comair, Kenya Airways	2	25	An Individual: Joint CEO, CEO
Non-declared	6	75	–
Total	8	100	

4.4. Observations on Segment Reporting in Asia-Pacific

4.4.1 The Nature and Number of Segments Reported by the Airlines

The sample of airlines from the Asia-Pacific region reveals that methods of deriving segments are based on "whole business," "business units," "pure geographic," and "operating entities" (Table 27). The "pure geographic" of Air AsiaX refers to Malaysia, Thailand, and Indonesia. Some airlines (Korean Air and Singapore Airlines) having more than two reportable segments, also have segment of type of "others."

4.4.2 Factors Used to Identify the Airline's Reportable Segments

The number of airlines declaring the factors used to identify the airlines' reportable segments reflects all airlines in the region. Factors, generally, refer to resource allocation and performance decision, internal reporting system, key business activities, category of customer for each type of service, each airline that owns the air operator certificate under the brand name as well as nature of operations and services provided.

4.4.3 Types of Products and Services from which Each Reportable Segment Derives its Revenues

Information related to the types of products and services from which each reportable segment derives its revenue was stated by all airlines in the region. Products and services constituting the segments are provided below (Fig. 10). In this

Table 27. Segmental Reporting Categories by Airlines from Asia-Pacific.

# of Segments	Airline	Whole Business	Business Units	Pure Geographic	Operating Entities	Total
1	Alliance	√				
	Air New Zealand	√				3
	Cebu Pacific	√				
2	Regional		√			2
	Sri Lanka		√			
3	Korean Air	√				1
3	Air AsiaX			√		1
4	Singapore				√	
5	Virgin Atlantic		√			2
	Qantas		√			

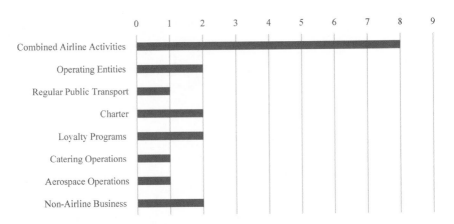

Fig. 10.   Types of Products and Services by Airlines from Asia-Pacific.

context, the composition of some of the products and services should be noted to provide a clear picture: (1) operating entities refer to the services provided by different entities which belong to Singapore Airlines and AirAsiaX; (2) aerospace operations include maintenance of aircraft and manufacture of aircraft parts; and (3) non-airline business includes hotel service, centralized management, and governance.

4.4.4 Proportion of Total Revenues Represented by Separately Reportable Segments

In the Asia-Pacific region, the total external revenue of identified reportable segments of the airlines with one or more reportable segments (excluding the segment type of "others") represents more than 75% of the airlines' total revenues (Fig. 11).

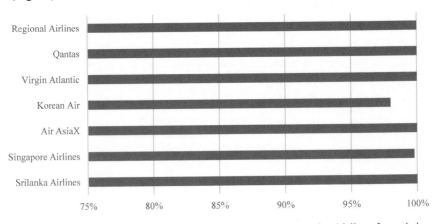

Fig. 11.   Proportion of Revenues from Reportable Segments by Airlines from Asia-Pacific.

4.4.5 Segmental Performance Measures

In the Asia-Pacific region, almost half of the airlines use one measure of segmental performance (Table 28). Airlines having one or more reportable segments (excluding segment type "others") (Korean Air, Air AsiaX, Virgin Atlantic, Qantas, and Regional Airlines) reported their profit or loss for each reportable segment using non-IFRS performance measures as the following: "operating profit," "operating income," "segment result," "net operating profit," "profit before taxation," "segment EBIT," "segment EBITDA," and "segment EBITDAR" (Table 28).

On the other hand, Sri Lankan Airlines reported "profit after tax" (net income) as an IFRS performance measure. In addition, Singapore Airlines declared one non-IFRS and one IFRS based performance measure as follows: "segment result" and "profit for the year" (net income).

4.4.6 Reporting Currency

Most airlines reported their segment related disclosures using a single currency in the region, including Australian Dollars, New Zealand Dollars, Singapore Dollars, except for Korean Air prefers reporting in Korean Won and US Dollars.

4.4.7 Total Assets, Total Liabilities, and Other Asset Items for Each Reportable Segment

Among the airlines having one or more reportable segments (excluding segment type "others") except for Virgin Atlantic Airlines and Qantas Airlines that did not declare their total segment assets and liabilities without any rationale, five airlines (Sri Lanka Airways, Singapore Airlines, Air AsiaX, Korean Air, and Regional Airlines) declared their total segment assets and total segment liabilities (Table 29).

Table 28. Analysis of Profitability Measures by Airlines from Asia-Pacific.

$N = 7$	1 Measure	%	2 Measures	%	3 Measures	%
Number of airlines	3	42	2	29	2	29
	Non-IFRS Measure		IFRS Measure		IFRS + Non-IFRS Measure	
Number of airlines	5	72	1	14	1	14

Table 29. Composition of Balance Sheet Items Disclosed by Airlines from Asia-Pacific.

Items Required Under IFRS 8 If Certain Conditions are Met	Number of Airlines Disclosing	Percentage of Airlines $N = 7$
Segment assets	5	71%
Segment liabilities	5	71%
Equity method investment	2	29%
Additions to non-current assets	3	43%

As an additional observation, two airlines (Singapore Airlines and Air AsiaX) declared the amount of investment in associates accounted for by the equity method and three airlines (Sri Lanka Airlines, Singapore Airlines, and Regional Airlines) reported the amounts of additions to non-current assets.

4.4.8 Income and Expense Items Disclosed

Among the airlines having one or more reportable segments (excluding segment type "others"), three airlines reported "between 6 and 10" and an additional three airlines reported "more than 11 or more" income and expense items as seen below in the context of required and non-required items (Table 30).

As an additional observation, the least frequently reported items are (1) interest in the profit or loss of associates accounted for by the equity method (Singapore Airlines and Qantas) and (2) income tax expenses (Sri Lankan, Singapore Airlines, Cebu Pacific Air, Virgin Atlantic, and Regional) (Table 31). In addition, six airlines (Sri Lankan, Singapore Airlines, Air AsiaX, Virgin Atlantic, Qantas, and Regional) reported material non-cash items other than depreciation and amortization such as impairment losses.

4.4.9 Segmental Cash Flow Information

None of the airlines reported segmental cash flows from operating, investing, and financing activities.

Table 30. Number of Income/Expense Items Reported by Airlines from Asia-Pacific.

Number of Income and Expense Items Disclosed	Number of Airlines Disclosing	Percentage of Airlines $N = 7$
5 or less	1	14%
Between 6 and 10	3	43%
11 or more	3	43%

Table 31. Number of Profit/Loss Items Reported by Airlines from Asia-Pacific.

Items Required Under IFRS 8 If Certain Conditions are Met	Number of Airlines Disclosing	Percentage of Airlines $N = 7$
Revenues from external customers	7	100%
Intersegment revenues	6	86%
Interest revenue	6	86%
Interest expense	6	86%
Depreciation and amortization	6	86%
Equity method income	2	29%
Income tax expense/benefit	4	57%
Material non-cash items other than depreciation and amortization (impairment)	6	86%

4.4.10 Entity-wide Disclosures

Revenue from external customers for products and services: All airlines reported revenue related information but reporting in the revenue disclosure or segment reporting does not dominate (Table 32).

Revenue by geographical areas: Six airlines (Sri Lankan, Singapore, Air New Zealand, Air AsiaX, Korean Air, and Virgin Atlantic) provided revenue related information by geographical areas (Fig. 12). However, two of them (Air AsiaX and Korean Air) did not state the method that they used to declare geographic areas as seen below. Four airlines did not report their revenues by geographical areas with no rationale.

Geographical allocation of assets: Two airlines (Air AsiaX and Korean Air) declared the geographical allocation of their non-current assets, but they did not state the method that they used in reporting (Fig. 13). On the other hand, five airlines (Sri Lankan, Singapore, Cebu Pacific Air, Air New Zealand, and Virgin Atlantic) stated that aircraft fleet assets are employed across their worldwide route network, thus there was no suitable basis to allocate those assets in the geographical context. Three airlines (Qantas, Alliance, and Regional) did not report geographical allocation of their non-current assets with no rationale.

Information About Major Customers: None of the airlines disclosed information about the major customers. In addition, Cebu Pacific Air and Qantas stated that there was no revenue from transactions with a single customer amounting to 10% or more of total revenue for the reporting period.

Table 32. Reporting of the Revenue from External Customers by Airlines from Asia-Pacific.

	Number of Airlines Disclosing	Percentage of Airlines $N = 10$
On the face of the income statement	2	20%
Disclosure of revenue	3	30%
Disclosure of segment reporting	4	40%
Disclosure combining revenue and segment reporting	1	10%

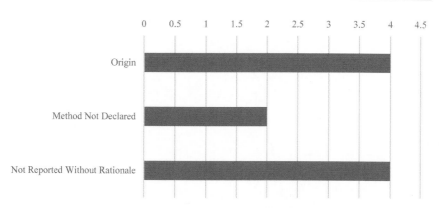

Fig. 12. Geographical Allocation of Revenue by Airlines from Asia-Pacific.

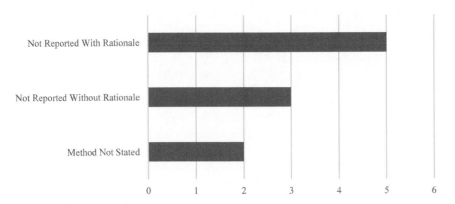

Fig. 13.   Geographical Allocation of Assets by Airlines from Asia-Pacific.

4.4.11 Disclosure of Identity of the CODM

Five airlines declared the identity of the CODM in the disclosures of segment reporting as seen below (Table 33). Half of the airlines did not declare the identity of CODM.

4.5. Observations on Segment Reporting in China and Northern Asia

4.5.1 The Nature and Number of Segments Reported by the Airlines

The sample of airlines from this region reveals that methods of deriving segments are based on "whole business" in the context of four airlines (China Southern, China Eastern, China Airlines, and Air China) that have one reportable segment versus "business units" in the context of one airline (Cathey Pacific) which has two reportable segments that refer to airline business and non-airline business segments (Table 34).

Table 33.   Identity of CODM by Airlines from Asia-Pacific.

Airlines	$N = 10$	%	CODM
Alliance Airlines	1	10	BoDs
Qantas Airways	1	10	Comprehensive: CEO, Group Management Committee, and BoDs
Virgin Atlantic, Air Asia X, and Cebu Pacific	3	30	An Individual: CEO, President, and CEO of the parent company
Non-declared	5	50	–
Total	10	100	

Table 34. Segmental Reporting Categories by Airlines from China and Northern Asia.

# of Segments	Airline	Whole Business	Business Units	Total
1	China Southern	√		
	China Eastern	√		4
	China Airlines	√		
	Air China	√		
2	Cathey Pacific		√	1

4.5.2 Factors Used to Identify the Airline's Reportable Segments

The factors used to identify the airlines' reportable segments were declared by three airlines (China Southern, Cathey Pacific, and Air China) in the region. They referred to the following issues such as internal organizational structure, internal reporting system, managerial needs, as well as nature of operations and services.

4.5.3 Types of Products and Services from which Each Reportable Segment Derives its Revenues

Information related to the types of products and services from which each reportable segment derives its revenue was stated by all airlines in the region. Products and services constituting the segments are provided below (Fig. 14).

4.5.4 Proportion of Total Revenues Represented by Separately Reportable Segments

In the region, the total external revenue of identified reportable segments of the airlines having one or more reportable segments (excluding segment type "others") represents more than 75% of the airlines' total revenues (Fig. 15).

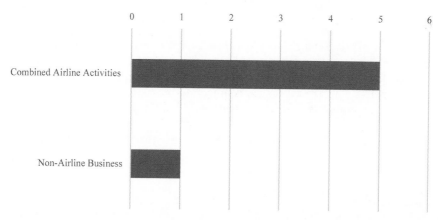

Fig. 14. Types of Products and Services by Airlines from China and Northern Asia.

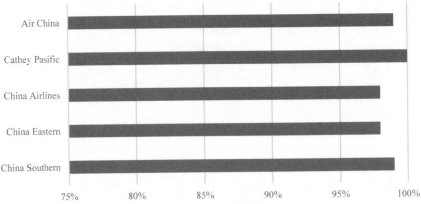

Fig. 15.   Proportion of Revenues from Reportable Segments by Airlines from China and Northern Asia.

4.5.5 Segmental Performance Measures

Most airlines use one measure of segmental performance (Table 35). Airlines having one or more reportable segments (excluding segment type "others") reported their profit or loss for each reportable segment using a single non-IFRS performance measure (Table 35). These included "reportable segment profit before taxation," "operating profit or loss," and "segment profit or loss." However, China Southern Airlines used a non-IFRS performance measure as "reportable segment profit before taxation" and an IFRS performance measure as "reportable segment profit after taxation (net income)."

4.5.6 Reporting Currency

Airlines reported their segment related disclosures using a single currency in the region, including US Dollars, Hong Kong Dollars, and the People's Renminbi (RMB).

4.5.7 Total Assets, Total Liabilities, and Other Asset Items for Each Reportable Segment

Among the airlines having one or more reportable segments (excluding segment type "others"), four airlines (China Southern, China Eastern, China Airlines, and Air China) declared their total segment assets while three of these four airlines

Table 35.   Analysis of Profitability Measures by Airlines from China and Northern Asia.

$N = 5$	One Measure	%	Two Measures	%
Number of airlines	4	80	1	20
	Non-IFRS Measure		Non-IFRS + IFRS Measure	
Number of airlines	4	80	1	20

(except for China Airlines) declared total segment liabilities as well (Table 36). On the other hand, one airline (Cathey Pacific) was not able to declare its total segment assets and liabilities, stating that there was no suitable basis to allocate assets and liabilities on a segment basis.

As an additional observation, two airlines (China Airlines and Cathey Pacific) declared the amount of investment in associates accounted for by the equity method and four airlines (except for China Airlines) reported the amounts of additions to non-current assets.

4.5.8 Number of Income and Expense Items Disclosed

Among the airlines having one or more reportable segments (excluding segment type "others"), most disclosed "between 6 and 10" income and expense items as seen below in the context of required and non-required items (Table 37).

As an additional observation, three airlines declared their interest in the profit or loss of associates accounted for by the equity method (China Southern, China Airlines, and Air China) as well as income tax expense (China Southern, Cathey Pacific, and Air China) (Table 38). In addition, three airlines (China Southern, China Eastern, and Air China) reported their impairment losses as part of material non-cash items as well as one airline (Cathey Pacific) which declared interest revenue and interest expense as net finance charges which would indicate that the CODM relies primarily on net interest revenue to assess the performance of the segment.

4.5.9 Segmental Cash Flow Information

None of the airlines reported net cash flows from operating, investing, and financing activities.

Table 36. Composition of Balance Sheet Items Disclosed by Airlines from China and Northern Asia.

Items Required Under IFRS 8 If Certain Conditions are Met	Number of Airlines Disclosing	Percentage of Airlines $N = 5$
Segment assets	4	80%
Segment liabilities	3	60%
Equity method investment	2	40%
Additions to non-current assets	4	80%

Table 37. Number of Income/Expense Items Reported by Airlines from China and Northern Asia.

Number of Income and Expense Items Disclosed	Number of Airlines Disclosing	Percentage of Airlines $N = 5$
5 or less	0	0%
Between 6 and 10	4	80%
11 or more	1	20%

Table 38. Number of Profit/Loss Items Reported by Airlines from China and Northern Asia.

Items Required Under IFRS 8 If Certain Conditions are Met	Number of Airlines Disclosing	Percentage of Airlines $N = 5$
Revenues from external customers	5	100%
Intersegment revenues	5	100%
Interest revenue	5	100%
Interest expense	5	100%
Depreciation and amortization	5	100%
Equity method income	3	60%
Income tax expense/benefit	3	60%
Material non-cash items other than depreciation and amortization (impairment)	3	60%

4.5.10 Entity-wide Disclosures

Revenue from external customers for products and services: All the airlines reported this information but most of them reported in the disclosure of revenue (Table 39).

Revenue by geographical areas: All the airlines provided revenue related information by geographical areas. However, four of them (except for China Airlines) declared the methods that they used to declare geographic areas as seen below (Fig. 16).

Geographical allocation of assets: China Airlines is the only airline declaring its geographical allocation of its non-current assets in the region, but the method used to declare geographical allocation of these assets was not stated (Fig. 17).

Table 39. Reporting of the Revenue from External Customers by Airlines from China and Northern Asia.

	Number of Airlines Disclosing	Percentage of Airlines $N = 5$
On the face of the income statement	0	–
Disclosure of revenue	4	80%
Disclosure of segment reporting	1	20%

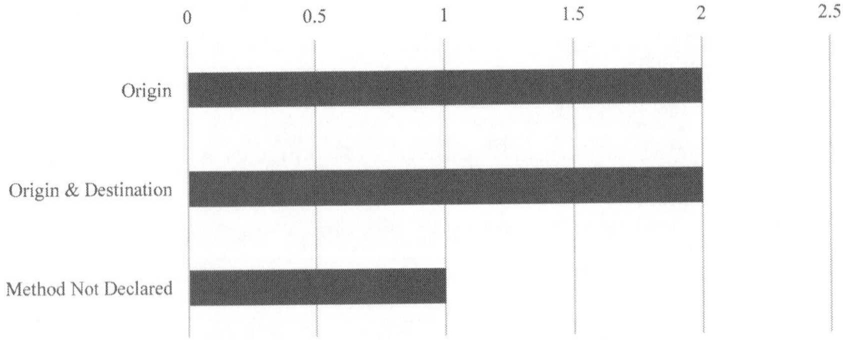

Fig. 16. Geographical Allocation of Revenue by Airlines from China and Northern Asia.

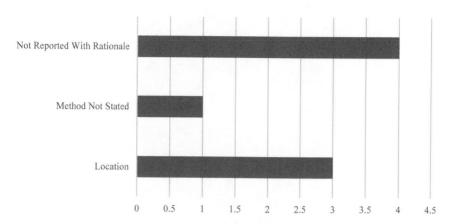

Fig. 17. Geographical Allocation of Assets by Airlines from China and Northern Asia.

On the other hand, four airlines (China Southern, China Eastern, Cathey Pacific, and Air China) declared that their major revenue earning asset is their aircraft fleet. Because these assets are employed across their worldwide route network, they stated that there was no suitable basis to allocate those assets in the geographical context.

As an additional observation, three of these four airlines (China Southern, China Eastern, and Air China) declared where their most non-current assets other than their aircraft assets and financial instruments (if any) are mainly located.

Information About Major Customers: None of the airlines disclosed any information about the major customers. In addition, Air China stated that there was no revenue from transactions with a single customer amounting to 10% or more of total revenue for the reporting period.

4.5.11 Disclosure of Identity of the CODM

None of the airlines declared the identity of the CODM in the disclosures of segment reporting.

4.6. Analysis of Segment Reporting in the Global Context

When the regional analysis of segment reporting is combined, this chapter reveals the following findings in the global context:

1. In a sample of 52 airlines, more than half of the airlines have a single reportable segment (Fig. 18).
2. The composition of the 25 airlines having multiple reportable segments is as follows (Fig. 19). Almost half of the airlines have two reportable segments.
3. Most airlines having a single reportable segment adopt the "whole business" method as the method of deriving segments in addition to the "matrix line of business" (Fig. 20). In this context, the matrix approach was observed in

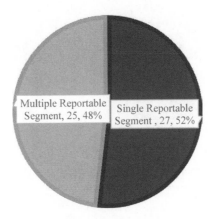

Fig. 18.   Global Composition of Airlines on a Segmental Basis.

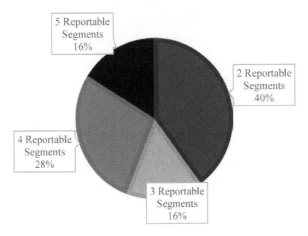

Fig. 19.   Global Composition of Airlines on Multiple Segmental Basis.

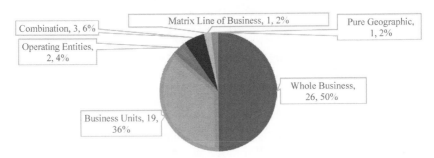

Fig. 20.   Methods of Driving Operating Segments in the Airline Industry.

the Americas. On the other hand, most airlines having multiple reportable segments adopt the "business units" method in addition to the "combination," "pure geographic," and "operating entities" methods. In this regard, the combination method was observed in Europe, the "operating entities" method was observed in Europe and Asia-Pacific, and the "pure geographic" method was observed in Asia-Pacific.

4. In the sample of 52 airlines, 83% reported the factors used to identify their reportable segments such as internal organizational structure, internal reporting system, and nature of operations, etc. In this context, these factors were mostly observed in the disclosures of airlines from Europe and Asia-Pacific.

5. Information related to the types of products and services from which each reportable segment derives its revenue was stated by all airlines having reportable operating segments. Products and services constituting the segments are provided below in the global context (Fig. 21). Most airlines have "combined airlines activities" which mainly include passenger and cargo services.

6. The total external revenue of identified reportable segments of 30 airlines having single or more than one reportable segment except the segment type of "others" represents 90% and above in the airline industry considering 75% rule under IFRS 8.

7. Half of 30 airlines having single or more than one reportable segment except the segment type of "others" use single segmental performance measure (Fig. 22). Nine airlines prefer two performance measures.

8. Observations show that most of 30 airlines having single or more than one reportable segment except the segment type of "others" use non-IFRS performance measures (Fig. 23), consistent with Nichols et al. (2012).

9. Two airlines from Europe and Asia-Pacific report their segment related disclosures using two currencies.

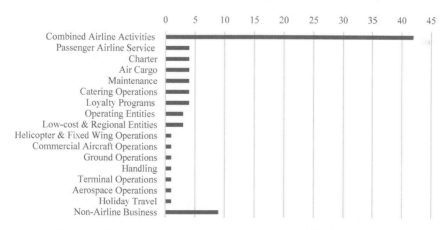

Fig. 21. Types of Global Products and Services Provided by Airlines.

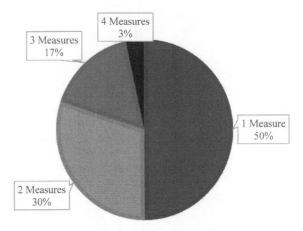

Fig. 22. Use of Single or Multiple Segmental Performance Measures by Airlines.

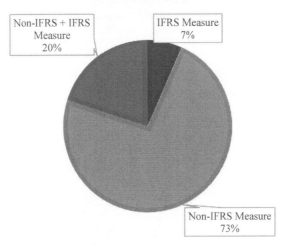

Fig. 23. Use of IFRS and/or Non-IFRS Performance Measures by Airlines.

10. In a sample of 30 airlines having single or more than one reportable seg-
    ment except the segment type of "others," "total segment assets" is the first,
    and "total segment liabilities" is the second most frequently reported balance
    sheet items (Table 40). The airlines that did not report these items either they
    declared their rationales or not. Additions to non-current assets is the third
    frequently reported item. Reporting of equity method investments is rare.

11. The number of income and expense items disclosed was declared by 29 air-
    lines having single or multiple segments except segment type of "others" (ex-
    cluding Jazeera Airways) (Table 41). In this context, most airlines (mostly
    from Europe, Asia-Pacific, and China) reported "between 6 and 10 revenue
    and expense items, including mostly required items versus 33% of airlines
    from all regions reports "11 items or more," including required and non-
    required items under IFRS 8.

Table 40. Composition of Balance Sheet Items Disclosed by Airlines.

Items Required Under IFRS 8 If Certain Conditions are Met	Number of Airlines Disclosing	Percentage of Airlines $N = 30$
Segment assets	22	73%
Segment liabilities	19	63%
Equity method investment	9	30%
Additions to non-current assets	17	57%

Table 41. Number of Profit/Loss Items Reported by Airlines.

Number of Income and Expense Items Disclosed	Number of Airlines Disclosing	Percentage of Airlines $N = 30$
0	1	4%
5 or less	6	20%
Between 6 and 10	13	43%
11 or more	10	33%

Table 42. Number of Profit/Loss Items Reported by Airlines.

Items Required Under IFRS 8 If Certain Conditions are Met	Number of Airlines Disclosing	Percentage of Airlines $N = 30$
Revenues from external customers	29	97%
Intersegment revenues	25	83%
Interest revenue	23	77%
Interest expense	24	80%
Depreciation and amortization	25	83%
Equity method income	16	53%
Income tax expense/benefit	17	56%
Material non-cash items other than depreciation and amortization (impairment)	15	50%

12. The composition of the reported income and expense items required by IFRS 8 is as follows in the global context (Table 42). Thirty airlines having single or multiple segments except segment type of "others" primarily report "revenues from external customers," "intersegment revenues" (if any), interest revenue, interest expense, and depreciation and amortization.

13. Observations show that Latam is the only airline reporting segmental cash flows from operating, investing, and financing activities.

14. There are three types of observations in the context of entity-wide disclosures as follows.

    Revenue from external customers for products and services: Except for the Air Transat, all airlines stated their revenues from external customers for each product and service (Table 43). This refers to 98% of the sample. Most airlines reported this information on the revenue disclosure reported under IFRS 15.

Table 43.   Reporting of the Revenue from External Customers by Airlines.

	Number of Airlines Disclosing	Percentage of Airlines $N = 52$
On the face of the income statement	9	17%
Disclosure of revenue	31	60%
Disclosure of segment reporting	10	19%
Disclosure combining revenue and segment information	1	2%
No disclosure	1	2%

Revenue by geographical areas: 80% of airlines (42 airlines) reported revenue related information by geographical areas versus 20% did not report, with or without rationale (Table 44). In addition, 76% declared the methods that they used to declare geographic areas as seen below. "Origin" method is mostly preferred in reporting the geographical allocation of revenue.

Geographical allocation of assets: 20% of airlines (10 airlines) reported geographical allocation of assets versus 80% did not report with or without rationale (Table 45). If declared, employment of the aircraft fleet assets across the airline's worldwide route network is usually the rationale, thus there is no suitable basis to allocate those assets in the geographical context. "Location" method is the preferred method in reporting geographical allocation of assets.

15. None of the airlines disclosed any information about the major customers. Some of them declared that there was no revenue from transactions with a single customer amounting to 10% or more of total revenue for the period.

Table 44.   Geographical Allocation of Revenue by Airlines.

	Number of Airlines Disclosing	Percentage of Airlines $N = 52$
Origin method	16	31%
Destination method	2	4%
Origin and destination methods	9	17%
Departure method	4	8%
Origin and departure methods	1	2%
Method not declared	10	19%
Not reported without rationale	6	11%
Not reported with rationale	4	8%

Table 45.   Geographical Allocation of Assets by Airlines.

	Number of Airlines Disclosing	Percentage of Airlines $N = 52$
Location method	6	12%
Method not stated	4	8%
Not reported without rationale	19	36%
Not reported with rationale	23	44%

Table 46. Analysis of the Identify of the CODM.

CODM	N = 52	%
An Individual: CEO, President, and CEO of the parent company, General Director	10	19
BoDs	6	12
Executive management (similar terminology: Executive Committee, Management Committee, Senior Management Team, Group Executive Board, Executive Directors and other key management personnel, and Group Management)	7	13
Comprehensive: CEO, Group Management Committee, and BoDs	1	2
Non-declared	28	54
Total	52	100

The results indicate that airline industry is not oriented toward a single customer, consistent with (IATA, 2016d). Therefore, it is not expected that revenue from a single customer exceeds 10% or more of the total revenue.

16. Observations show that more than 50% of the airlines did not report the identity of the CODM. Among the reporting airlines, 42% of the CODM consists of an individual like a CEO or General Director (Table 46).

5. CONCLUSION

This chapter revisits the research of IATA (2016d), by also considering the study by Nichols et al. (2012). Findings reveal that diversity exists at different levels in the airline industry when the 11 sections are analyzed. However, it looks like that one of the major areas where the diversity exists is related to the calculation of segmental performance. Therefore, further research should focus on the calculation of segmental non-IFRS and IFRS metrics to declare comparative performance information from one airline to another.

Another major area to analyze for further research is based on the studies by Cereola, Nichols, and Street (2017) which analyses geographic disclosures of IFRS 8 in the European, Australian, and New Zealand context. Cereola et al. (2017) states that companies are inclined to report (1) country specific segments which include country of domicile and material country data; and (2) mixed segments which include countries and regions rather than broad geographic regions after the adoption of IFRS 8, leading to disaggregated revenues at the individual country level. In this context, further research would be to analyze geographical disclosures of IFRS 8 in the airline industry to observe whether airlines are inclined to report country specific or mixed segments rather than broad segments, consistent with Cereola et al. (2017).

PART II

INTERNATIONAL AUDITING

CHAPTER 5

SOME OBSERVATIONS ON INTERNATIONAL AUDITING: THE CASE OF THE AIRLINE INDUSTRY

ABSTRACT

This chapter focuses on the international aspects of auditing in the context of the airline industry for the year 2018. This chapter finds that International Standards on Auditing have been widely adopted in the global context. This chapter also analyses several observations related to the composition of audit firms (Big 4 vs. non-Big 4), types of audit opinions, emphasis of matter, other matters, material uncertainty related to going-concern, and types of auditors (single or joint auditor). This chapter covers the frequency of the four elements of describing key audit matters (KAM) in the audit reports in the global and auditor context as well as the KAMs observed in the airline industry and classifies them as industry-specific KAMs and entity-specific KAMs. In addition, this chapter analyses the requirements of the expanded audit report of the UK which includes the declaration of materiality threshold and scope of the audit in connection with the materiality and KAMs considering UK and non-UK airlines.

Keywords: Auditing; Airline Industry; ISA 570; ISA 700; ISA 701; ISA 705; ISA 706

Perspectives on International Financial Reporting and Auditing in the Airline Industry
Studies in Managerial and Financial Accounting, Volume 35, 127–157
ISSN: 1479-3512/doi:10.1108/S1479-351220220000035005

1. INTRODUCTION

Financial statements and disclosures of publicly accountable entities must be audited by independent audit firms for the purpose of stating whether their financial statements and disclosures, fairly present the financial position, financial performance, and cash flows of these entities for the benefit of investors, creditors, and shareholders. In this context, most countries have adopted International Financial Reporting Standards (IFRS) so that publicly accountable entities can prepare and present their financial statements and disclosures in a globally accepted, transparent, and comparative manner.

In line with the widespread adoption of IFRS, most countries have also adopted International Standards on Auditing (ISAs) issued by International Auditing and Assurance Standards Board (IAASB) or developed their own standards on auditing aligned with ISAs so that the audit process can have a common denominator in external auditing in the global context as it is in the case of IFRS adoption. When the 57 audit reports of airlines that are mostly publicly accountable and consist of the sample of this chapter are analyzed, this chapter points out that the following findings for the year 2018, which verifies direct or indirect adoption of ISAs in the global context considering audit reports of airlines and the Global Impact Map of the International Federation of Accountants (IFAC, 2018):

(1) In the Americas, audit reports of four airlines clearly state that the audit was conducted in accordance with ISAs. In the audit reports, the following titles were used.

- ISAs
- ISAs & Brazilian Standards on Auditing

However, audit report of five airlines state that the audit was conducted following Canadian or Chilean Generally Accepted Auditing Standards. In this context, it should be noted that both standards conform with ISAs, but they were stated using a different title in the audit reports. On the other hand, one airline's financial statement audit was conducted following the standards of Public Company Accounting Oversight Board (PCAOB) of the United States.

(2) In Europe, the audit reports of 17 airlines clearly state that the audit was conducted in accordance with ISAs. Either the version of ISAs used in the financial statement audit of airlines are fully in compliance with the ISAs issued by IAASB or the version of the ISAs used in the financial statement audit of airlines is slightly different from the ISAs issued by IAASB as is in the case of ISAs UK and ISAs Ireland. In the audit reports, the following titles were used.

- ISAs.
- ISAs UK: They are based on ISAs issued by the IAASB, with some additions to account for UK Company law.

- ISAs Ireland: They are based on ISAs issued by the IAASB with specific additions.
- ISAs & German Generally Accepted Standards for Financial Statement Audits.
- ISAs & Generally Accepted Auditing Standards in Sweden.
- ISAs & Generally Accepted Auditing Standards and Practices in Norway.

On the other hand, audit report of five airlines state that the audit was conducted in accordance with auditing practices, but their audit reports do not explicitly state the use of ISAs. Therefore, the users of financial information are not able to know whether the audit was conducted following ISAs or not.

- *Israeli Auditing Standards:* ISAs are in process of adoption in Israel. Therefore, they are partially adopted.
- *Good auditing practice in Finland:* The Auditing Act of Finland (1141/2015) states that audits must be conducted in accordance with the ISAs as adopted by the European Commission (EC) in line with the EU Directive 2006/43/EC, Directive 2014/56/EU, and Regulation (EU) No. 537/2014 but an auditor shall observe any particular instructions given by the partners or by the shareholders' meeting or equivalent governing body, insofar as these instructions are not in conflict with the law, the articles of association, the rules, the deed of partnership, international auditing standards, good auditing practice, or the principles of professional ethics (Finland Ministry of Economic Affairs and Employment, 2015).
- *Professional standards applicable in France:* National legislation in France is in process of adopting EU Directive 2006/43/EC, Directive 2014/56/EU and Regulation (EU) No. 537/2014. French standards are based on ISAs.
- *Prevailing audit regulations in Spain:* This refers to Spanish Generally Accepted Auditing Standards that are ISAs adapted for their application in Spain.
- *Turkish Auditing Standards (TAS):* TAS is fully compliance with ISAs.

In Europe, research clarifies that European airlines' financial statements except for the case of El Al from Israel were audited in compliance with ISAs. However, audit reports prepared in Finland, France, Spain, and Turkey should clearly state the title of ISAs rather than using national titles.

(3) In Africa – Middle East, research reveals that the financial statements audit of airlines was conducted in accordance with ISAs and this is explicitly stated in the audit reports.

(4) In Asia-Pacific, audit report of two airlines clearly state that the audit was conducted in accordance with ISAs. In the audit reports, the following titles were used.

- ISAs & Approved Standards on Auditing in Malaysia.
- ISAs issued by the New Zealand Auditing and Assurance Standards Board & Auditor-General's Auditing Standards.

On the other hand, audit report of seven airlines state that the audit was conducted in accordance with auditing practices, but their audit report does not explicitly state the adoption of ISAs. Therefore, the users of financial information are not able to know whether the audit was conducted following ISAs or not.

- *Australian Auditing Standards:* They conform with ISAs but with some additions and amendments related to Australian legislative environment and to maintain audit quality where the Auditing and Assurance Standards Board has considered there are compelling reasons to do so.
- *Korean Standards on Auditing:* They conform with ISAs.
- *Philippine Standards on Auditing:* They conform with ISAs with additional country-specific standards to address issues not covered by IAASB pronouncements.
- *Singapore Standards on Auditing:* They conform with ISAs with amendments to reflect national requirements in Singapore.
- *Sri Lanka Auditing Standards*: They are in line with ISAs with amendments to reflect national legal and regulatory requirements in Sri Lanka.

In Asia-Pacific, auditing standards in Australia, Korea, Phippilines, Singapore, and Sri Lanka are based on ISAs but most of them also include some additions and amendments. Even if this is the case, auditing standards should state both national titles and ISAs in the audit report.

(5) In China and Northern Asia, audit reports of two airlines clearly state that the audit was conducted in accordance with ISAs. However, audit reports of three airlines state that the audit was conducted following Auditing Standards Generally Accepted in the Republic of China or Hong Kong Standards on Auditing. In this context, it should be noted that both standards on auditing conform with ISAs.

As a result of this worldwide adoption of ISAs, the objective of this chapter is to focus on some observations related to international auditing considering ISA 570 *Going-Concern*, ISA 700 *Forming an Opinion and Reporting on Financial Statements*, ISA 701 *Communicating Key Audit Matters in The Independent Auditor's Report*, 705 *Modifications to The Opinion in the Independent Auditor's Report*, and 706 *Emphasis of Matter Paragraphs and Other Matter Paragraphs in The Independent Auditor's Report* in the context of airline industry. The basis for the related observations is discussed below.

Observations related to the audit firms and types of auditors: This chapter observes the patterns of Big 4 and non-Big 4 audit firms in the airline industry such as in the case of Akdoğan, Aktaş, and Gülhan (2015) for Turkey and check whether the audit reports are signed by a single auditor or joint auditors depending on the country-specific regulation adopted. In this context, it should be noted that in the joint audit, financial statements are audited by two or more independent auditors considering (a) coordination of audit planning, (b) shared audit effort, (c) cross reviews, and (d) mutual quality controls (Ratzinger-Sakel,

Audousset-Coulier, Kettunen, & Lesage, 2013). At the final stage of the audit process, one single audit report is issued by auditors that are jointly liable. In this context, Ratzinger-Sakel et al. (2013) show that there are mandatory and voluntary joint audit regimes in the global context. Considering the prior research by Ratzinger-Sakel et al. (2013), this chapter focuses on the following observations in the context of the airline industry:

- The patterns of airlines whose audit report was signed by joint auditors.
- The patterns of airlines whose audit report is subject to mandatory or voluntary joint audit regime.

Observations related to auditors' opinions and related paragraphs of the audit report considering ISA 700, ISA 705, and ISA 706: This chapter observes the patterns of auditors' opinions in general and auditors' opinions with emphasis of matter or another matter paragraph in particular, in the airline industry considering the prior research stated below.

In line with the prior Australian research of Craswell (1986) and Aitken and Simnett (1991), Carson, Ferguson, and Simnett (2006) analyzes the information on auditors' opinions for publicly accountable entities in Australia over the period 1996–2003. Their paper considers the year 1996 as the starting point because Australian Standards on Auditing started to align with ISAs through the inclusion of the emphasis of matter paragraph in the audit report and shows a picture of the patterns of audit reports in terms of (1) audit opinions (unqualified opinion, unqualified opinion with emphasis of matter, qualified opinion, qualified opinion with emphasis of matter, adverse opinion, and disclaimer of opinion); (2) types of audit opinions by Australian audit firms (Big 4 or non-Big 4); and (3) types of audit opinions by industry. The particular emphasis of this paper is the wide adoption of the unqualified opinion with emphasis of matter within this period by the Australian audit firms due to the alignment with ISAs.

Like prior research, Grosu, Robu, and Istrate (2015) analyze the information on auditors' opinion for publicly accountable entities in Romania over the period 2011–2014 but from a different perspective. This paper takes the year 2011 as the starting point because Romanian Accounting Standards (RAS) was in force in 2011 and IFRS had been adopted in Romania starting from 2012. It considers the patterns of audit opinions with respect to (1) audit opinions; (2) the use of accounting framework (RAS or IFRS); (3) types of audit opinions by Big 4 or non-Big 4 audit firms; and (4) types of audit opinions by industry. The particular emphasis of this paper is the increase in unqualified opinions with emphasis of matter versus the decrease in qualified opinion due to the increase in the quality of the information after IFRS adoption.

In addition, the audit reports of publicly accountable entities in Turkey are examined by Akdoğan et al. (2015) for the period 2009–2013, by Akdoğan et al. (2018) for the period of 2014–2016, and by Akdoğan (2020) for the period of 2017–2018 after the adoption of ISAs in Turkey to show a picture of the patterns of the following issues: (1) the concentration of Turkish audit firms (Big 4 or non-Big 4); (2) the composition of auditors' opinions; (3) the rationale behind the audit opinions in case of a qualified opinion, adverse opinion, or disclaimer of opinion; (4) emphasis of matter in the case of unqualified opinion; (5) change of audit opinion from one year to another; and (6) whether there is a relationship between the change of auditor and audit opinion if an entity has a qualified audit opinion and changes its audit opinion to unqualified after the change of auditor. The particular emphasis of this research reveals that auditors' opinions other than unqualified audit opinion increased in the period of 2014–2016 compared to 2009–2013 but decreased in the period 2017–2018 compared to 2014–2016.

In the context of sector-specific analysis of the matters stated in prior research, it should be noted that Carson et al. (2006) and Grosu et al. (2015) analyze auditors' opinions by industry, but the industry classification of Carson et al. (2006) do not include the transportation as well as the airline industry. The industry classification of Grosu et al. (2015) includes service entities but does not classify transportation entities and airlines. In addition, Akdoğan et al. (2015, 2018) and Akdoğan (2020) do not analyze auditors' opinions by industry.

Considering prior studies by Carson et al. (2006), Grosu et al. (2015), Akdoğan et al. (2015, 2018), and Akdoğan (2020), this chapter focuses on the following observations for the year 2018 in the context of the airline industry:

- The patterns of auditors' opinions.
- The patterns of the audit reports including emphasis of matter paragraph, and other matter paragraph.

Observations on material uncertainty related to going concern considering ISA 570: Material uncertainty refers to the uncertainties related to events or conditions which may cast significant doubt on the entity's ability to continue as a going-concern that should be disclosed in the financial report (IAASB, 2015a). In this context, Demirkol (2019) analyzed the audit reports of publicly accountable entities of construction and public works listed in Borsa Istanbul of Turkey for the period 2013–2017 to observe whether there are cases of material uncertainty related to going-concern. Considering prior research of Demirkol (2019), this chapter focuses on the following observations for the year 2018 in the context of the airline industry:

- The patterns of material uncertainty related to going-concern in the audit reports.
- The rationale behind the material uncertainty related to going-concern within the framework of the examples of financial, operating, and other events or conditions stated in ISA 570 (IAASB, 2015a). They consist of events or conditions that individually or collectively, may cast significant doubt on the entity's ability to continue as a going-concern.

Key audit matters (KAMs), are the matters that, were of most significance in the audit of the financial statements of the current period in the context of auditor's professional judgment (IAASB, 2015b). There are three purposes of communicating KAMs in the audit report: (1) to improve the communicative value of the auditor's report leading to greater transparency about the performed audit; (2) to provide additional information to the users of the financial statements to assist them in understanding those matters that were of most significance in the audit of the financial statements of the current period in the context of the auditor's professional judgment; and (3) to assist the users of the financial statements in understanding the entity and areas of significant management judgment in the audited financial statements. Observations related to KAMs consist of two sections: (1) observations related to the elements of describing KAMs; and (2) observations related to the content of the KAMs.

Observations related to the elements of describing KAMs in the audit report considering ISA 701: ISA 701 states that professional judgment is required to determine the amount of detail to be provided in the auditor's report to describe how a KAM was addressed in the audit (IAASB, 2015b). In this context, the auditor may include each or some combination of the following elements into the audit report: (a) aspects of the auditor's response or approach that were most relevant to the matter or specific to the assessed risk of material misstatement (*element A*); (b) an overview of procedures performed (*element B*); (c) an indication of the outcome of the auditor's procedures (*element C*); or (d) key observations with respect to the matter (*element D*). Considering the elements stated above, this chapter focuses on the following observations for the year 2018 in the context of the airline industry:

- The patterns of the elements of describing KAMs in the audit report.

Observations related to the content analysis of KAMs in the audit report considering ISA 701: This chapter observes the patterns of KAMs declared in the airline industry considering prior research stated below.

Vik and Walter (2017) analyzed KAMs in Norway by preparing a sample of publicly accountable entities for the year 2016. This research focuses on KAMs in the country, considering the differences in the reporting of KAMs between the big five audit firms in Norway (BDO, Deloitte, EY, KPMG, and PWC).

Pinto and Morais (2019) analyzed the determinants of KAMs in Europe by establishing a sample of publicly accountable entities listed in the CAC 40 from France, in the AEX 25 from Netherlands, and in the FTSE 100 from UK. This research considered the audit reports for the year 2016. Therefore, audit reports do not include first time adopters. It classifies KAMs in the context of IFRS related KAMs and non-IFRS related KAMs and does not determine which KAMs are industry-specific in Europe.

Iwanowicz and Iwanowicz (2019) observed the composition of KAMs by designing a sample of audit reports from publicly accountable Polish plus British entities for the period 2017. Akdoğan and Bülbül (2019) examined the composition of KAMs in Turkey by establishing a sample of publicly accountable entities listed in BIST 100 for the first adoption of KAMs in year 2017. In addition,

Arzova and Şahin (2020) established a sample of publicly accountable financial entities (banks and leasing entities) listed in BIST 30, BIST 50, BIST 100 in Turkey to analyze KAMs for the period 2017 and 2018 as well as Kend and Nguyen (2020) established a sample from Australian publicly accountable entities to observe KAMs for the period 2017–2018. In the same context, Karapınar and Dölen (2020) examined the content of KAMs in Turkey for the period 2018 classifying KAMs in terms of manufacturing entities, financial entities, holdings, and wholesale entities by determining the most frequently observed KAMs under each classification.

While Vik and Walter (2017), Pinto and Morais (2019), Iwanowicz and Iwanowicz (2019), Akdoğan and Bülbül (2019), Arzova and Şahin (2020), Kend and Nguyen (2020), and Karapınar and Dölen (2020) classify KAMs as country-specific and do not determine which KAMs are industry-specific, Abdullatif and Al-Rahahleh (2019) and İşseveroğlu (2019) adopt an industry-specific approach as to whether observed KAMs are industry-specific or entity-specific.

Abdullatif and Al-Rahahleh (2019) examined the composition of KAMs in Jordan by designing a sample of audit reports from publicly accountable entities for the period 2017–2018. This research classified KAMs as country-specific, industry-specific, and entity-specific. It determined which KAMs are industry-specific in Jordan and emphasized that auditors tend to report industry-specific KAMs rather than entity-specific KAMs.

İşseveroğlu (2019) designed a sample of publicly accountable insurance entities listed in BIST 100 in Turkey for the period 2017 and 2018 and declared that KAMs of the insurance entities are industry-specific.

Considering the prior research related to KAMs, this chapter focuses on the following observations in the context of airline industry:

- KAMs observed in the airline industry for the year 2018.
- In line with the prior research of Abdullatif and Al-Rahahleh (2019), and İşseveroğlu (2019) stating that KAMs would be industry-specific, the composition of KAMs in the airline industry, considering key takeaways of the airline industry (Lavi, 2016), including revenue recognition on tickets sold, customer loyalty programs, determining useful lives of aircraft related assets and other property, plant, and equipment (PPE), and their residual values, impairment of assets, leases, provisions, employee benefits, pensions, goodwill and intangible assets, and derivative instruments.

Observations on communicating the concept of materiality in planning and performing the audit under ISA 701 of the UK: The audit report prepared under ISA 701 of the UK issued by the Financial Reporting Council (FRC) is slightly different from the audit report prepared under ISA 701 issued by IAASB. ISA 701 of the UK requires an expanded auditor's report prepared by premium entities listed in the London stock exchange (Gutierrez, Minutti-Meza, Tatum, & Vulcheva, 2018).

In the expanded auditor's report, before the adoption of the reporting KAMs, the former ISA 700 of the UK (2013) required auditors (1) to describe the risks of material misstatements that had the greatest effect on the audit; (2) to disclose how the auditor applied the concept of materiality, including a materiality threshold for the statements as a whole; and (3) to explain the scope of the audit, including how it relates to the risks of material misstatements and materiality in the audit report (FRC, 2013, pp. 6–7).

After the adoption of KAMs, however, this requirement was transferred to ISA 701 of the UK (2016) from the former ISA 700 of the UK (2013) and a bridge has been established between material misstatement and KAMs. In this context, ISA 701 of the UK, similarly require auditors (1) to explain how they applied the concept of materiality in planning and performing the audit; (2) to specify the materiality threshold used by the auditor as being materiality for the financial statements as a whole; and (3) an overview of the scope of the audit, considering risks of material misstatement and KAMs (FRC, 2016, pp. 5–6). The current version of ISA 701 of the UK (2020) also requires the reporting of performance materiality in the expanded auditor's report which was optional in the ISA 701 of the UK (2016) (FRC, 2016, p. 22, 2020, p. 5).

Considering expanded auditor's report of the UK, this chapter focuses on the following observations in the context of the airline industry:

- The patterns of the UK and non-UK airlines declaring materiality threshold for the financial statements as a whole.
- The pattern of the airlines whose audit report declares performance materiality on a voluntary basis.
- The patterns of the declaration of the rationale behind the materiality threshold in the context of the airlines stating a materiality threshold.
- The patterns of the declaration of the materiality threshold as a monetary value, percentage, or both in the context of the airlines stating a materiality threshold.

This chapter has the following structure: Section 2 presents a literature review on international auditing in the airline industry; Section 3 explains the data and the research methodology; Section 4 discusses the findings on international auditing in the airline industry. Finally, Section 5 presents concluding remarks along with main findings.

2. LITERATURE REVIEW ON INTERNATIONAL AUDITING IN THE AIRLINE INDUSTRY

In the literature of international auditing in the airline industry, the research of Özçelik (2020) focuses on the KAMs observed in the airline industry. The author establishes a sample of airlines from members of IATA and Star Alliance whose audit reports include KAMs for the period 2017–2018. The sample consists of

40 airlines with a particular focus on Europe, Middle East & Africa, Asia-Pacific, and China & Northern Asia. In this regard, the research determines KAMs for the stated consecutive periods in a comparative manner but does not make an explicit statement whether KAMs of the airline industry are industry-specific, entity-specific, or a mixture of both.

Compared to Özçelik (2020), the current chapter extends the contribution to the academic literature on international auditing regarding the airline industry not only by focusing on KAMs reported in the airline industry but also by examining different aspects of international auditing other than KAMs such as types of audit opinions, emphasis of matter, other matters, types of auditors, material uncertainty related to going-concern, whether KAMs are industry-specific or entity-specific or both, materiality threshold, performance materiality, and elements of describing KAMs in the audit report. Even if the chapter is based on one year of observations, it is the starting point for further research in international auditing regarding the airline industry by providing a greater perspective in the context of ISA 570, ISA 700, ISA 701, ISA 705, ISA 706, and ISA 701 of the UK.

3. DATA AND RESEARCH METHODOLOGY

3.1 Data

This chapter uses two sets of data. It has been developed in the regional and global context. The first set of data has been collected from the 2018 audit reports of the 57 airlines whose financial statements are based on IFRS for the analysis of the composition of audit firms (Big 4 vs. non-Big 4), type of auditors (single or joint auditors), audit opinions, emphasis of matter, other matters, and material uncertainty related to going-concern (Table 1).

The second set of data has been collected from the audit reports of 45 out of 57 airlines where KAMs are provided for the year 2018. The data reveal that around 79% of airlines report KAMs in their audit reports. This finding shows that ISA 701 was adopted by most of the airlines' countries of incorporation that either explicitly or implicitly adopts ISAs (Fig. 1). However, 21% of airlines do not report KAMs in their audit reports because of the following constraints:

In the UK and Ireland, two non-listed airlines (Virgin Atlantic Group and Aer Lingus) do not report KAMs in their audit report because declaration of KAMs is required for publicly listed entities in these countries (FRC, 2016, pp. 2–3). In Canada, ISA 701 has been in force since December 31, 2020 (RSM, 2020). In Chile and Portugal, ISA 701 was not effective as of the year 2018. In Sri Lanka, the auditor of Sri Lankan Airlines delayed the adoption of KAMs in 2018 even if reporting of KAMs has been in force since March 31, 2018 (KPMG, 2019). Israel is in process of adopting ISAs. Financial statement audit of Copa Airlines was conducted following the standards of PCAOB of the United States which started to include the reporting of KAMs in the audit report as critical audit matters starting from 2019 (PCAOB, 2018).

Table 1. List of Airlines.

Americas	
GOL Linhas Aereas	Turkish Airlines
Azul Brazilian Airlines	Pegasus Airlines
Air Transat	Norwegian Air
WestJet	*Africa – Middle East*
Air Canada	Royal Jordanian
Cargojet Airways	Kenya Airways
LATAM Airlines Group	Jazeera Airways
Aeromexico	Air Mauritius
Volaris	Qatar Airways
COPA Airlines	Comair
Europe	Emirates
Croatia Airlines	Air Arabia
Finnair – Finnair Group	Abu Dhabi Aviation
Air France – KLM Group	*Asia-Pacific*
Lufthansa Group	Regional Express
Aegean Group	Alliance Airlines
Aer Lingus	Qantas
Ryanair	Virgin Australia
Wizz Air	Korean Air
TAP Group	Asiana Airlines
SAS – SAS Group	Air Asia X
International Airlines Group	Air New Zealand
Virgin Atlantic Group	Cebu Pacific Air
Air Partner	Singapore Airlines
Easy Jet	Sri Lankan Airlines
British Airways	*China & Northern Asia*
Fast Jet	Cathay Pacific Airlines
Icelandair	Air China Group
Norwegian Air	China Southern Airlines
El Al	China Eastern Airlines
Aeroflot	China Airlines

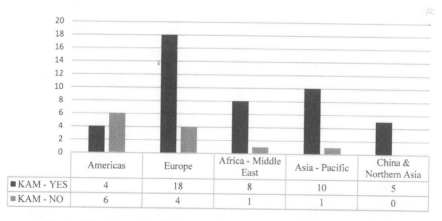

	Americas	Europe	Africa - Middle East	Asia - Pacific	China & Northern Asia
■ KAM - YES	4	18	8	10	5
▪ KAM - NO	6	4	1	1	0

Fig. 1. Number of Audit Reports Reporting and Non-reporting KAMs.

3.2 Research Methodology

This research assesses those collected data using the frequency of distribution method and content analysis regarding international auditing in the airline industry.

4. FINDINGS AND DISCUSSION

4.1 Audit Firms in the Audit Reports of Airlines

This chapter points out the following findings related to audit firms, and audit types in the airline industry:

(1) Data reveals that around 97% of airlines' financial statements were audited by international audit firms in year 2018 of which 93% of airlines were audited by Big 4 audit firms (KPMG, E&Y, PWC, and Deloitte) (Fig. 2). The composition of Big 4 audit firms refers to 29% of by KPMG, 25% by E&Y, 22% by PWC, and 17% by Deloitte. Due to the rotation mechanism in auditing that is variable from one country to another, the weight of each Big 4 audit firm within the airline industry is subject to change from one period to another.

On the other hand, 3% of airlines' financial statements were audited by a national audit firm or by a government department. In this context, the financial statements of Cebu Pacific Air from Philippines were audited by SGV that is a national audit firm in Philippines but has been a member firm of E&Y since 2002 versus the financial statements of Sri Lankan Airlines which was audited by the National Audit Office which is a government department in Sri Lanka.

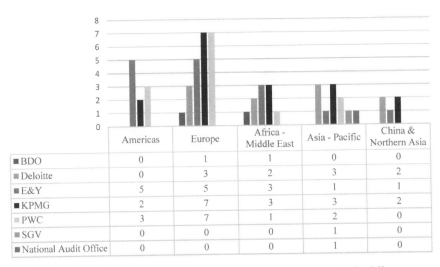

	Americas	Europe	Africa - Middle East	Asia - Pacific	China & Northern Asia
■ BDO	0	1	1	0	0
■ Deloitte	0	3	2	3	2
■ E&Y	5	5	3	1	1
■ KPMG	2	7	3	3	2
■ PWC	3	7	1	2	0
■ SGV	0	0	0	1	0
■ National Audit Office	0	0	0	1	0

Fig. 2.   Composition of Audit Firms in the Audit Reports of Airlines.

(2) To explain the dominance of Big 4 audit firms in the audit of financial statements in the airline industry, the concepts of "audit quality" and "financial
reporting credibility" in the context of Big 4 audit firms should be considered
(Khurana & Raman, 2004a). Prior research indicates that (1) the Big 4 audit
firms are different from other auditors because they invest more in reputation capital (Beatty, 1989); (2) Big 4's reputation capital refers to the view of
providing higher quality audits based on (a) competence which is generated
from their heavy spending on auditor training and (b) independence which is
generated from their size and large portfolio of clients (Khurana & Raman,
2004a); (3) the Big 4 audit firms are perceived as providing higher quality
audits and improving credibility of financial statements relative to non-Big
4 audit firms in the United States by reporting more credible earnings for
their auditees (Teoh & Wong, 1993); (4) Big 4 audit firms provide higher
quality audits in the United States to avoid litigation and to protect the firm's
reputation (Francis & Krishnan, 1999); and (5) Big 4 audit firms are considered to be essential component of the international financial infrastructure
to increase the reliability and globalization of capital markets and to attract
international investors (Khurana & Raman, 2004b).

Considering the findings of prior research, the reasons why airlines would
prefer the Big 4 audit firms for the audit of their financial statements would be
evident. In addition, it should be noted that airlines are the major customers of
aircraft leasing and manufacturing entities. These entities analyze the financial
statements of airlines to determine their sale or lease policies in the context of
airlines' financial position, financial performance, and cash flows. Consistent with
the prior research, therefore, aircraft leasing and manufacturing entities would
consider financial statements audited by Big 4 more credible than the financial
statements audited by national audit firms or a government department.

4.2 Types of Auditors in the Audit Reports of Airlines

Findings reveal that 96% of audit reports were signed by single auditors. However,
two airlines' financial statements (Air France – KLM and Air Mauritius) were
audited in accordance with a joint audit. In the joint audit, financial statements
are audited by two or more independent auditors considering (a) coordination of
the audit planning; (b) shared audit effort; (c) cross reviews; and (d) mutual quality controls (Ratzinger-Sakel et al., 2013). At the final stage of the audit process,
one single audit report is issued by auditors who are jointly liable.

Literature review of Ratzinger-Sakel et al. (2013) show that there are mandatory and voluntary joint audit regimes in the global context.

The case of Air France – KLM is an example of mandatory joint audit. The
joint audit process took place between KPMG and Deloitte. In the context of
France, the appointment of two independent auditors has been in force since
1966 according to the provision of the 1966 *loi des sociétés* (Baker, Mikol, &
Quick, 2001; Francis, Richard, & Vanstraelen, 2009). It has been required for
all consolidated financial statements in France since 1984 (Ratzinger-Sakel
et al., 2013). According to Bennecib (2004), the French joint audit requirement is

explained by two rationales: (1) if one of the joint auditors defaults, the defaulting auditor can only be replaced by a decision of the Court of Commerce; and (2) a joint audit can improve the auditors' independence, which would enhance the credibility and prestige of the auditing profession in France.

On the other hand, the case of Air Mauritius is an example of voluntary joint audit because the Mauritius Financial Reporting Act (Financial Reporting Council of Mauritius, 2004) requires the appointment of a single auditor (Article 62). The joint audit process took place between KPMG and E&Y. Preference given to joint audit in Air Mauritius would be due to the credibility and prestige that are intended to be given to airline's financial statements consistent with Bennecib (2004).

4.3 Audit Opinions in Audit Reports of Airlines

Considering ISA 700 and ISA 705 (IAASB, 2015d, 2015e), this research reveals that independent audit report of all airlines regardless of the type of audit firm issued unqualified (unmodified, clean) audit opinions for the year 2018.

4.4 Emphasis of Matter and Other Matter Paragraphs in the Audit Reports of Airlines

An emphasis of matter paragraph that is included in the audit report refers to a matter appropriately presented or disclosed in the financial report that, in the auditor's judgment, is of such importance that it is fundamental to users' understanding of the financial report (IAASB, 2015c). Examples of emphasis of matters for the year 2018 are provided in the context of Gol Linhas Aereas (2018), Westjet (2018), and Air France – KLM (2018), considering paragraph A5 of the ISA 706 in the context of "Early application (where permitted) of a new accounting standard that has a material effect on the financial report" (Table 2).

In addition, paragraph A6 of the ISA 710 *Comparative Information-Corresponding Figures and Comparative Financial Reports* states that the auditor's report may include an Emphasis of Matter paragraph describing the circumstances and referring to, where relevant, disclosures that fully describe the matter that can be found in the financial report, when a prior period financial report that is misstated has not been amended and an auditor's report has not been reissued, but the corresponding figures have been properly restated or appropriate disclosures have been made in the current period financial report (IAASB, 2018). In this context, this research observes that the auditors of Asiana Airlines experienced such a case for the year 2018 and prepared an Emphasis of Matter paragraph in connection with ISA 706 (Asiana Airlines, 2018) (Table 3).

Table 2. Examples of ISA 706 as an Emphasis of Matter in the Audit Reports of Airlines.

Gol Linhas Aéreas	Restated values and comparative information under IFRS 15
West Jet	Restated values and comparative information under IFRS 15
Air France – KLM:	Restated values and comparative information under IFRS 9, IFRS 15, and IFRS 16

Table 3. Example of ISA 710 as an Emphasis of Matter in the Audit Reports of Airlines.

Asiana Airlines	Paragraph A6 Misstatement in Prior Period Financial Report: (1) Restatement of current year financial statements to correct the overstatement of sales related to deferred income from mileage, understatement of provision for repairs and maintenance of leased aircraft, impairment loss on investments, and assets and liabilities related to investments in associates; (2) Restatement of prior year financial statements to correct errors on the understatement of property, aircraft and equipment, cost of sales (depreciation for aircraft), and overstatement of other expenses (loss on disposal of property, aircraft, and equipment) in the statement of financial statements for the year ended December 31, 2017, and errors on the understatement of property, aircraft, and equipment

On the other hand, an "other matter" paragraph that is included in the auditor's report refers to a matter other than those presented or disclosed in the financial report that, in the auditor's judgment, is relevant to users' understanding of the audit, the auditor's responsibilities, or the auditor's report (IAASB, 2018). An example of an "other matter" is provided in the audit report of Virgin Atlantic Group (2018) (Table 4).

4.5 Material Uncertainty related to Going-concern in the Audit Reports of Airlines

In this research, four cases including Fast Jet (2018), Kenya Airways (2018), Asiana Airlines (2018), and Sri Lankan Airlines (2019) were determined to have material uncertainty related to going-concern for the year 2018. An example of a case of material uncertainty related to going-concern is provided below (Table 5).

Table 4. Example of ISA 706 as an Other Matter in the Audit Reports of Airlines.

Virgin Atlantic Group	Uncertainties related to the effects of Brexit are relevant to understanding our audit of the financial statements. All audits assess and challenge the reasonableness of estimates made by the Directors and the appropriateness of the going-concern basis of preparation of the financial statements. All of these depend on assessments of the future economic environment and the Company's and Group's future prospects and performance
	Brexit is one of the most significant economic events for the UK, and at the date of this report its effects are subject to unprecedented levels of uncertainty of outcomes, with the full range of possible effects unknown. We applied a standardized firm-wide approach in response to that uncertainty when assessing the company's and group's future prospects and performance. However, no audit should be expected to predict the unknowable factors or all possible future implications for a company and this is particularly the case in relation to Brexit

Table 5.   Example of ISA 570 in the Audit Reports of Airlines.

Kenya Airways	We draw your attention to note 2(e) in the financial statements, which indicates that the Group and Company incurred a loss of KShs 7,558 million for the year (for the nine-month period ended December 31, 2017: KShs 6,418 million) and KShs 7,812 (December 31, 2017: KShs 6,639 million), respectively, during the year ended December 31, 2018 and, as of that date, the Group's and Company's current liabilities exceeded current assets by KShs 101,536 million (2017: KShs 106,422 million) and KShs 104,803 million (2017: KShs 109,066 million), respectively. As stated in note 2(e), these events or conditions, along with other matters as set forth therein, indicate that a material uncertainty exists that may cast significant doubt on the Group's and Company's ability to continue as going-concerns. Our opinion is not modified in respect of this matter

The reasons behind the material uncertainty related to going-concern are based on financial events or conditions provided below consistent with ISA 570 (IAASB, 2015a) (Table 6).

4.6 Analysis of the Elements of Describing KAMs in the Audit Report

To describe KAMs, paragraph A46 of the ISA 701 states that the auditor may include each or some combination of the following elements into the audit report (IAASB, 2015b): (a) aspects of the auditor's response or approach that were most relevant to the matter or specific to the assessed risk of material misstatement (*element A*); (b) an overview of procedures performed (*element B*); (c) an indication of the outcome of the auditor's procedures (*element C*); or (d) key observations with respect to the matter (*element D*), or some combination of these elements.

To observe each of these elements, two examples of KAMs are provided below. The audit report of Azul Brazilian Airlines reflects some combination of these elements, but Kenya Airways (2018) reflects all the elements.

In the audit report of Azul Brazilian Airlines (2018), passenger revenue consists of one of the KAMs. To meet the describing requirement of *element A* and *element B*, the reason why passenger revenue is a KAM of this airline was stated on the "key audit matter" column (left column) and the procedures performed were declared on the "How our audit addressed the Key audit matter" column

Table 6.   Rationale Behind the Material Uncertainty Related to Going-Concern.

Fast Jet	Net current liability position: Current Liabilities > Current Assets
Kenya Airways	Substantial operating losses as well as Current Liabilities > Current Assets
Asiana Airlines	Current Liabilities > Current Assets
Sri Lankan Airlines	Substantial operating losses as well as Current Liabilities > Current Assets

(right column) of (Table 7a). To meet the reporting requirement of *element C*, the auditor declares the outcome of the procedures using the following sentence *Based on the results of the audit procedures performed, … we consider ….* at the bottom of table. In addition, the auditor does not use key observations related to this KAM.

In the audit report of Kenya Airways, impairment of aircraft and related equipment consists of the one of the KAMs. To meet the describing requirement of *element A* and *element B*, the reason why impairment of aircraft and related equipment is a KAM of this airline was stated in the "key audit matter" column (left column) and the procedures performed was declared on the "How our audit addressed the Key audit matter" column (right column) of (Table 7b). To meet the reporting requirement of *element C*, the auditor declares the outcome of the procedures using the following sentence *Based on the procedures completed, we concluded that …"* at the bottom of table. In addition, the auditor uses key observations related to this KAM such as monetary values which refer to *aircraft and related equipment amounted to KShs 90,044 million and KShs 89,965 million as at 31 December 2018* and percentage values which refer to *aircraft and related equipment constitute 66% and 60% of the total assets of the Group and the Company*.

4.6.1 Patterns of Elements of Describing KAMs in the Global Context
In terms of the elements of describing KAMs, this research reveals that the auditors of all airlines include the *element A* and *element B* in the audit report in the

Table 7a. Describing KAMs in the Audit Report of Azul Brazilian Airlines.

Azul Brazilian Airlines

KAM: Passenger Revenue	How our audit addressed the KAM
Flight revenue is recognized upon effective rendering of the transportation service. Tickets sold and not used, corresponding to advanced ticket sales (air traffic liability), are recorded in current liabilities and are recognized when used, on an accrual basis. The recognition of certain revenues takes into account estimates with a high degree of professional judgment by management, such as the expectation of expiration of unused tickets, these assumptions are evaluated by management based on historical data. Additionally, the process of ticket sales and flight revenue recognition is highly dependent on information technology (IT) systems. Considering the facts listed above and the magnitude of these balances on the financial statements as a whole, we consider this a KAM	The audit procedures included, among others (i) the analysis of the adequacy of manual journal entries included in the revenue accounts; (ii) comparison of a sample of flights with reports issued by the aviation regulatory agency (ANAC); (iii) observation of a sample of passenger boarding the airplanes in order to verify the respective revenue; (iv) analytical review of revenue balances considering our expectations and market indicators; and (v) analysis of revenue recognition over expired credits (breakage); and (vi) evaluation of financial statements disclosures, included in notes 3.17 and 22, were appropriate

Based on the results of the audit procedures performed, which is consistent with management's assessment, we consider the Company's passenger revenue recognition policies are acceptable to support the judgments, estimates, and information included in the financial statements taken as a whole

Table 7b. Describing KAMs in the Audit Report of Kenya Airways.

Kenya Airways	
KAM: Impairment of aircraft and related equipment	How our audit addressed the KAM
As disclosed in note 15 of the consolidated and company financial statements as at December 31, 2018, the Group's and Company's aircraft and related equipment amounted to KShs 90,044 million and KShs 89,965 million as at December 31, 2018, respectively; constitutes 66% and 60% of the total assets of the Group and the Company, respectively	Our procedures to address the risk relating to impairment of aircrafts and related equipment included:
As required by IAS 36: Impairment of assets, the Directors conduct annual impairment tests to assess the recoverability of the carrying value of its aircraft and related equipment. This is performed using discounted cash flow models	• Evaluating the design and implementation of controls over the assessment of aircraft impairment, in particular around the review of assumptions and outputs • Assessing whether there are any indicators of impairment of the aircrafts as per the requirements of IAS 36: Impairment of assets • Engaging our in-house fair value specialist in reviewing and recomputing the discount rate used in the model
The determination of impairment is based on the Directors' assumptions and significant judgment and thus may be subject to bias. The key assumptions include passenger revenue and cost growth, fuel recovery, and the discount rate. Accordingly, impairment of aircraft and related equipment is considered as a KAM	• Assessing and challenging the impairment model used including the identification of the cash-generating units • Analyzing the projected cash flows by assessing the key assumptions against historical performance to test the reasonableness of the Directors' assumption
Based on procedures completed, we concluded that the assumptions used by the Directors in assessment of impairment were appropriate and had been applied. In addition, the disclosures pertaining to the impairment of aircraft and related equipment were found to be appropriate in the financial statements	

global context (Fig. 3). However, *element C* and *element D* are not observed in all audit reports. This situation indicates diversity in elements of KAMs. In this regard, around 24% of the audit reports includes *element C* which refers to the least frequent element and around 82% of the audit reports include *element D* which is the third most frequent element of describing KAMs.

4.6.2 Patterns of Diversified Elements of Describing KAMs in the Auditor Context

Regarding the elements of describing KAMs, diversity in elements C and D is globally analyzed below in the context of auditors for the year 2018 (Fig. 4).

With respect to the *element C*, PWC reports this element in around 56% of the audit reports, but it is even less than this percentage for other Big 4 auditors: E&Y at 30%, KPMG at 15%, and Deloitte at 12.50%.

In terms of the *element D*, PWC reports this element in all reports, but it is observed at 88% of audit reports of Deloitte, 80% of audit reports of E&Y, and 69% of audit reports of KPMG.

In this regard, PWC is the most frequently reporting auditor of elements C and D for the year 2018. On the other hand, these percentages stated above are

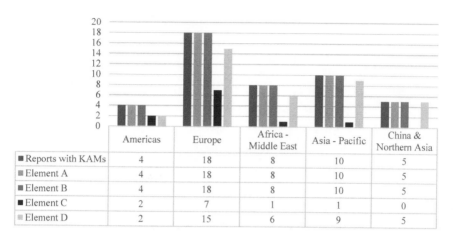

	Americas	Europe	Africa - Middle East	Asia - Pacific	China & Northern Asia
■ Reports with KAMs	4	18	8	10	5
■ Element A	4	18	8	10	5
■ Element B	4	18	8	10	5
■ Element C	2	7	1	1	0
■ Element D	2	15	6	9	5

Fig. 3. Patterns of Elements of Describing KAMs in the Global Context.

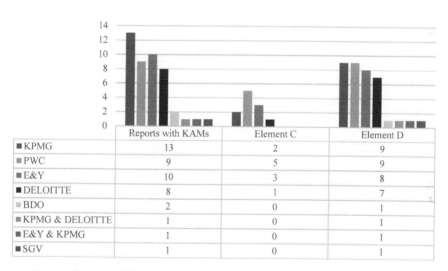

	Reports with KAMs	Element C	Element D
■ KPMG	13	2	9
■ PWC	9	5	9
■ E&Y	10	3	8
■ DELOITTE	8	1	7
■ BDO	2	0	1
■ KPMG & DELOITTE	1	0	1
■ E&Y & KPMG	1	0	1
■ SGV	1	0	1

Fig. 4. Patterns of Diversified Elements of Describing KAMs in the Auditor Context.

indicators of the diversity in reporting elements C and D in the intraregional and interregional context due to the reporting flexibility provided by the ISA 701 stating *describing some combination of these elements.* If the audit reports of the same auditor such as Deloitte are observed in the regional context, it should be noted that element C or D is reported in the audit report of one airline of the same region while it is not in the audit report of another airline of the same or different region.

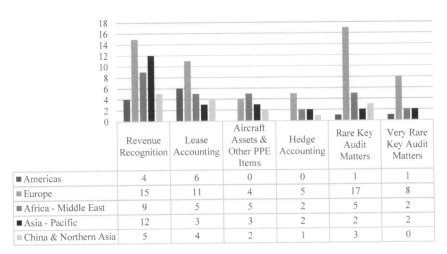

	Revenue Recognition	Lease Accounting	Aircraft Assets & Other PPE Items	Hedge Accounting	Rare Key Audit Matters	Very Rare Key Audit Matters
■ Americas	4	6	0	0	1	1
■ Europe	15	11	4	5	17	8
■ Africa - Middle East	9	5	5	2	5	2
■ Asia - Pacific	12	3	3	2	2	2
▥ China & Northern Asia	5	4	2	1	3	0

Fig. 5.   Frequent, Rare, and Very Rare KAMs in the Airline Industry.

4.7. Content Analysis of Reporting KAMs in the Audit Report of Airlines

This research points out the following findings for the year 2018 related to KAMs in the airline industry. Research reveals 139 observations of KAMs. In this regard, there are four KAMs that are frequently observed in the global context (Fig. 5): (1) revenue recognition; (2) lease accounting; (3) aircraft assets and other PPE; and (4) hedge accounting. These are industry-specific KAMs and consist of 70% of observations, consistent with key takeaways stated by Lavi (2016). The remaining 30% of observations refers to rare and very rare KAMs which cover industry- and entity-specific KAMs.

4.7.1 KAMs Related to Revenue Recognition

Revenue recognition which consists of 32% of observations is the most frequently observed KAM because revenue recognition for the year 2018 is based on the first adoption of the new revenue standard IFRS 15. Therefore, auditors evaluated the accurate adoption of the accounting policies related to recognition of revenue from passenger and cargo services, breakage revenue related to passenger tickets and miles, customer loyalty programs and the use of complex IT systems in revenue recognition from passenger services.

Considering the content analysis of the KAMs section of the airlines' audit reports, the following findings were collected toward the composition of the revenue recognition as a KAM (Fig. 6): (1) 45% of the observations related to revenue recognition is related to the revenue from passenger and cargo services; (2) 21% of the observations related to revenue recognition consists of the accurate determination of revenue from passenger services through the use of complex IT systems; and (3) 19% of the observations related to revenue recognition include the accurate recognition of customer loyalty programs such as frequent

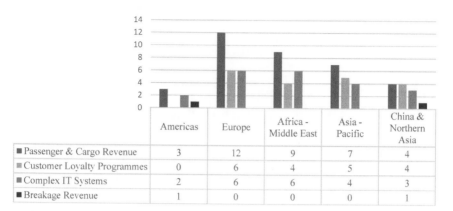

	Americas	Europe	Africa - Middle East	Asia - Pacific	China & Northern Asia
■ Passenger & Cargo Revenue	3	12	9	7	4
■ Customer Loyalty Programmes	0	6	4	5	4
■ Complex IT Systems	2	6	6	4	3
■ Breakage Revenue	1	0	0	0	1

Fig. 6. Classification of Revenue Recognition as a KAM in the Airline Industry.

flyer programs in the airline industry. In addition, two airlines (Gol Linhas Aéreas and China Southern Airlines) declared breakage revenue as a separate KAM by explicitly stating this revenue that is typically part of IFRS 15. However, it should be noted that the classification of passenger and cargo revenue may also include the analysis of breakage revenue as a KAM even if it was not explicitly stated in the audit reports.

4.7.2 KAMs Related to Lease Accounting
Lease accounting consisting of 21% of observations is the second most frequently observed KAM because operating and financing leases are quite intensive in the airline industry (IASB, 2016t). In 2018, IAS 17 was still in force, but two airlines early adopted the new lease standard IFRS 16. In this context, auditors evaluated the accuracy of lease classifications, aircraft maintenance provisions (also called as provision for return condition obligations or aircraft lease return costs), pre-paid maintenance assets (aircraft maintenance deposits), early adoption of IFRS 16 by Air France – KLM and Easy Jet, and expected effect of IFRS 16.

Considering the content analysis of the KAMs section of the airlines' audit reports, the following findings were collected toward the composition of the lease accounting as a KAM (Fig. 7): (1) 62% of the observations related to lease accounting refers to the accurate determination of aircraft maintenance provisions; (2) 17% of the observations related to lease accounting consists of the accurate determination of the classification of operating and finance leases; and (3) 10% of the observations related to lease accounting include the determination of aircraft maintenance deposits.

4.7.3 KAMs Related to Aircraft Assets and Other PPE Items
Aircraft assets and other PPE items which refer to 10% of observations is the third most frequently observed KAM because this asset class includes depreciable

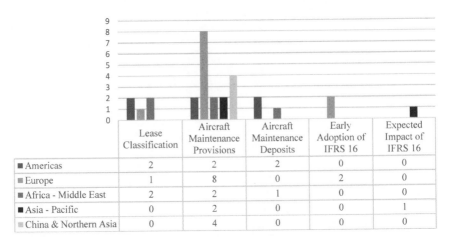

	Lease Classification	Aircraft Maintenance Provisions	Aircraft Maintenance Deposits	Early Adoption of IFRS 16	Expected Impact of IFRS 16
▪ Americas	2	2	2	0	0
▪ Europe	1	8	0	2	0
▪ Africa - Middle East	2	2	1	0	0
▪ Asia - Pacific	0	2	0	0	1
▪ China & Northern Asia	0	4	0	0	0

Fig. 7. Classification of Lease Accounting as a KAM in the Airline Industry.

assets, particularly aircraft, aircraft related assets, and other PPE items thus leading to the analysis of component accounting, accurate determination of depreciation rates (useful lives), and residual values under IAS 16 and accurate determination of their recoverability (impairment) under IAS 36.

Considering the content analysis of the KAMs section of the airlines' audit reports, the following findings were collected toward the composition of the aircraft assets and other PPE items as a KAM (Fig. 8): (1) 35% of observations related to aircraft and PPE items refers to accurate determination of residual values; (2) 31% of observations related to aircraft and PPE items refers to accurate determination of useful lives; and (3) 35% of observations related to aircraft and PPE items refers to accurate determination of whether they are impaired, and if any their impaired values.

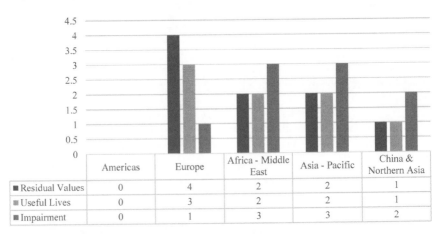

	Americas	Europe	Africa - Middle East	Asia - Pacific	China & Northern Asia
▪ Residual Values	0	4	2	2	1
▪ Useful Lives	0	3	2	2	1
▪ Impairment	0	1	3	3	2

Fig. 8. Classification of Aircraft Assets and Other PPE as a KAM in the Airline Industry.

4.7.4 KAMs Related to Hedge Accounting

Recognition of hedge accounting including derivative financial instruments which consists of 7% of observations is the least frequently observed KAM. Airlines try to avoid foreign exchange risk, fuel price risk, and interest rate risk (Lavi, 2016).

Considering the content analysis of the KAMs section of the airlines' audit reports, the following findings were collected toward the composition of the hedge accounting as a KAM (Fig. 9): (1) 40% of observations related to hedge accounting focuses on hedging the fuel price risk; 35% of observations related to hedge accounting refers to hedging foreign currency risk; and (3) 25% of observations related to hedge accounting consists of hedging interest rate risk.

4.7.5 Rare KAMs

The "rare KAMs" consist of industry-specific matters such as provisions for taxation, litigation, and claims under IAS 37, impairment of goodwill and intangible assets under IAS 38 such as landing rights and timeslots, consistent with key takeaways stated by Lavi (2016) versus entity-specific matters such as deferred tax assets and liabilities, defined benefit plan obligations, first adoption of IFRS 9, carrying value of inventory, including allowance for obsolete and slow-moving inventories, pension plans, and new aircraft purchases including its purchase and financing (Fig. 10).

4.7.6. Very Rare KAMs

The "very rare KAMs" are entity-specific. They include convertible bond, going-concern assumption, change in accounting policy, accounting for one-off items, accuracy of opening balances, EU 261 provision, acquisition accounting, disposal of trade operations, functional currency, carrying value of receivables, loan classification, asset retirement obligation, and accounting for low-cost airlines cash generating unit. They are observed once in different regions.

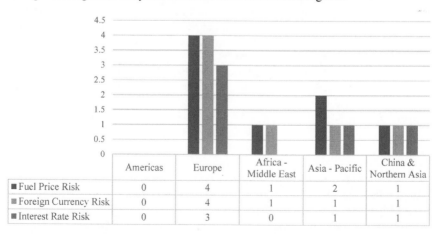

	Americas	Europe	Africa - Middle East	Asia - Pacific	China & Northern Asia
■ Fuel Price Risk	0	4	1	2	1
■ Foreign Currency Risk	0	4	1	1	1
■ Interest Rate Risk	0	3	0	1	1

Fig. 9. Classification of Hedge Accounting as a KAM in the Airline Industry.

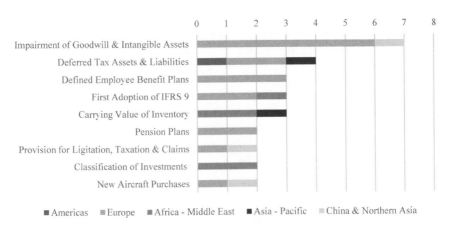

Fig. 10.   Rare KAMs in the Airline Industry.

4.8 Materiality in the Audit Reports of Airlines

Providing materiality related information in the audit report is not required under ISA 701 (IAASB, 2015b). However, paragraph 16.1 of the ISA 701 of the UK requires the declaration of materiality threshold and an overview of the scope of the audit in connection with materiality and KAMs (FRC, 2016). Therefore, the auditors of the UK's, Ireland's, and Jersey's listed airlines adopting ISA (UK), mandatorily report the materiality threshold and the scope of audit in the audit report versus the auditors of the listed airlines from Finland, Russia, UAE, Australia, and New Zealand, voluntarily report the materiality threshold and/or the scope of audit in the audit report.

In Finland, the auditing process is subject to good auditing practice as stated before, but it is in line with ISAs. As part of good auditing practice, auditing act of Finland (1141/2015) states that an auditor can observe any particular instructions given by the partners or by the shareholders' meeting or equivalent governing body (Chapter 4, Section 3). Therefore, the declaration of the materiality threshold within the audit report of Finnair (2018) would be considered as part of good auditing practice in Finland.

In Australia and New Zealand, the ASA 701 of the Australia and ISA (NZ) 701 of the New Zealand do not include such an additional accounting policy (AASB, 2015; NZ AASB, 2015). Therefore, the audit report of Alliance Airlines (2019) and Air New Zealand (2019) declares the materiality threshold on a voluntary basis.

4.8.1 Declaration of Materiality Related Information in the Audit Reports

Audit reports of 11 airlines from Australia, Finland, Ireland, Jersey, Russia, New Zealand, UAE, and the UK declare that materiality concept was considered in designing the audit process. However, audit reports of 10 airlines declare the group materiality, audit reports of four airlines also declare the parent company materiality, and audit reports of two airlines declare performance materiality (Fig. 11). Scope of audit is provided by 11 airlines.

4.8.2 Declaration of Group and Company Materiality in Audit Reports
Declaration of group and company materiality takes place through the benchmarks. The group materiality benchmarks declared in the audit reports of airlines reveal a diverse structure in the context of the analysis of materiality made by the audit firms. Even if the sample size is small, 40% of audit reports declare "profit before tax" as a benchmark, 30% of audit reports declare "revenues" as a benchmark (Fig. 12). In addition, there are unique cases of benchmark: (1) one airline's audit report shows "operating profit before exceptional items" as a benchmark of

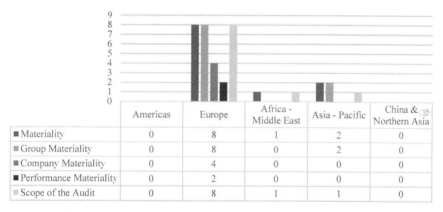

	Americas	Europe	Africa - Middle East	Asia - Pacific	China & Northern Asia
■ Materiality	0	8	1	2	0
▦ Group Materiality	0	8	0	2	0
■ Company Materiality	0	4	0	0	0
■ Performance Materiality	0	2	0	0	0
▨ Scope of the Audit	0	8	1	1	0

Fig. 11. Declaration of Materiality and Scope of the Audit in the Airline Industry.

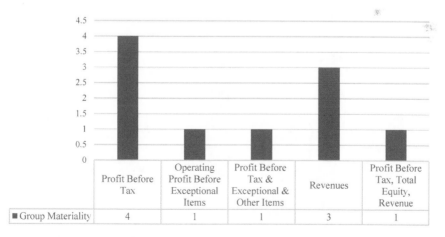

	Profit Before Tax	Operating Profit Before Exceptional Items	Profit Before Tax & Exceptional & Other Items	Revenues	Profit Before Tax, Total Equity, Revenue
■ Group Materiality	4	1	1	3	1

Fig. 12. Patterns of the Benchmarks of the Group Materiality in the Airline Industry.

which exceptional items refer to items need to be disclosed by virtue of their size or incidence considering management's view; (2) one airline's audit report indicates "profit before tax and exceptional and other items" as a benchmark by adding back exceptional and other items which was deducted to calculate operating profit; and (3) one airline's report declares three materiality benchmarks that are collectively considered in analysis of materiality: profit before tax, total equity, and revenue.

Compared to the declaration of group materiality in the audit reports of 10 airlines, this research reveals that audit reports of five airlines declare company level materiality (Fig. 13). As it is in the case of group materiality, the benchmark used by the audit firms reveals a diverse structure to analyze the materiality on the parent company's financial statements and disclosures.

4.8.3 Analysis of the Rationales Behind the Group and Company Materiality Benchmarks

Considering the audit reports of 10 airlines, Table 8 reports that the audit reports of all airlines declare the rationales of the group materiality benchmarks versus two of the five airlines declare their rationales behind the company materiality benchmarks. These rationales are provided below.

Considering the audit reports of five airlines stating company materiality benchmarks, Table 9 provides the rationales of the company materiality benchmarks.

4.8.4 Declaration of Performance Materiality in Audit Reports

Under ISA 701 of the UK, declaration of performance materiality was optional as of the year 2018 (FRC, 2016). Therefore, audit reports of two UK airlines declare the performance materiality and the rationale behind the performance materiality (Table 10).

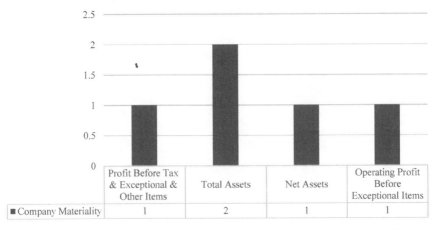

Fig. 13.   Patterns of the Benchmarks of the Company Materiality in the Airline Industry.

Table 8. Rationales Behind the Group Materiality Benchmarks.

Group Materiality Benchmark	Rationale Behind the Benchmark
Operating profit before exceptional items	*British Airways:* Audit firm states that the group uses this benchmark as its key profit measure and performance indicator internally and in reporting results externally (British Airways, 2018)
Profit before tax	*Easy Jet:* Audit firm states that this benchmark is a generally accepted auditing practice when there is no alternative benchmark that would be appropriate given that profitability is the primary measure used by the shareholders in assessing the underlying financial performance of the group (Easy Jet, 2019).
	Ryanair: Audit firm states that this is one of the principal benchmarks in assessing the financial performance of the group (Ryanair, 2019).
	Wizz Air: Audit firm states that this is the primary measure used by shareholders in assessing the financial performance of the group (Wizz Air, 2019)
	Alliance Airlines: Audit firm declares that this is the benchmark most used to measure the financial performance of the group (Alliance Airlines, 2019)
Profit before tax and exceptional and other items	*Air Partner:* Audit firm states that this is a generally accepted auditing benchmark and is the primary measure used by the shareholders in assessing the financial performance of the group (Air Partner, 2019)
Revenues	*Finnair:* Audit firm states that there are two reasons to choose revenue as a benchmark: (1) it provides with a consistent year-on-year basis for determining materiality, reflecting the group's growth and investment plans due to the volatile profitability of the group significantly impacted by items affecting comparability; and (2) this is commonly used benchmark to measure the performance of the by users (Finnair, 2018)
	Fastjet: Audit firm considers this benchmark because it provides a more stable measure year-on-year than group loss before tax in the current period of restructuring and stabilization (Fastjet, 2018)
	Aeroflot: Audit firm states that revenue represents a more appropriate measure of the size of the business and risks of misstatement than profit before tax due to the volatile structure of the financial results of the group (Aeroflot, 2018)
Profit before tax, total equity, revenue	*Air New Zealand:* Audit firm declares that these benchmarks were chosen considering the cyclical nature of the airline industry (Air New Zealand, 2019)

Table 9.   Rationales Behind the Company Materiality Benchmarks.

Company Materiality Benchmark	Rationale Behind the Benchmark
Profit before tax and exceptional and other items	*Air Partner:* Audit firm states that this is a generally accepted auditing benchmark and is the primary measure used by the shareholders in assessing the financial performance of the group (Air Partner, 2019)
Total assets	*Easy Jet:* Audit firm states that this benchmark is a generally accepted auditing practice when there is no alternative benchmark that would be appropriate given that the company does not generate revenues of its own (Easy Jet, 2019)

Table 10.   Rationales Behind the Performance Materiality.

Airlines	Rationale Behind the Performance Materiality
British Airways	Audit firm states that the performance materiality was set through understanding of the entity and past experience that does not indicate a higher risk of misstatements (British Airways, 2018)
Fastjet	Audit firm states that performance materiality was set considering the fact that (1) it is a first-year audit; (2) expected value of known and likely misstatements; (3) the number of material estimates and judgments; (4) how homogeneous processes are within the group; and (5) the expected use of sample testing (Fastjet, 2018)

4.8.5 Monetary and Percentage Value of Group, Company, and Performance Materiality

In the context of the declaration of the monetary value, and percentage of the benchmarks of group materiality, company materiality, and performance materiality, research reveals that audit reports declare the monetary value and percentage for each type of materiality (Table 11).

4.8.6 Scope of the Audit

Information related to the scope of the audit in connection with the materiality is provided by 10 airlines except Air New Zealand. However, the scope of the audit is diversified from one audit report to another in the form of a long or short paragraph but what is expected from the scope of the audit is truly reflected in the audit reports of the UK airlines. In this context, two examples related to the scope of the audit are provided below (Tables 12a and 12b).

5. CONCLUSION

This chapter focuses on the different perspectives of international auditing in the context of the airline industry. It is the starting point for further research

Table 11. Monetary and Percentage Values of Materiality.

	Group Materiality	Company Materiality	Performance Materiality
British Airways (British Airways, 2018)	£90 Million 5% of operating profit before exceptional items	£90 Million 5% of operating profit before exceptional items	£68 Million 75% of the group materiality
Fastjet (Fastjet, 2018)	$0.39 Million 1% of revenue	$0.1 Million 1.5% of total assets	– 50% of the group materiality
Air Partner (Air Partner, 2019)	£290,000 5% of profit before tax and exceptional and other items	£226,000 5% of profit before tax and exceptional and other items	–
Easy Jet (Easy Jet, 2019)	£21.5 Million 5% of profit before tax	£21.3 Million 1% of total assets	–
Ryanair (Ryanair, 2019)	€47.3 Million 5% of profit before tax	€10 Million 1% of net assets	–
Wizz Air (Wizz Air, 2019)	€15 Million 5% of profit before tax	–	–
Finnair (Finnair, 2018)	€14 Million 0.5 % of revenues	–	–
Aeroflot (Aeroflot, 2018)	RUB 6,110 million 1% of the revenue	–	–
Alliance Airlines (Alliance Airlines, 2019)	$1.64 Million 5% of the profit before tax	–	–
Air New Zealand (Air New Zealand, 2019)	$25 Million 6.7% of profit before tax 1.2% of total equity 0.4% of revenue	–	–

Table 12a. Example of Scope of the Audit in the context of Air Partner.

Airlines	Scope of Audit
Air Partner	We performed full scope audit procedures on four trading entities (Air Partner, 2019). We then extended our testing in relation to revenue and costs for one further trading entity to ensure that we achieved required levels of audit coverage. Overall, these audit procedures provided coverage of 85% of consolidated gross profit and 95% of consolidated profit before income tax and exceptional and other items

Of the four full scope audits, three audits were performed by the group engagement team based in the UK. For one entity, Air Partner SAS, a separate Deloitte component audit team based in France performed the audit under instruction from the group team. The risks for Air Partner SAS were agreed with the component team prior to the work commencing. The group engagement team reviewed the work of the Deloitte component audit team in France during the course of their audit and attended the clearance meeting to discuss the audit work and findings. As part of the review and supervision of the French component audit team, senior members of the group engagement team visited France on a number of occasions to evaluate the work performed, including reviewing relevant audit working papers

Specified procedures were then completed on revenue and costs for Air Partner GmbH to provide additional coverage. This work was performed by the group engagement team

Additionally, the group engagement team performed additional audit work over tax balances, share based payments, business combinations including consideration of management's goodwill impairment review and the group consolidation as these items are controlled centrally |

Table 12b. Example of Scope of the Audit in the context of Easy Jet.

Easy Jet	We performed audit procedures over six reporting components in the Group, including all individually significant components (Easy Jet, 2019)
	• Separate audit procedures were carried out over the Company and in relation to consolidation adjustments
	• This provided coverage of 100% external revenue and profit before tax
	We tailored the scope of our audit to ensure that we performed enough work to be able to give an opinion on the financial statements as a whole, taking into account the structure of the Group and the Company, the accounting processes and controls, and the industry in which they operate
	The Group operates through the Company and its twelve subsidiary undertakings of which six were actively trading through the year
	The remaining subsidiaries are either holding companies, dormant or have been newly established during the year and not yet started to actively trade. The accounting for these components is largely centralized in the UK
	We determined the most effective approach to scoping was to perform full scope procedures over five components registered in the UK and Austria, together with performing procedures over all material financial statement line items for easyJet Switzerland SA. Under our direction and supervision some financial statement line items identified in our scope were audited by a component team from PwC Switzerland
	We determined the appropriate level of our involvement in the underlying work to ensure we could conclude that sufficient appropriate audit evidence had been obtained for the Group financial statements as a whole. We issued written instructions to the component auditor and had regular communications with them throughout the audit cycle. Additional audit procedures were performed in relation to consolidation adjustments. The testing approach ensured that appropriate audit evidence had been obtained over all financial statement line items in order to support our opinion on the Consolidated financial statements as a whole. Based on the detailed audit work performed across the Group, we have gained coverage of 100% of both external consolidated revenue and profit before tax

regarding audit report related research in the airline industry. The chapter points out that financial statements and disclosures of most airlines are audited by international audit firms and specifically by Big 4 audit firms. For the year 2018, the chapter reveals that the financial statements and disclosures of the airlines, fairly present the financial position, financial performance, and cash flows under IFRS. There are rare cases of emphasis of matter, other matters, and material uncertainty related to going-concern in the airline industry for the year 2018. In addition, elements of describing KAMs particularly are based on element A, B, and D. Most KAMs in the airline industry focus on industry-specific matters. In the context of the materiality threshold on the audit report, benchmarks are diversified. However, analysis of the rationales behind the benchmarks reveals that audit firms are inclined to select indicators related to profitability stating that they are primary benchmarks in assessing financial performance. However, profitability indicators are replaced by revenue if the audit firm determines that the financial performance of the auditee is volatile. This research could be replicated for 2019 and 2020 to further observe the patterns of the airline industry in terms of international auditing.

REFERENCES

Abdullatif, M., & Al-Rahahleh, A. S. (2020). Applying a new audit regulation: Reporting key audit matters in Jordan. *International Journal of Auditing*, 24(2), 268–291.

Acar, V., & Bayramoğlu, G. (2020). Evaluation of IFRS 15 revenue from contracts with customer within the scope of customer loyalty programs. *Uluslararası İşletme, Ekonomi ve Yönetim Perspektifleri Dergisi*, 4(1), 125–135.

Aer Lingus. (2005). *Aer Lingus group plc annual report 2005*. Retrieved from https://www.iairgroup.com/~/media/Files/I/IAG/annual-reports/aer-lingus-annual-reports/en/Aer%20Lingus%20Annual%20Report%202005.pdf

Aer Lingus. (2006). *Aer Lingus group plc annual report 2006*. Retrieved from https://www.iairgroup.com/~/media/Files/I/IAG/annual-reports/aer-lingus-annual-reports/en/Aer%20Lingus%20Annual%20Report%202006.pdf

Aeroflot. (2018). *Aeroflot 2018 annual report*. Retrieved from https://ir.aeroflot.com/fileadmin/user_upload/files/eng/companys_reporting/annual_reports/aeroflot_ar18_eng.pdf

American Institute of Certified Public Accountants (AICPA). (2016). *Audit and accounting guide: Airlines*. New York, NY: John Wiley & Sons.

Air France – KLM. (2017). *Registration document 2017 including the annual financial report*. Retrieved from https://www.airfranceklm.com/en/system/files/ddr_air_france-klm_2017_va_0_1_0.pdf

Air France – KLM. (2018). *Registration document 2018 including the annual financial report*. Retrieved from https://www.airfranceklm.com/en/system/files/registration_document_air_france-klm_2018_va_def.pdf

Air New Zealand. (2019). *Air New Zealand annual financial results 2019*. Retrieved from https://p-airnz.com/cms/assets/PDFs/airnz-2019-financial-results.pdf

Air Partner. (2019). *Air Partner 2019 annual report*. Retrieved from https://www.airpartnergroup.com/media/jwufzcn5/2019-annual-report.pdf

Air Transport Action Group (ATAG). (2018). *Aviation: Benefits without borders*. Retrieved from https://www.aviationbenefits.org/media/166713/abbb18_factsheet_global.pdf

Air Transport Action Group (ATAG). (2020). *Aviation: Fact and figures*. Retrieved from https://www.atag.org/facts-figures.html

Aitken, M., & Simnett, R. (1991). Australian audit reports: 1980–89. *Australian Accounting Review*, 1(1), 12–19.

Akbulut, D. H. (2018). Faaliyet kiralaması işlemlerinin aktifleştirilmesinin finansal tablolara ve finansal oranlara etkisi üzerine bir telekomünikasyon şirketinin vak'a incelemesi. *Journal of Accounting & Finance*, (78), 17–36.

Akdoğan, N. (2020). Borsa İstanbul (BİST) şirketlerinin 2017 ve 2018 yıllarındaki denetim görüşleri ile bağımsız denetçi raporlarında verilen görüşün dayanağının incelenmesine yönelik bir araştırma. *Muhasebe ve Denetime Bakış, 19*(59), 1–18.

Akdoğan, N., Aktaş, M., & Gülhan, O. (2015). Borsa İstanbul'da bağimsiz denetim şirketleri ve bağımsız denetim görüşleri üzerine bir inceleme. *Muhasebe Bilim Dünyası Dergisi*, 17(1), 19–32.

Akdoğan, N., & Bülbül, S. (2019). Bağımsız denetçi raporlarında kilit denetim konularının bildirilmesinde BİST 100 şirketlerindeki ilk uygulama sonuçlarının değerlendirmesine yönelik bir araştırma. *Muhasebe ve Denetime Bakış, 18*(56), 1–24.

Akdoğan, N., & Erhan, D. U. (2020). TFRS 16 kiralamalar standardının finansal tablolar üzerine etkisi ve perakendecilik sektörü üzerine bir araştırma. *Muhasebe Bilim Dünyası Dergisi*, 22(1), 164–191.

Akdoğan, N., Güdü, E. S., Işık, A., Sevindik, İ., Şahin, D., & Özkan, G. (2018). 2014–2016 Yılları arasında BIST şirketleri ile ilgili denetim görüşleri. *Muhasebe ve Denetime Bakış, 18*(54), 1–18.

Akdoğan, N., & Öztürk, C. (2015). A country specific approach to IFRS accounting policy choice in the European, Australian, and Turkish context. *EMAJ: Emerging Markets Journal, 5*(1), 60–81.

Aktaş, R., Karğın, S., & Arıcı, N. D. (2017). Changes new leases standard IFRS 16 has brought and evaluation of its possible effects on financial reports and financial ratios of corporations. *Journal of Business Research–Turk, 9*(4), 858–881.

Alabood, E., Abuaddous, M., & Bataineh, H. (2019). The impact of IFRS 16 on airline companies: An exploratory study in the Middle East. *International Journal of Economics and Business Research, 18*(1), 112–128.

Ali, S. A. M. (2021). Compliance with IFRS 16 mandatory presentation and disclosure requirements and company characteristics: Evidence from an emerging market. *Scientific Journal for Financial and Commercial Studies and Researches, 2*(1), 182–227.

Alliance Airlines. (2019). *Alliance Aviation Services Limited annual report year ended 30 June 2019*. Retrieved from https://www.allianceairlines.com.au/docs/default-source/default-document-library/asx-alliance-aviation-(aqz)--financial-statements-30-june-2019.pdf?sfvrsn=74771c9e_0

André, P., & Kalogirou, F. (2020). IFRS adoption by UK unlisted firms: Subsidiary-versus group-level incentives. *Accounting Forum, 44*(3), 215–237.

Arzova, S. B., & Şahin, B. Ş. (2020). ISA 701 (BDS 701) kilit denetim konuları: BİST 30, BİST 50 ve BİST 100 endekslerinde yer alan finans kurumlarına yönelik analiz. *Muhasebe ve Denetime Bakış, 20*(60), 75–94.

Asiana Airlines. (2018). *Asiana Airlines, Inc. separate financial statements December 31, 2018 and* 2017. Retrieved from https://flyasiana.com/C/US/EN/company/investor-relations/n-detail/audit/CM201905230001139374

Australian Accounting & Auditing Standards Board. (2015). *Auditing standard ASA 701 communicating key audit matters in the independent auditor's report*. Retrieved from https://www.auasb.gov.au/admin/file/content102/c3/ASA_701_2015.pdf

Azul Brazilian Airlines. (2018). *Azul S.A. consolidated financial statements December 31, 2018, and 2017 with registered public accounting firm.* Retrieved from https://mz-filemanager.s3.amazonaws.com/ed78542a-4e01-429a-8926-03d69ccfa307/file_manager/40d1b882-1a04-4f60-89c3-90633d311415/4q18_financial_statements.pdf

Baker, C. R., Ding, Y., & Stolowy, H. (2005). Using "statement of intermediate balances" as tool for international financial statement analysis in airline industry. *Advances in International Accounting, 18*, 169–198.

Baker, C. R., Mikol, A., & Quick, R. (2001). Regulation of the statutory auditor in the European Union: A comparative survey of the United Kingdom, France, and Germany. *European Accounting Review, 10*(4), 763–786.

Beattie, V., Edwards, K., & Goodacre, A. (1998). The impact of constructive operating lease capitalisation on key accounting ratios. *Accounting and Business Research, 28*(4), 233–254.

Beatty, R. P. (1989). Auditor reputation and the pricing of initial public offerings. *Accounting Review, 64*, 693–709.

Belesis, N., Sorros, J., Karagiorgos, A., & Kousounadis, P. (2021). Cumulative effect of IFRS 15 and IFRS 16 on maritime company financial statements: A hypothetical case. *SN Business & Economics, 1*(3), 1–20.

Belobaba, P. (2015). Introduction and overview. In P. Belobaba, A. Odoni, & C. Barnhart (Eds.), *The global airline industry* (2nd ed., pp. 1–18). New York, NY: John Wiley & Sons.

Bennecib, F. (2004). *Le co-commissariat aux comptes: sa contribution à l'accroissement de l'indépendance de l'auditeur.* Doctorat en sciences de gestion, Université Paris Dauphine, Paris.

Boujelben, S., & Kobbi-Fakhfakh, S. (2020). Compliance with IFRS 15 mandatory disclosures: An exploratory study in telecom and construction sectors. *Journal of Financial Reporting and Accounting, 18*(4), 707–728.

British Airways. (2005). *British Airways Plc annual report and accounts year ended 31* March 2005. Retrieved from https://www.iairgroup.com/~/media/Files/I/IAG/annual-reports/ba/en/Reports%20%20Accounts%202004%20%2005.pdf

British Airways. (2006). *British Airways Plc annual report and accounts year ended 31* March 2006. Retrieved from https://www.iairgroup.com/~/media/Files/I/IAG/annual-reports/ba/en/Report%20and%20Accounts%20for%20the%20year%20ending%2031%20March%202006.pdf

British Airways. (2018). *British Airways Plc annual report and accounts year ended 31* December 2018. Retrieved from https://www.iairgroup.com/~/media/Files/I/IAG/annual-reports/ba/en/british-airways-plc-annual-report-and-accounts-2018.pdf

Bujaki, M., & Durocher, S. (2014). Depreciation in the Canadian airline industry. *Accounting Perspectives, 13*(3), 209–218.

Cairns, D., Massoudi, D., Taplin, R., & Tarca, A. (2011). IFRS fair value measurement and accounting policy choice in the United Kingdom and Australia. *The British Accounting Review, 43*(1), 1–21.

Carson, E., Ferguson, A., & Simnett, R. (2006). Australian audit reports: 1996–2003. *Australian Accounting Review, 16*(40), 89–96.

Cereola, S. J., Nichols, N. B., & Street, D. L. (2017). Geographic segment disclosures under IFRS 8: Changes in materiality and fineness by European, Australian and New Zealand blue chip companies. *Research in Accounting Regulation, 29*(2), 119–128.

Choi, F. D., & Levich, R. M. (1991). International accounting diversity: Does it affect market participants? *Financial Analysts Journal, 47*(4), 73–82.

Christensen, H. B., & Nikolaev, V. V. (2013). Does fair value accounting for non-financial assets pass the market test? *Review of Accounting Studies, 18*(3), 734–775.

Coetsee, D., Mohammadali-Haji, A., & van Wyk, M. (2021). Revenue recognition practices in South Africa: An analysis of the decision usefulness of IFRS 15 disclosures. *South African Journal of Accounting Research.* https://doi.org/10.1080/10291954.2020.1855886

Cole, V., Branson, J., & Breesch, D. (2011). *Determinants influencing the de facto comparability of European IFRS financial statements.* Retrieved from https://dx.doi.org/10.2139/ssrn.1967001

Craswell, A. (1986). *Audit qualifications in Australia, 1950 to 1979.* Spokane, WA: Garland Pub.

Croatia Airlines. (2018). *Croatia Airlines consolidated and separate annual report for the year ended 31.12.2018.* Retrieved from https://www.croatiaairlines.com/About-us/Financial-information/Financial-reports

De Souza, F. Ê. A., & Lemes, S. (2016). Comparability of accounting choices in subsequent measurement of fixed assets, intangible assets, and investment property in South American companies. *Revista Contabilidade & Finanças-USP, 27*(71), 169–184.

Demirkol, Ö. F. (2019). BDS 570 işletmenin sürekliliği standardının uygulama süreci ve bağımsız denetim raporlarına etkisi: BİST inşaat ve bayındırlık sektöründe uygulama. *İşletme Araştırmaları Dergisi, 11*(1), 478–489.

Doupnik, T. S., & Perera, M. H. B. (2014). *International accounting.* New York, NY: McGraw-Hill.

Duke, J. C., Franz, D., & Hsieh, S. J. (2012). Evaluating constructive lease capitalization and off-balance-sheet financing: An instructional case with FedEx and UPS. *Accounting Perspectives, 11*(1), 57–69.

Duke, J. C., Hsieh, S. J., & Su, Y. (2009). Operating and synthetic leases: Exploiting financial benefits in the post-Enron era. *Advances in Accounting, 25*(1), 28–39.

Easy Jet. (2019). *East Jet plc annual report and accounts 2019.* Retrieved from https://corporate.easyjet.com/~/media/Files/E/Easyjet/pdf/investors/results-centre/2019/eas040-annual-report-2019-web.pdf

European Union (EU). (2002). *Regulation (EC) No 1606/2002 of the European Parliament and of the Council of* 19 July 2002 *on the application of international accounting standards.* Retrieved from https://eur-lex.europa.eu/legal-content/EN/TXT/PDF/?uri=CELEX:32002R1606&from=EN

Fastjet. (2018). *Fastjet Plc and its subsidiary undertakings annual report and financial statements for the year ended 31 December 2018.* Retrieved from https://www.fastjet.com/upload/RNS%20articles/RNS%202019/Fastjet%20Annual%20Report%202018.pdf

Financial Reporting Council of Mauritius (FRC of Mauritius). (2004). *Financial reporting act of Mauritius.* Retrieved from https://frc.govmu.org/24032021_frc/wp-content/uploads/2020/11/THE-FINANCIAL-REPORTING-ACT-2004-Amended-2020.pdf

Financial Reporting Council of the UK (FRC). (2013). *International standard on auditing (UK and Ireland) 700 The independent auditor's report on financial statements.* Retrieved from https://www.frc.org.uk/getattachment/501de004-b616-43c3-8d65-aeaebde19f8d/ISA-700-(UK-and-Ireland)-700-(Revised)-Independent-auditors-report-June-2013.pdf

Financial Reporting Council of the UK. (FRC) (2016). *International standard on auditing (UK) 701 Communicating key audit matters in the independent auditor's report.* Retrieved from https://www.frc.org.uk/getattachment/b250cf61-407f-4b1e-9f1c-e959174e1426/ISA-(UK)-701.pdf

Financial Reporting Council of the UK (FRC). (2020). *International standard on auditing (UK) 701 (revised November 2019) (updated January 2020): Communicating key audit matters in the independent auditor's report.* Retrieved from https://www.frc.org.uk/getattachment/4af1deff-9145-4758-b033-ff637da24117/ISA-(UK)-701_Revised-November-2019_Updated-January-2020_final-With-Covers.pdf

Finland Ministry of Economic Affairs and Employment. (2015). *Auditing act (1141/2015).* Retrieved from https://finlex.fi/sv/laki/kaannokset/2015/en20151141.pdf

Finnair. (2018). *Finnair financial information 2018.* Retrieved from https://investors.finnair.com/~/media/Files/F/Finnair-IR/documents/en/financial/fina-2018-en.pdf

Francis, J. R., & Krishnan, J. (1999). Accounting accruals and auditor reporting conservatism. *Contemporary Accounting Research, 16*(1), 135–165.

Francis, J. R., Richard, C., & Vanstraelen, A. (2009). Assessing France's joint audit requirement: Are two heads better than one? *Auditing: A Journal of Practice & Theory, 28*(2), 35–63.

Glaum, M., Schmidt, P., Street, D. L., & Vogel, S. (2013). Compliance with IFRS 3-and IAS 36-required disclosures across 17 European countries: company- and country-level determinants. *Accounting and Business Research, 43*(3), 163–204.

Gol Linhas Aereas. (2018). *GOL Linhas Aéreas Inteligentes S.A. individual and consolidated financial statements december 31, 2018 with review report of independent auditors.* Retrieved from https://ri.voegol.com.br/conteudo_en.asp?idioma=1&conta=44&tipo=54312&ano=2018

Gouveia, D. (2019). *The effects of the new accounting standard for leases on firms: A practical case of TAP's financial statement reformulation for IFRS 16.* Ph.D. thesis, NOVO School Business and Economics. Retrieved from https://run.unl.pt/bitstream/10362/70305/1/Gouveia_2019.pdf

Grosu, M., Robu, I. B., & Istrate, C. (2015). Exploratory study regarding the impact of IFRS on the audit opinion in the case of Romanian listed companies. *Audit Financiar*, *13*(127), 81–93.

Guerreiro, M. S., Rodrigues, L. L., & Craig, R. (2012). Voluntary adoption of International Financial Reporting Standards by large unlisted companies in Portugal–Institutional logics and strategic responses. *Accounting, Organizations and Society*, *37*(7), 482–499.

Gutierrez, E., Minutti-Meza, M., Tatum, K. W., & Vulcheva, M. (2018). Consequences of adopting an expanded auditor's report in the United Kingdom. *Review of Accounting Studies*, *23*(4), 1543–1587.

Güleç, Ö. F., Bektaş, T. (2019). Cash Flow Ratio Analysis: The Case of Turkey. *Muhasebe ve Finansman Dergisi*, special issue, 247–262.

Hanlon, J. P. (2007). *Global airlines: competition in a transnational industry*. Burlington, MA: Routledge.

Imhoff, E. A., Jr, Lipe, R. C., & Wright, D. W. (1991). Operating leases: Impact of constructive capitalization. *Accounting Horizons*, *5*(1), 51–63.

Imhoff, E. A., Jr, Lipe, R. C., & Wright, D. W. (1997). Operating leases: Income effects of constructive capitalization. *Accounting Horizons*, *11*(2), 12–32.

International Accounting Standards Board (IASB). (2014). *IFRS 15 Revenue from contracts with customers: Project summary and feedback statement.* Retrieved from https://www.ifrs.org/content/dam/ifrs/project/revenue-from-contracts-with-customers/project-summary-feedback-statement.pdf

International Accounting Standards Board (IASB). (2016a). *Who uses IFRS standards? Chile.* Retrieved from https://cdn.ifrs.org/-/media/feature/around-the-world/jurisdiction-profiles/chile-ifrs-profile.pdf

International Accounting Standards Board (IASB). (2016b). *Who uses IFRS standards? Mexico.* Retrieved from https://cdn.ifrs.org/-/media/feature/around-the-world/jurisdiction-profiles/mexico-ifrs-profile.pdf

International Accounting Standards Board (IASB). (2016c). *Who uses IFRS standards? Panama.* Retrieved from https://cdn.ifrs.org/-/media/feature/around-the-world/jurisdiction-profiles/panama-ifrs-profile.pdf

International Accounting Standards Board (IASB). (2016d). *Who uses IFRS standards? Chinese Taipei.* Retrieved from https://cdn.ifrs.org/-/media/feature/around-the-world/jurisdiction-profiles/chinese-taipei-ifrs-profile.pdf

International Accounting Standards Board (IASB). (2016e). *Who uses IFRS standards? Croatia.* Retrieved from https://cdn.ifrs.org/-/media/feature/around-the-world/jurisdiction-profiles/croatia-ifrs-profile.pdf

International Accounting Standards Board (IASB). (2016f). *Who uses IFRS standards? Israel.* Retrieved from https://cdn.ifrs.org/-/media/feature/around-the-world/jurisdiction-profiles/israel-ifrs-profile.pdf

International Accounting Standards Board. (2016g). *Who uses IFRS standards? Russia.* Retrieved from https://cdn.ifrs.org/-/media/feature/around-the-world/jurisdiction-profiles/russia-ifrs-profile.pdf

International Accounting Standards Board (IASB). (2016h). *Who uses IFRS standards? Jordan.* Retrieved from https://cdn.ifrs.org/-/media/feature/around-the-world/jurisdiction-profiles/jordan-ifrs-profile.pdf

International Accounting Standards Board (IASB). (2016i). *Who uses IFRS standards? Kenya.* Retrieved from https://cdn.ifrs.org/-/media/feature/around-the-world/jurisdiction-profiles/kenya-ifrs-profile.pdf

International Accounting Standards Board (IASB). (2016j). *Who uses IFRS standards? Tanzania.* Retrieved from https://cdn.ifrs.org/-/media/feature/around-the-world/jurisdiction-profiles/tanzania-ifrs-profile.pdf

International Accounting Standards Board (IASB). (2016k). *Who uses IFRS standards? Uganda.* Retrieved from https://cdn.ifrs.org/-/media/feature/around-the-world/jurisdiction-profiles/uganda-ifrs-profile.pdf

International Accounting Standards Board (IASB). (2016l). *Who uses IFRS standards? Kuwait.* Retrieved from https://cdn.ifrs.org/-/media/feature/around-the-world/jurisdiction-profiles/kuwait-ifrs-profile.pdf

International Accounting Standards Board (IASB). (2016m). *Who uses IFRS standards? Mauritius.* Retrieved from https://cdn.ifrs.org/-/media/feature/around-the-world/jurisdiction-profiles/mauritius-ifrs-profile.pdf

International Accounting Standards Board (IASB). (2016n). *Who uses IFRS standards? South Africa.* Retrieved from https://cdn.ifrs.org/-/media/feature/around-the-world/jurisdiction-profiles/south-africa-ifrs-profile.pdf

International Accounting Standards Board (IASB). (2016o). *Who uses IFRS standards? United Arab Emirates.* Retrieved from https://cdn.ifrs.org/-/media/feature/around-the-world/jurisdiction-profiles/united-arab-emirates-ifrs-profile.pdf

International Accounting Standards Board (IASB). (2016p). *Who uses IFRS standards? Qatar.* Retrieved from https://cdn.ifrs.org/-/media/feature/around-the-world/jurisdiction-profiles/qatar-ifrs-profile.pdf

International Accounting Standards Board (IASB). (2016q). *Who uses IFRS standards? Vietnam.* Retrieved from https://cdn.ifrs.org/-/media/feature/around-the-world/jurisdiction-profiles/vietnam-ifrs-profile.pdf

International Accounting Standards Board (IASB). (2016r). *Who uses IFRS standards? Sri Lanka.* Retrieved from https://cdn.ifrs.org/-/media/feature/around-the-world/jurisdiction-profiles/sri-lanka-ifrs-profile.pdf

International Accounting Standards Board (IASB). (2016s). *Who uses IFRS standards? Singapore.* Retrieved from https://cdn.ifrs.org/-/media/feature/around-the-world/jurisdiction-profiles/singapore-ifrs-profile.pdf

International Accounting Standards Board (IASB). (2016t). *Effects Analysis: International Financial Reporting Standard 16, Leases.* Retrieved from https://www.ifrs.org/content/dam/ifrs/project/leases/ifrs/published-documents/ifrs16-effects-analysis.pdf

International Accounting Standards Board (IASB). (2016u). *Project summary and feedback statement: International Financial Reporting Standard 16, Leases.* Retrieved from https://www.ifrs.org/content/dam/ifrs/project/leases/ifrs/published-documents/ifrs16-project-summary.pdf

International Accounting Standards Board (IASB). (2017a). *Who uses IFRS standards? Canada.* Retrieved from https://cdn.ifrs.org/-/media/feature/around-the-world/jurisdiction-profiles/canada-ifrs-profile.pdf

International Accounting Standards Board (IASB). (2017b). *Who uses IFRS standards? Brazil*. Retrieved from https://cdn.ifrs.org/-/media/feature/around-the-world/jurisdiction-profiles/brazil-ifrs-profile.pdf

International Accounting Standards Board (IASB). (2017c). *Who uses IFRS standards? United States*. Retrieved from https://cdn.ifrs.org/-/media/feature/around-the-world/jurisdiction-profiles/united-states-ifrs-profile.pdf

International Accounting Standards Board (IASB). (2017d). *Who uses IFRS standards? Indonesia*. Retrieved from https://cdn.ifrs.org/-/media/feature/around-the-world/jurisdiction-profiles/indonesia-ifrs-profile.pdf

International Accounting Standards Board (IASB). (2017e). *Who uses IFRS standards? Thailand*. Retrieved from https://cdn.ifrs.org/-/media/feature/around-the-world/jurisdiction-profiles/thailand-ifrs-profile.pdf

International Accounting Standards Board (IASB). (2017f). *Who uses IFRS standards? Australia*. Retrieved from https://cdn.ifrs.org/-/media/feature/around-the-world/jurisdiction-profiles/australia-ifrs-profile.pdf

International Accounting Standards Board (IASB). (2017g). *Who uses IFRS standards? Korea*. Retrieved from https://cdn.ifrs.org/-/media/feature/around-the-world/jurisdiction-profiles/south-korea-ifrs-profile.pdf

International Accounting Standards Board (IASB). (2018a). *Who uses IFRS standards? China*. Retrieved from https://cdn.ifrs.org/-/media/feature/around-the-world/jurisdiction-profiles/china-ifrs-profile.pdf

International Accounting Standards Board (IASB). (2018b). *Who uses IFRS standards? Hong Kong*. Retrieved from https://cdn.ifrs.org/-/media/feature/around-the-world/jurisdiction-profiles/hong-kong-sar-ifrs-profile.pdf

International Accounting Standards Board (IASB). (2018c). *Who uses IFRS standards? European Union*. Retrieved from https://www.ifrs.org/use-around-the-world/use-of-ifrs-standards-by-jurisdiction/european-union/

International Accounting Standards Board (IASB). (2018d). *Who uses IFRS standards? Turkey*. Retrieved from https://cdn.ifrs.org/-/media/feature/around-the-world/jurisdiction-profiles/turkey-ifrs-profile.pdf

International Accounting Standards Board (IASB). (2018e). *International accounting standard 1: Presentation of financial statements*. London: IFRS Foundation.

International Accounting Standards Board (IASB). (2018f). *International accounting standard 2: Inventory*. London: IFRS Foundation.

International Accounting Standards Board (IASB). (2018g). *International accounting standard 7: Statement of cash flows*. London: IFRS Foundation.

International Accounting Standards Board (IASB). (2018h). *International accounting standard 8: Accounting policies, changes in accounting estimates and errors*. London: IFRS Foundation.

International Accounting Standards Board (IASB). (2018i). *International accounting standard 16: Property, plant, and equipment*. London: IFRS Foundation.

International Accounting Standards Board (IASB). (2018j). *International accounting standard 27: Separate financial statements*. London: IFRS Foundation.

International Accounting Standards Board (IASB). (2018k). *International accounting standard 38: Intangible assets*. London: IFRS Foundation.

International Accounting Standards Board (IASB). (2018l). *International accounting standard 40: Investment property*. London: IFRS Foundation.

International Accounting Standards Board (IASB). (2018m). *International accounting standard 21: The effects of changes in foreign exchange rates*. London: IFRS Foundation.

International Accounting Standards Board (IASB). (2018n). *International financial reporting standard 11: Joint arrangements*. London: IFRS Foundation.

International Accounting Standards Board (IASB). (2018o). *International financial reporting standard 8: Operating segments*. London: IFRS Foundation.

International Accounting Standards Board (IASB). (2018p). *International financial reporting standard 15: Revenue from contracts with customers*. London: IFRS Foundation.

International Accounting Standards Board (IASB). (2018q). *International financial reporting standard 16: Leases*. London: IFRS Foundation.

International Accounting Standards Board (IASB). (2019a). *Who uses IFRS standards? India*. Retrieved from https://cdn.ifrs.org/-/media/feature/around-the-world/jurisdiction-profiles/india-ifrs-profile.pdf

International Accounting Standards Board (IASB). (2019b). *Who uses IFRS standards? Japan*. Retrieved from https://cdn.ifrs.org/-/media/feature/around-the-world/jurisdiction-profiles/japan-ifrs-profile.pdf

International Accounting Standards Board (IASB). (2019c). *Who uses IFRS standards? New Zealand*. Retrieved from https://cdn.ifrs.org/-/media/feature/around-the-world/jurisdiction-profiles/new-zealand-ifrs-profile.pdf

International Accounting Standards Board (IASB). (2019d). *Who uses IFRS standards? Philippines*. Retrieved from https://cdn.ifrs.org/-/media/feature/around-the-world/jurisdiction-profiles/philippines-ifrs-profile.pdf

International Accounting Standards Board (IASB). (2019e). *Who uses IFRS standards? Malaysia*. Retrieved from https://cdn.ifrs.org/-/media/feature/around-the-world/jurisdiction-profiles/malaysia-ifrs-profile.pdf

International Air Transport Association (IATA). (2016a). *Airline disclosure guide: Hedge accounting under IFRS 9*. Retrieved from https://www.iata.org/contentassets/4a4b100c43794398baf73dcea6b5ad42/airline-disclosure-guide-hedge-accounting.pdf

International Air Transport Association (IATA). (2016b). *Airline disclosure guide: Maintenance accounting*. Retrieved from https://www.iata.org/contentassets/4a4b100c43794398baf73dcea6b5ad42/airline-disclosure-guide-maintenance-accounting.pdf

International Air Transport Association (IATA). (2016c). *Airline disclosure guide: Aircraft acquisition cost and depreciation*. Retrieved from https://www.iata.org/contentassets/4a4b100c43794398baf73dcea6b5ad42/airline-disclosure-guide-aircraft-acquisition.pdf

International Air Transport Association (IATA). (2016d). *Airline disclosure guide: Segment reporting*. Retrieved from https://www.iata.org/contentassets/4a4b100c43794398baf73dcea6b5ad42/airline-disclosure-guide-segment-reporting.pdf

International Air Transport Association (IATA). (2019a). *Industry statistics fact sheet: December 2019.* Retrieved from www.iata.org

International Air Transport Association (IATA). (2019b). *Economic performance of the airline industry: 2019 End-year report.* Retrieved from www.iata.org

International Air Transport Association (IATA). (2020a). *Industry statistics fact sheet: June 2020.* Retrieved from www.iata.org

International Air Transport Association (IATA). (2020b). *Economic performance of the airline industry: 2020 Mid-year report.* Retrieved from www.iata.org

International Air Transport Association (IATA). (2020c). *IATA industry accounting working group guidance IFRS 9: Financial instruments.* Retrieved from https://www.iata.org/contentassets/e65a4360f04e41b1a6c45063060d1939/iawg-guidance-ifrs-9.pdf

International Air Transport Association (IATA). (2020d). *IATA industry accounting working group guidance IFRS 15: Revenue from contracts with customers.* Retrieved from https://www.iata.org/contentassets/e65a4360f04e41b1a6c45063060d1939/iawg-guidance-ifrs-15.pdf

International Air Transport Association (IATA). (2020e). *IATA industry accounting working group guidance IFRS 16: Leases.* Retrieved from https://www.iata.org/contentassets/e65a4360f04e41b1a6c45063060d1939/iawg-guidance-ifrs-16.pdf

International Auditing and Assurance Standards Board (IAASB). (2015a). *International standard on auditing (ISA) 570 (revised), going concern.* Retrieved from https://www.iaasb.org/publications/international-standard-auditing-isa-570-revised-going-concern-3

International Auditing and Assurance Standards Board (IAASB). (2015b). *International standard on auditing (ISA) 701 (new), communicating key audit matters in the independent auditor's report.* Retrieved from https://www.iaasb.org/publications/international-standard-auditing-isa-701-new-communicating-key-audit-matters-independent-auditors-4

International Auditing and Assurance Standards Board (IAASB). (2015c). *International standard on auditing (ISA) 706 (revised), emphasis of matter paragraphs and other matter paragraphs in the independent auditor's report.* Retrieved from https://www.iaasb.org/publications/international-standard-auditing-isa-706-revised-emphasis-matter-paragraphs-and-other-matter-4

International Auditing and Assurance Standards Board (IAASB). (2015d). *International standard on auditing 700 (revised) forming an opinion and reporting on financial statements.* Retrieved from https://www.ifac.org/system/files/publications/files/ISA-700-Revised_8.pdf

International Auditing and Assurance Standards Board (IAASB). (2015e). *International standard on auditing 705 (revised) modifications to the opinion in the independent auditor's report.* Retrieved from https://www.ifac.org/system/files/publications/files/ISA-705-Revised_0.pdf

International Auditing and Assurance Standards Board (IAASB). (2018). *International standard on auditing (ISA) 710 comparative information— Corresponding figures and comparative financial statements.* Retrieved from https://www.iaasb.org/publications/2018-handbook-international-quality-control-auditing-review-other-assurance-and-related-services-26

International Federation of Accountants (IFAC). (2018). *Global impact map: Country profiles*. Retrieved from https://www.ifac.org/what-we-do/global-impact-map/country-profiles

Irvine, H. (2008, June). The global institutionalization of financial reporting: The case of the United Arab Emirates. *Accounting Forum, 32*(2), 125–142.

Isack, I., & Tan, R. C. W. (2008). Transparent blue skies for the global airline industry: A study of key accounting disclosures. *Journal of the Asia-Pacific Centre for Environmental Accountability, 14*(1), 12–23.

İşseveroğlu, G. (2019). Bağımsız denetim raporunda kilit denetim konuları: BIST sigorta şirketlerinin 2017–2018 yılları analizi. *Muhasebe ve Finansman Dergisi*, (84), 49–64.

Iwanowicz, T., & Iwanowicz, B. (2019). ISA 701 and materiality disclosure as methods to minimize the audit expectation gap. *Journal of Risk and Financial Management, 12*(4), 161. Retrieved from https://www.mdpi.com/1911-8074/12/4/161/pdf

Jaafar, A., & McLeay, S. (2007). Country effects and sector effects on the harmonization of accounting policy choice. *Abacus, 43*(2), 156–189.

Joubert, M., Garvie, L., & Parle, G. (2017). Implications of the new accounting standard for leases AASB 16 (IFRS 16) with the inclusion of operating leases in the balance sheet. *The Journal of New Business Ideas & Trends, 15*(2), 1–11.

Karapınar, A., & Dölen, T. (2020). Bağımsız denetim raporlarında kilit denetim konusu açıklamaları: Türkiye örneği. *Muhasebe Bilim Dünyası Dergisi, 22*(4), 763–780.

Kend, M., & Nguyen, L. A. (2020). Investigating recent audit reform in the Australian context: An analysis of the KAM disclosures in audit reports 2017–2018. *International Journal of Auditing, 24*(3), 412–430.

Kenya Airways. (2018). *Kenya Airways limited (KQ.ke) 2018 annual report.* Retrieved from https://africanfinancials.com/document/ke-kq-2018-ar-00/

Khurana, I. K., & Raman, K. K. (2004a). Litigation risk and the financial reporting credibility of Big 4 versus non-Big 4 audits: Evidence from Anglo-American countries. *The Accounting Review, 79*(2), 473–495.

Khurana, I. K., & Raman, K. K. (2004b). Are big four audits in ASEAN countries of higher quality than non-big four audits? *Asia-Pacific Journal of Accounting & Economics, 11*(2), 139–165.

Kieso, D. E., Weygandt, J. J., & Warfield, T. D. (2020). *Intermediate accounting IFRS edition.* Hoboken, NJ: John Wiley & Sons.

Kobbi-Fakhfakh, S., Shabou, R. M., & Pigé, B. (2018). Determinants of segment reporting quality: evidence from EU. *Journal of Financial Reporting and Accounting, 16*(1), 84–107.

Korean Air. (2018). *Korean Airlines co., ltd. and its subsidiaries consolidated financial statements as of and for the years ended December 31, 2018, and 2017.* Retrieved from https://www.koreanair.com/content/dam/koreanair/

en/footer/about-us/inverstor-relation s/financial-information/details/2018_ consolidated.pdf

KPMG. (2019). *Key audit matters: Auditor's report snapshot in Sri Lanka.* Retrieved from https://assets.kpmg/content/dam/kpmg/lk/pdf/key-audit-matters-aug-2019.pdf

KPMG, & von Keitz, I. (2006). *The application of IFRS: choices in practice.* London: KPMG.

Kvaal, E., & Nobes, C. (2010). International differences in IFRS policy choice: A research note. *Accounting and Business Research, 40*(2), 173–187.

Lavi, M. R. (2016). The impact of IFRS on industry. Hoboken, NJ: John Wiley & Sons.

Le Manh, A. (2017). The role and current status of IFRS in the completion of national accounting rules – Evidence from France. *Accounting in Europe, 14*(1–2), 94–101.

Lourenço, I. C., Sarquis, R., Branco, M. C., & Magro, N. (2018). International differences in accounting practices under IFRS and the influence of the US. *Australian Accounting Review, 28*(4), 468–481.

Lourenço, I. C., Sarquis, R., Branco, M. C., & Pais, C. (2015). Extending the classification of European countries by their IFRS practices: A research note. *Accounting in Europe, 12*(2), 223–232.

Lucchese, M., & Di Carlo, F. (2016). The impact of IFRS 8 on segment disclosure practice: Panel evidence from Italy. *International Journal of Accounting and Financial Reporting, 6*(1), 96–126.

Lyth, P. (1996). *Introduction. Aspects of commercial air transport history. Lyth, Peter J.(Hg.): Air transport* (Studies in Transport History). Aldershot: Routledge.

Maali, B. (2018) The effect of applying the new IFRS 16 "Leases" on financial statements: An empirical analysis on the airline industry in the Middle East. *Organisational Studies and Innovation Review, 4*(1), 1–9.

Marşap, B. (2001). *İşletmelerde finansal bilgilerin bölümlere göre raporlanması.* Ankara: Tutibay Yayınları.

Marşap, B., & Yanık, S. (2018). IFRS 16 kapsamında kiralama işlemlerinin finansal raporlamaya etkisinin incelenmesi. *Muhasebe ve Finansman Dergisi,* (80), 23–42.

Mohrman, M. B. (2009). Depreciation of airplanes and garbage trucks: information value and fraud prevention in financial reporting. *Issues in Accounting Education, 24*(1), 105–107.

Morales-Díaz, J., & Zamora-Ramírez, C. (2018). The impact of IFRS 16 on key financial ratios: A new methodological approach. *Accounting in Europe, 15*(1), 105–133.

Najar, L. L., da Costa Marques, J. A. V., da Silva Carvalho, M., & Mello, L. B. (2019). Principais impactos da nova norma international de arrendamento mercantil sobre os indicadores econômico-financeiros das empresas aéreas GOL e LATAM. *Revista Contabilidade e Controladoria, 10*(3), 86–106.

Napier, C. J., & Stadler, C. (2020). The real effects of a new accounting standard: The case of IFRS 15 Revenue from Contracts with Customers. *Accounting and Business Research, 50*(5), 474–503.

New Zealand Auditing and Assurance Standards Board (NZ AASB). (2015). *ISA (NZ) 701 communicating key audit matters in the independent auditor's report.* Retrieved from https://www.xrb.govt.nz/assurance-standards/auditing-standards/isa-nz-701/

Nichols, N. B., Street, D. L., & Cereola, S. J. (2012). An analysis of the impact of adopting IFRS 8 on the segment disclosures of European blue-chip companies. *Journal of International Accounting, Auditing and Taxation, 21*(2), 79–105.

Nobes, C. (1992). *International classification of financial reporting.* London: Routledge.

Nobes, C. (1998). Towards a general model of the reason for international differences in financial reporting. *ABACUS, 34*(2), 162–187.

Nobes, C. (2006). The survival of international differences under IFRS: Towards a research agenda. *Accounting and Business Research, 36*(3), 233–245.

Nobes, C. (2013). The continued survival of international differences under IFRS. *Accounting and Business Research, 43*(2), 83–111.

Özçelik, H. (2020). BDS 701 Kilit denetim konuları: Uluslararası havayolu işletmeleri üzerine bir araştırma. In K. Ganite & C. Y. Özbek (Eds.), *Denetimde Seçme Konular 3* (pp. 149–173). Ankara: Gazi Kitabevi.

Özdoğan, B., & Uygun, U. (2020). TMS 17 kiralama işlemleri standardından TFRS 16 kiralamalar standardına geçişte bist şirketlerine yönelik sektörel etkilerin karşılaştırmalı analizi. *Manisa Celal Bayar Üniversitesi Sosyal Bilimler Dergisi, 18*(2), 209–227.

Özerhan, Y., Marşap, B., & Yanık, S. S. (2015). IFRS 15 müşterilerle yapılan sözleşmelerden doğan hasılat standardının irdelenmesi. *Muhasebe Bilim Dünyası Dergisi, 17*(2), 193–226.

Öztürk, C. (2011). *Examination of the accounting policies presented in the disclosures of the financial statements in the context of International Financial Reporting Standards.* Unpublished Ph.D. thesis, Başkent University, Ankara.

Öztürk, C. (2016). UFRS 16 Kiralama İşlemleri standardının eski UMS 17 standardı ile karşılaştırılması ve Almanya ve Türkiye'de hisse senetleri halka açık olan hava yolu şirketlerinin finansal durumuna etkisi. *Muhasebe Bilim Dünyası Dergisi, 18*(1), 1–50.

Öztürk, M., & Serçemeli, M. (2016). Impact of new standard "IFRS 16 Leases" on statement of financial position and key ratios: A case study on an airline company in Turkey. *Business and Economics Research Journal, 7*(4), 143–157.

Pacter, P. (2005). What exactly is convergence?. *International Journal of Accounting, Auditing and Performance Evaluation, 2*(1–2), 67–83.

Pinto, I., & Morais, A. I. (2019). What matters in disclosures of key audit matters: Evidence from Europe. *Journal of International Financial Management & Accounting, 30*(2), 145–162.

Public Company Accounting Oversight Board (PCAOB). (2018). *Staff guidance: Implementation of critical audit matters: The basics.* Retrieved from https://pcaobus.org/Standards/Documents/Implementation-of-Critical-Audit-Matters-The-Basics.pdf

Qatar Airways. (2019). *Qatar* Airways *Group Q.C.S.C. consolidated financial statements 31* March 2019. Retrieved from https://www.qatarairways. com/content/dam/documents/annual-reports/2019/Qatar%20Airways%20 FS%2031%20March%202019%20(EN).pdf

Ratzinger-Sakel, N. V., Audousset-Coulier, S., Kettunen, J., & Lesage, C. (2013). Joint audit: Issues and challenges for researchers and policy-makers. *Accounting in Europe, 10*(2), 175–199.

Riccardi, L. (2016). Accounting Standards for Business Enterprises No. 30— Presentation of Financial Statements. In *China Accounting Standards* (pp. 227–238). Singapore: Springer.

RSM. (2020). *What to expect from key audit matters in Canada.* Retrieved from https://rsmcanada.com/our-insights/audit-insights/what-to-expect-from-key-audit-matters-in-canada.html

Ryanair. (2019). *Ryanair 2019 annual report.* Retrieved from https://investor. ryanair.com/wp-content/uploads/2019/07/Ryanair-2019-Annual-Report. pdf

Sarı, E. S., Altıntaş, T., & Taş, N. (2016). The effect of the IFRS 16: Constructive capitalization of operating leases in the Turkish retailing sector. *Journal of Business Economics and Finance, 5*(1), 138–147.

Securities and Exchange Commission (SEC). (2007). *Acceptance from foreign private issuers of financial statements prepared in accordance with International Financial Reporting Standards without reconciliation to U.S. GAAP.* Retrieved from https://www.sec.gov/rules/final/2007/33-8879.pdf

Sri Lankan Airlines. (2019). *Sri Lankan Airlines annual report 2018/19.* Retrieved from https://www.srilankan.com/pdf/annual-report/SriLankan_Airlines_ Annual_Report_2018-19_English.pdf

Straszheim, M. R. (1969). The international airline industry. Washington, DC: Brookings Institution, Transport Research Program.

Street, D. L., & Stanga, K. G. (1989). The relevance of a segment cash flow statement in lending decisions: An empirical study. *Accounting and Business Research, 19*(76), 353–361.

Tai, B. Y. (2013). Constructive capitalization of operating leases in the Hong Kong fast-food industry. *International Journal of Accounting and Financial Reporting, 3*(1), 128–142.

Tan, C. W., Tower, G., Hancock, P., & Taplin, R. (2002). Empires of the sky: Determinants of global airlines' accounting-policy choices. *The International Journal of Accounting, 37*(3), 277–299.

Taplin, R., Verona, R., & Doni, F. (2011). The process of global convergence IFRS/US-GAAP. An empirical analysis on IFRS-compliant and US GAAP-compliant financial statements. In *Accounting Renaissance: Lessons from the crisis and looking into the future.* Venice, Italy.

Teoh, S. H., & Wong, T. J. (1993). Perceived auditor quality and the earnings response coefficient. *Accounting Review, 68*(2), 346–366.

Tsalavoutas, I., André, P., & Dionysiou, D. (2014). Worldwide application of IFRS 3, IAS 38 and IAS 36, related disclosures, and determinants of non-compliance. *ACCA research report,* 134. Retrieved from https://www.

accaglobal.com/ie/en/technical-activities/technical-resources-search/2014/may/worldwide-application-of-ifrs.html

Tsalavoutas, I., Tsoligkas, F., & Evans, L. (2020). Compliance with IFRS mandatory disclosure requirements: A structured literature review. *Journal of International Accounting, Auditing and Taxation*, 40. https://doi.org/10.1016/j.intaccaudtax.2020.100338

Veverková, A. (2019). IFRS 16 and its impacts on aviation industry. *Acta Universitatis Agriculturae et Silviculturae Mendelianae Brunensis*, *67*(5), 1369–1377.

Vik, C., & Walter, M. C. (2017). *The reporting practices of key audit matters in the Big five audit firms in Norway*. Master's thesis, BI Norwegian Business School, Oslo.

Virgin Atlantic Group. (2018). *Virgin Atlantic annual report 2018*. Retrieved from https://flywith.virginatlantic.com/content/dam/corporate/VIR007_2018%20Annual%20Report%20%26%20Accounts.pdf

Westjet. (2018). *Westjet 2018 annual report*. Retrieved from https://www.westjet.com/assets/wj-web/documents/en/investorMedia/WestJet-2018-Annual-Report.pdf

Wizz Air. (2019). *Wizz Air 2019 annual report and accounts*. Retrieved from https://wizzair.com/static/docs/default-source/downloadable-documents/corporate-website-transfer-documents/annual-reports/ar-f19-final-(web-indexed)_6afd66af.pdf

Yergin, D., Evans, P. C., & Vietor, R. H. (2000). Fettered flight: Globalization and the airline industry (pp. 1–61). Cambridge: Cambridge Energy Research Associates.

Yu, J. (2019). Investigation of IFRS 16 effect on the airlines. *Journal of Finance and Accounting*, *7*(5), 132–135.

Zeff, S. A. (2007). Some obstacles to global financial reporting comparability and convergence at a high level of quality. *The British Accounting Review*, *39*(4), 290–302.

INDEX